The Environment of Br
First Millennium

The Environment of Britain in the First Millennium AD

Petra Dark

Duckworth

First published in 2000 by
Gerald Duckworth & Co. Ltd.
61 Frith Street, London W1V 5TA
Tel: 0207 434 4242
Fax: 0207 434 4420
Email: enquiries@duckworth-publishers.co.uk
www.duckw.com

A catalogue record for this book is available
from the British Library

ISBN 0 7156 2909 3

Typeset by Ray Davies
Printed in Great Britain by
Redwood Books Ltd, Trowbridge

Contents

Preface

The nature of the environment is of key importance to the archaeology of any period, but the focus of attention has concentrated on prehistory. Issues such as the resources available to Mesolithic hunter-gatherers, the environmental impact of the spread of agriculture, and the date at which Britain's original natural woodland cover was removed have been discussed in many publications, including the well-known *Environment in British Prehistory* (I.G. Simmons & Tooley 1981).

Aspects of the environment of the Roman and later periods have received much less attention. This is despite the obvious importance of historic periods, both in their own right, and because they provide the link to understanding the origin of our contemporary landscape. The only substantial attempt to review the post-prehistoric environment, *The Environment of Man: the Iron Age to the Anglo-Saxon Period* (M. Jones & Dimbleby 1981) is now largely out of date due to the wealth of subsequent data. Some of these data have been discussed in *The Landscape of Roman Britain* (K. Dark & Dark 1997) and *Environment and Economy in Anglo-Saxon England* (J. Rackham 1994), but there is no recent book providing a detailed examination of environmental change throughout the first millennium AD.

Possibly the neglect of historic-period environments has come partly from a perception that there is less need for environmental archaeology for periods with written evidence. Yet for first-millennium AD Britain textual sources shed little light on the nature of the environment overall. Reconstruction of the environment is, therefore, largely reliant on the same types of evidence used for prehistory – principally the remains of plant and animal communities, soils and sediments.

The aim of this book is to examine the results of recent research on the environment of Britain from the end of the Iron Age to the end of the Anglo-Saxon period, using evidence from biological remains, soils and sediments, recovered from archaeological sites and 'off-site' contexts such as lake sediments and peat deposits. Probably the most important source of information for the general character of the environment in terms of vegetation cover is pollen analysis, so pollen data play a key part in this book. In particular, a detailed examination has been undertaken of all well-dated pollen sequences relating to each period of the first millennium AD.

While some of the most obvious changes in vegetation, animal communities and soils during this period have resulted from human activity, natural environmental changes – particularly climate and sea-level fluctuations – are also fundamental to our understanding of the first millennium AD. These aspects are also discussed, drawing on evidence from a variety of sources.

A note on archaeological terminology

The structure of much of this book is based on the main archaeological periods, but this approach faces the problem that such periods do not necessarily apply to the whole of Britain at the same time, if at all. They are used here merely to provided a chronological framework for discussion of the data. This discussion begins with the late Iron Age, which here refers to the period *c.* 100 BC to AD 43 (Chapter 3), although outside the areas encompasssed within the Roman Empire Iron Age ways of life continued beyond this date. The Roman period is taken as AD 43-410 (Chapter 4), but it should be remembered that some communities, especially in the west and north of Britain, appear to have retained many aspects of Roman culture after this. These communities, and the people grouped conventionally under the name 'Anglo-Saxons', form the subject of Chapter 5. 'Medieval' is here taken to refer to the period after the Norman Conquest of England – the period immediately following the first millennium AD. In this book, Britain is understood as the island of Britain (today, England, Scotland and Wales).

Acknowledgments

It is a pleasure to acknowledge all those who have discussed various questions relating to the subject of this book with me, especially Martin Bell, Keith Bennett, Jennifer Foster, Martin Jones, and Winifred Pennington. I would also like to thank everyone who has helped by providing illustrations (see individual captions). My research on the environmental context of Hadrian's Wall, aspects of which are published here for the first time, was funded by the award of a Postdoctoral Fellowship by the Science and Engineering Research Council, with support for radiocarbon dates provided through the Natural Environment Research Council Radiocarbon Laboratory.

Greatest thanks go to my husband, Ken, who has been a constant source of advice and encouragement. I dedicate this book to him.

List of figures

1

Reconstructing environments of the first millennium AD

The range of methods applied to environmental reconstruction is constantly increasing, and it is obviously beyond the scope of this book to describe all of them in detail. The aim of this chapter is to introduce the main methods that have been used to reconstruct the environment of the first millennium AD in Britain. These, which include biological and sedimentological analyses and dating methods, provide the data discussed in Chapters 3-6. Greatest attention is here given to pollen analysis, because this provides the principal method for reconstructing the effects of human activity on environmental change over long time-scales. Methods for reconstructing climate and sea level are discussed separately in Chapter 2.

Details of the range of techniques used more widely in environmental archaeology and palaeoecology are to be found in Lowe and Walker (1997) and Bell and Walker (1992), and are not discussed here.

Textual sources

The start of the first millennium AD coincides approximately with the earliest written references to Britain, but there are few texts that shed any light on the nature of the environment. For example, while Roman accounts of military campaigns often mention woodland, the woods are rarely identifiable or described in any detail. These references may, in any case, reflect no more than 'colouring' of the text for rhetorical purposes (Rivet & Smith 1979, p. 44). However, not all information of this sort can be summarily dismissed, and even literary texts may contain useful environmental data. For example, the Caledonian Forest, referred to by a number of Roman writers (including Ptolemy and Pliny) and by later 'Celtic' poets (Rivet & Smith 1979, pp. 44-5), seems to have been a major feature of the south-west Scottish landscape throughout the period covered by this book.

Anglo-Saxon charters often contain descriptions of the boundaries of an area of land ('perambulations'), with references to landscape features such as streams, woods and roads (O. Rackham 1980, 1986, 1990; Hooke 1981, 1985, 1998). Unfortunately the location of such landmarks is usually impossible to identify with certainty in the modern landscape, although they can still give a general impression of the landscape of named areas. Anglo-Saxon place-names may also provide topographical information, including hints of the presence of woodland (Gelling 1974, 1984; Hooke 1985, 1998; O. Rackham 1976, 1980). Perhaps the most widely used place-name element taken to infer the presence of woodland is Old English *leah* (-ley) (Gelling 1974), in names such as Wheatley and Cowley. The term can mean 'wood, glade or clearing', but also came to mean 'pasture' or 'meadow' (Gelling 1984), thus limiting its value for landscape reconstruction.

Pollen analysis

Many flowering plants produce abundant pollen grains, which may be widely dispersed by the wind before falling as a 'pollen rain'. The pollen may be preserved in a variety of sediments, peat deposits and sometimes soils, and provides one of the main sources for reconstructing past environments (for details see Birks & Birks 1980; Faegri & Iversen 1989; Moore, Webb & Collinson 1991). Spores of ferns and mosses may be similarly widely dispersed, and are usually included in analysis of pollen assemblages.

Lake sediments and peats may accumulate undisturbed for thousands of years, providing the opportunity to use their pollen content to reconstruct changes in the surrounding vegetation over long time scales. Smaller areas of organic deposition, such as wells and ditches on archaeological sites, also accumulate pollen, but usually over short periods. Such deposits are likely to be disturbed by human activity, such as ditch cleaning, so rarely provide good pollen sequences. Sometimes, pollen may be preserved in soils sealed under large earthworks, where a lack of oxygen inhibits decay, or in highly acidic soils, which contain few of the organisms that normally precipitate destruction of the pollen (Dimbleby 1985). Pollen from most soils will be poorly preserved and the composition of the assemblage may be skewed by different rates of decay of the various pollen types (Cushing 1967). Furthermore, the original stratification of the pollen may be lost due to mixing of the soil layers by earthworms and other soil organisms. The best deposits for providing a long-term reconstruction of environmental change are therefore waterlogged lake sediments and peat deposits. Such deposits are termed 'off-site' sequences, because they are not usually directly associated with archaeological sites, in contrast to 'on-site' sequences from archaeological contexts.

Samples for pollen analysis may be obtained from trenches, open section or by coring. Only a small amount of deposit (*c.* 1cm^3) is needed for each level to be analysed. The samples are chemically treated to remove as much of the mineral and non-pollen organic component of the deposit as possible. This leaves a pollen-rich residue which is examined under a light microscope, usually at a magnification of x400.

Pollen grains are identified by reference to published pollen 'keys' (Faegri & Iversen 1989; Moore, Webb & Collinson 1991) and by comparison with pollen from living plants (Figure 1.1). It is rarely possible to identify closely which species a pollen grain represents, and usually pollen

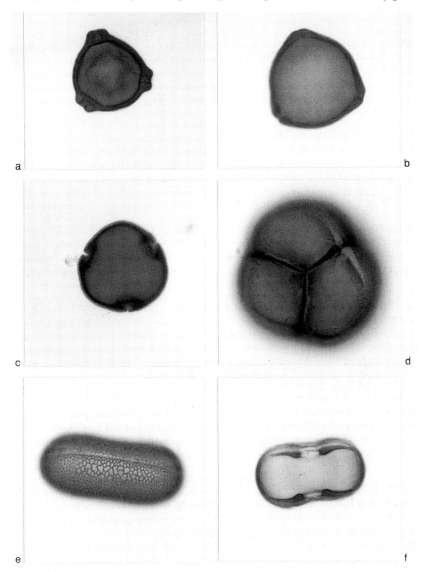

1.1: Pollen grains of (a) Dwarf birch, *Betula nana*, (b) Hazel, *Corylus avellana*, (c) Small-leaved lime, *Tilia cordata*, (d) Bell heather, *Erica cinerea*, (e) Sainfoin, *Onobrychis viciifolia*, (f) Bush vetch, *Vicia sepium*. All photographed at a magnification of x1000.

is identified to groups or families of plants. For example, there are two native species of oak (*Quercus*) in Britain, but their pollen cannot, at present, be distinguished. Pollen of most grasses looks very similar, so identification to family level (Poaceae) is all that is usually achieved. The pollen grains of cereals can, however, usually be separated from wild grasses due to a variety of characteristics, including their larger size (Andersen 1979). Pollen of rye (*Secale cereale*) can be identified to species level, but other cereals are only identifiable to groups or types that include several species. For example, 'Avena-Triticum group' (also known as 'Avena type') includes spelt wheat (*Triticum spelta*), emmer wheat (*T. dicoccum*), bread wheat (*T. aestivum*) and club wheat (*T. compactum*), as well as wild and cultivated oats (*Avena fatua* and *A. sativa*) (Andersen 1979; K.D. Bennett 1994a).

For each pollen sample around 500 pollen grains are counted, and the relative abundance of each type is usually expressed as a percentage of the total pollen count in that sample. Where a stratigraphic series of pollen samples has been analysed, the results are given as a pollen diagram showing how the percentages of each pollen type change through the sequence. Such percentage diagrams suffer from the interdependence of the pollen curves, so that an increase of one taxon will cause a reduction in percentage of the others, whether or not they have become less abundant in the vegetation. One way to overcome this problem is by calculating pollen concentrations to produce an 'absolute' pollen diagram. The usual method for doing this is by adding a known quantity of exotic pollen or spores to the sample, and using the ratio of exotic to 'fossil' pollen to calculate the number of 'fossil' pollen grains present in a unit volume or weight of deposit. In practice, such diagrams suffer from problems of variable pollen concentration caused by changes in accumulation rate, and percentage diagrams remain the main means of data presentation.

To aid in interpretation of pollen diagrams, they are usually divided into a series of 'pollen zones', each characterised by their distinctive pollen content. Zonation is usually performed by a computer program such as 'psimpoll' (K.D. Bennett 1994b), based on multivariate analysis of the dataset, although subjective zonation was used before the widespread availability of computers.

Probably the most difficult aspect of pollen analysis is interpretating the pollen diagram to provide a reconstruction of vegetation. There are many factors involved in formation of the pollen assemblage, and its relationship to the original vegetation (see discussions in Faegri & Iversen 1989; Moore, Webb & Collinson 1991). First, it is necessary to remember that not all plants likely to have been growing in an area are represented in the pollen record. Some plants release little or no pollen into the atmosphere, so their pollen is unlikely to occur in peat or sediment deposits. In general, wind-pollinated plants such as pine (*Pinus sylvestris*), birch (*Betula*), and most grasses, are well represented in the pollen record

4

due to their high pollen production. Conversely, insect-pollinated plants, such as members of the rose family (Rosaceae), and self-pollinated plants, such as wheat (*Triticum*), are under-represented. Some plants that produce abundant pollen, such as the rushes (Juncaceae), are rarely represented in the pollen record because their pollen is unusually fragile and so unlikely to be preserved. As we have seen, the limitations of pollen identification also impose some constraints. Pollen identifiable only to family level may represent a range of plants from different types of vegetation. For example, grasses grow in a variety of environments, ranging from reedswamps to pasture, to open woodland.

Another key aspect for the interpretation of a pollen sequence is the area of vegetation it reflects – the pollen source area. This will vary with the type of deposit sampled, and its size. On a peat bog, for example, plants growing on the peat surface, as well as more distant vegetation, will contribute pollen to the deposits. This can be problematic because the non-specific identification of many herb pollen types means that it is uncertain which pollen is from local sources. In lakes, aquatic plants contribute some pollen to the deposits, but fortunately most aquatic pollen is readily identifiable. Lake-edge communities may be less easily separated from the regional vegetation, however. The size of the lake or peat bog also influences the relative importance of pollen inputs from different sources. In general, the larger the size of the lake or peat bog sampled, the larger the pollen source area. A lake 1km across may reflect the vegetation from an area of several kilometres, while the pollen assemblages from a small peat deposit a few metres across may derive predominantly from plants growing within a few tens of metres (Jacobson & Bradshaw 1981). Pollen samples from archaeological contexts usually reflect predominantly local vegetation and require especially careful interpretation because of the potential for bias by on-site activities such as crop processing (M. Robinson & Hubbard 1977).

Even for a single site, different types of pollen will have travelled different distances from their source, depending on their means of dispersal. The pollen of wind-pollinated plants is likely to reflect a much wider area of vegetation than that of insect-pollinated plants. For example, pine pollen is so widely dispersed that it is generally assumed that pine may only have been present nearby if its pollen exceeds 20% of the total count (K.D. Bennett 1984). This contrasts strongly with the situation for the insect-pollinated lime (*Tilia*), the pollen of which seems largely to be deposited within a few hundred metres of the parent tree (Pigott & Huntley 1980). In this case a pollen count of 20% would suggest that local woodland was dominated by lime (Huntley & Birks 1983).

The next stage in interpretation of a pollen sequence is to ask which plant communities were present. 'Indicator species' may provide clues to the presence of some types of vegetation, based on the assumption that the present conditions under which such plants grow can be used an indicator of their past occurrence. The classic example is the ribwort plantain, *Plantago lanceolata*, which has for long been regarded as an indicator of pastureland. Caution must be exercised in this approach, however, as our present agricultural landscape, of tidy single-crop fields, treated with fertilisers, pesticides and herbicides, could hardly be regarded as presenting a similar range of habitats to the less intensively managed farming systems of the past (Behre 1981). Ribwort plantain could be linked indirectly with arable activity as well as pasture, as it grows on fallow land.

Evidence of arable farming may, of course, be provided by the presence of pollen of crops, although few have distinctive pollen. Of the cereals, only rye can be identified with certainty. Other crops with distinctive pollen are flax (*Linum usitatissimum*) and hemp (*Cannabis sativa*), both of which were grown in the past as a source of fibre. Hemp pollen may, however, be difficult to separate from that of hop (*Humulus lupulus*), which grows naturally in fens and hedges (Godwin 1967; Punt & Malotaux 1984; French & Moore 1986; Whittington & Gordon 1987; Whittington & Edwards 1989). Unfortunately, most crops produce little pollen and so are strongly under-represented in the pollen record. An absence of pollen of cereals, for example, should certainly not be taken to indicate that there was no cereal cultivation in an area.

In addition to pollen of the crops themselves, other plants have been argued to be indicative of arable land, such as the mugwort (*Artemisia*) and the Chenopodiaceae family (J. Turner 1964). Some attempts have been made to establish the relative proportion of arable and pastoral land by calculation of arable/pastoral ratios from the presence of indicator species (J. Turner 1964). The problems in assigning specific ecological requirements to particular species, and their differences in pollen production and dispersal, limit the value of this approach, however (Behre 1981).

As well as detecting the presence of human activity, it is desirable to obtain an estimate of the extent of the catchment affected. The main type of human activity visible in the pollen record is woodland clearance. The extent to which clearance has occurred can broadly be reconstructed from changes in the ratio of arboreal (tree and shrub) to non-arboreal (herb) pollen, especially of grasses. Comparisons of modern pollen assemblages with the surrounding vegetation suggest that tree and shrub pollen frequencies greater than 50% indicate a predominantly wooded landscape, while arboreal pollen frequencies less than 20% reflect an open environment (Tinsley & Smith 1974). The way the extent of clearance is defined depends on which pollen types are included in the sum used in calculations. Turner (1965) defined 'extensive clearance' as occurring when the grass pollen frequency reached approximately 100% of the total tree pollen. More recently, Tipping (1997) defined 'extensive clearance' as occurring when grass pollen occurred at 25-50% of total land pollen, and 'complete clearance' as when grass pollen exceeded 50% of total land pollen. Here I take extensive clearance to be reflected by arboreal pollen

6

frequencies at or below 50% of a pollen sum including all pollen and spores of vascular plants, apart from obligate aquatics, and total clearance to have occurred when arboreal pollen frequencies fall to 25% or less of this sum. Because many analysts have used different sums for calculations of their data, it has been necessary to recalculate percentages for sites where a different pollen sum was originally used.

Finally, if we are to relate the pollen record of vegetational change to the archaeological record of human activity it is essential to have a means of dating the pollen sequence. A chronology is usually based on radiocarbon dating of the sediment or peat (see later). Sometimes individual plant remains, such as hazel nuts, may be dated instead, if accelerator mass spectrometry (AMS) is an option. The ability of AMS to date small samples has recently advanced to the stage where it is becoming possible to date the pollen grains themselves (T.A. Brown *et al.* 1989; A. Long, Davis & de Lanois 1992)! The reliance of pollen analysis, and indeed most methods of environmental reconstruction, on radiocarbon dating imposes severe constraints when attempts are made to understand environmental change in relation to archaeological and historical sources, as will be discussed later.

Linked with the chronology of the sequence is the degree of temporal resolution it provides. This depends on the number of pollen samples taken per unit depth/time. Typically, sequences are sampled at intervals of 4 or 8cm, which usually represents a temporal resolution of approximately one sample/50-100 years. Recently there has been increasing application of 'fine resolution pollen analysis' where samples may be at 1cm or even 1mm intervals, providing an approximately decadal to annual sampling resolution. This approach has been most commonly applied to examination of the environmental impacts of Mesolithic hunter-gatherers, which tend to be small-scale and short-lived in comparison to those of farming communities (e.g. P. Dark 1998b), but there are a few examples from Roman and later deposits. The temporal resolution of the sequence obviously governs the type of question it can be used to answer. If samples are two hundred years apart it will not be possible to reconstruct the effects of activities spanning a few years or decades.

Charcoal

Microscopic charcoal particles commonly occur in the deposits used for pollen analysis, providing the opportunity to recontruct the history of burning as well as vegetation (Figure 1.2). From off-site deposits such charcoal may provide a valuable additional indicator of human activity that can help in interpretation of the pollen record. This is possible because natural fires are rare in Britain, especially in wooded environments, due to the difficulty of burning most native British trees (O. Rackham 1980). Pine is the exception, but was a minor aspect of most British woodland by the first millennium AD. This means that where

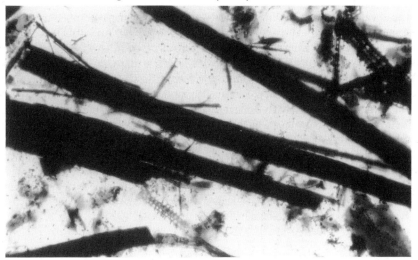

a

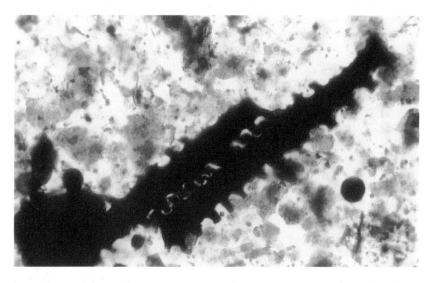

b

1.2: Microscopic charcoal particles from burning of (a) wood and (b) grasses Photographed at a magnification of (a) x400 (b) x1000.

charcoal occurs it is most likely to reflect human activity, although not necessarily the deliberate burning of vegetation.

As discussed earlier, one of the main ways in which human activity may be reflected in the pollen record is by a decline in the abundance of tree and shrub pollen and an increase in that of herbaceous plants. Human

8

activity does not provide the only possible cause of such events, however –
storms or wild animals, such as beaver (*Castor fiber*), may be involved. If
the changes in the pollen curves are accompanied by charcoal, this suggests a human presence. As mentioned above, direct burning of woodland
seems improbable – woodland clearance is more likely to have been
achieved by the axe than by fire. Most charcoal in lake sediments and peat
deposits probably derives from the domestic hearths of local settlements
(K.D. Bennett, Simonson & Peglar 1990) and from burning of other more
combustible vegetation types such as heathland and grassland (P. Dark
1998a).

Interpretation of charcoal sequences involves a number of problems,
and has been less widely studied than pollen analysis (see review by
Patterson, Edwards & Maguire 1987). Once again, a key question is how
far the charcoal has travelled from its source. At the most basic level it is
reasonable to assume that microscopic charcoal particles travel further
than larger, macroscopic, particles. There have been suggestions, based on
theoretical considerations, that the microscopic charcoal on pollen slides
has very large, and possibly global, source areas (J.S. Clark 1988). This
might be the case where large forest fires are involved, because these may
generate sufficient energy to inject charcoal particles high into the atmosphere where they are dispersed by the wind. In a British context such fires
will have been rare. Microscopic charcoal particles from domestic hearths
(K.D. Bennett, Simonson & Peglar 1990) or from burning of low-stature
non-woodland vegetation types (P. Dark 1998a) probably travel over distances of kilometres, at most, because such fires generate much less heat
than forest fires.

One approach to locating the source of the fire is to try to identify which
plants were being burned. Unfortunately microscopic charcoal particles
rarely have diagnostic features, but sometimes distinctive characteristics
may appear, such as surface cell patterns of grass leaves (e.g. P. Dark
1998a) (Figure 1.2).

Where charcoal comes directly from archaeological sites the source of
the fire is obviously less of a problem, and the larger fragments can usually
be identified with ease. What can assemblages of charcoal from archaeological sites tell us about the nature of the environment? Such charcoal
will often represent the remains of plant deliberately brought to the site
for specific purposes. For example, much of the charcoal from hearths is
likely to represent wood brought for fuel, while charred grain may be
retrieved from granaries destroyed by fire. The relationship of these plants
to the surrounding environment is uncertain. While the occupants of a site
are unlikely to have travelled far to gather wood for fuel, crops may have
been traded over large distances. Charred plant remains from archaeological sites must thus be interpreted with caution, as they may not derive
from the surrounding landscape, and if they do they will almost certainly
be a biassed selection.

Macroscopic plant remains

Analysis of larger (macroscopic) plant remains has an advantage over pollen analysis in that identification to species level is often possible. The most diagnostic and commonly preserved remains are the fruits and seeds of flowering plants, and pieces of wood, ranging from twig fragments to entire trees. These are usually preserved by waterlogging or charring (see above). Macroscopic plant remains in lake sediments and peat deposits tend to have very local sources – reflecting the vegetation growing on the peat surface or at the edge of the lake. Their use in environmental reconstruction is thus limited, although where combined with pollen analysis they can assist greatly in interpretation of the pollen record (by indicating which pollen types may have come from the local vegetation).

Macroscopic plant remains recovered from archaeological sites may derive from a variety of sources, including crop processing (crops and associated weeds), weeds growing on the site, and plants used for structural purposes such as thatch, timbers and wattle-work. As discussed in relation to charcoal, such remains are of limited value in terms of general environmental reconstruction, but critical in reconstruction of site economy. Wood has a special importance, however, in that tree rings provide a record linked to climate change and a means of dating (see later), and can also give clues to woodland management practices such as coppicing.

Animal remains

Animal remains, especially bones, have been recovered from many archaeological sites dating to the first millennium AD but, like on-site plant remains, most tell us more about site economy and diet than about the local environment (e.g. Maltby 1981). They are therefore not discussed here in detail, but regional reviews of the evidence are provided by Keeley (1984, 1987), Caseldine (1990) and Huntley and Stallibrass (1995).

Most ecological information is provided by the smaller animal remains that are unlikely to have been collected for food. Insects, for example, can provide important information about climate, human hygiene and crop storage (Kenward 1982). Unfortunately, insect remains are rarely recovered from archaeological sites, as they are preserved mainly by waterlogging, but they have been especially useful in illustrating the character of urban environments in the first millennium AD (Chapters 4 and 6).

Molluscs may be recovered from a wider range of contexts, as they are preserved in waterlogged and dry deposits (although acidic conditions cause deterioration). They usually reflect only local conditions, but edible types may have been widely traded. An example is the oyster (*Ostrea edulis*), commonly found on archaeological sites of the Roman and later periods, often at considerable distances from the coast.

Soils, sediments and peat deposits

Soils and sediments may provide clues to the nature of the environment in addition to the biological remains they contain. The present distribution of soil types is often used in discussing the potential of an area for agricultural activity in the past, but in most areas today's soils are likely to bear little relation to those of the past due to the effects of erosion, leaching of nutrients etc. 'Ancient' soils may, however, be preserved under earthworks or erosion deposits, where they are sealed from the effects of weathering and agricultural activity.

The vulnerability of soils to change is largely dependent on their parent material. Upland soils on acid rocks tend to be thin and poor in nutrients. The leaching effect of rainwater causes nutrients and metal ions to move down through the soil profile, where the latter may be deposited as an impermeable 'iron pan'. This can lead to waterlogging, which in turn causes death of trees and their replacement by plants tolerant of wet nutrient-poor conditions, such as *Sphagnum* moss, resulting in the accumulation of peat.

Peat deposits are widespread in many parts of northern and western Britain, where they are often considerd to be a 'natural' part of the landscape. In some areas peat formation probably results from climatic change in the prehistoric and later periods, but examination of the base of the peat often provides evidence for human activity, such as charcoal or changes in the pollen curves suggestive of woodland clearance (e.g. I.G. Simmons 1996). In many cases it seems that the onset of peat formation may be linked with a rise in the water table triggered by such clearance (Moore 1985, 1988, 1993). Removal of trees both increases the amount of rainfall reaching the ground and reduces uptake of water from the soil, so that the water table rises. Peat formation is especially likely to be triggered in an area where the rainfall is already high. Peat formation has begun at widely different dates in different areas, reflecting the interplay of local conditions of topography, climate and human activity.

As well as causing changes in the water balance of an area, woodland clearance and agricultural activity may also lead to soil erosion. The study of the products of this erosion can provide important insights into the scale and timing of agricultural activity (e.g. Bell 1981, 1992c). Arable cultivation exposes the bare soil surface to the rain, triggering movement of soil down-slope, where it may be deposited as hill-wash (or colluvium) towards the base of slopes or as lynchets where soil movement is restricted by field boundaries.

Eroded soil may enter rivers, and ultimately be deposited as alluvium. Deposition of alluvium can again reflect either climate change or human activity (A.G. Brown 1997). Lake sediments and basin peat deposits may also preserve a record of soil erosion by the presence of layers of mineral material. These may be visible to the naked eye in some cases, but more subtle variations in mineral inputs can be detected by loss-on-ignition analysis. Determination of loss-on-ignition involves burning off the organic material in a furnace, leaving behind the mineral component of the sediment which is often composed largely of eroded soil material.

Further information on soil erosion may be derived from the magnetic properties of a sediment (Thompson & Oldfield 1986; Oldfield 1991). Most of the magnetic minerals in a lake sediment or peat deposit will have entered the site through soil erosion, so variations in the concentration of magnetic minerals through a sequence provide an indication of soil inputs that at least partly reflects land use (e.g. Thompson *et al.* 1975). Rocks and soils vary in the quantity and types of magnetic minerals they contain, so magnetic measurements may be used to determine the source of material eroded into a lake (e.g. David, Dearing & Roberts 1998).

Another method that has been applied especially to the study of archaeological soils is soil micromorphology (Courty, Goldberg & Macphail 1989). This involves microscopic examination of the structure of the soil and identification of its components, as clues to the origin of the soil and processes of soil formation. This information may then assist in understanding site function, patterns of land use etc.

Dating methods

Radiocarbon dating

Radiocarbon dating provides the principal chronological tool used in environmental reconstruction (see Aitken 1990; Bowman 1990 for detailed accounts). A wide variety of organic remains may be dated, including bone, charcoal, waterlogged plant remains, peat and lake sediment. For off-site pollen sequences it is usual to radiocarbon date the peat or mud at intervals throughout the sequence, at points where major changes in the pollen assemblages occur. Because of the expense involved in radiocarbon dating (which is, however, small in relation to the time of the analyst involved in counting the pollen!), typically there would be around one radiocarbon date/thousand years. Dates for intermediate levels are then estimated by interpolation between the radiocarbon dates, assuming a constant accumulation rate.

It is now well known that radiocarbon dates have to be 'calibrated' before they can be compared with calendar dates, because radiocarbon years are not equivalent to calendar years. Past fluctuations in the carbon-14 content of the atmosphere mean that the length of radiocarbon years has varied over time. This became apparent when wood samples dated by dendrochronology (see below) were radiocarbon dated, and 'calibration curves' constructed (Figure 1.3). Calibration curves are now available for the whole of the last 10,000 years (Stuiver & Reimer 1993), providing the key to linking the environmental and archaeological records.

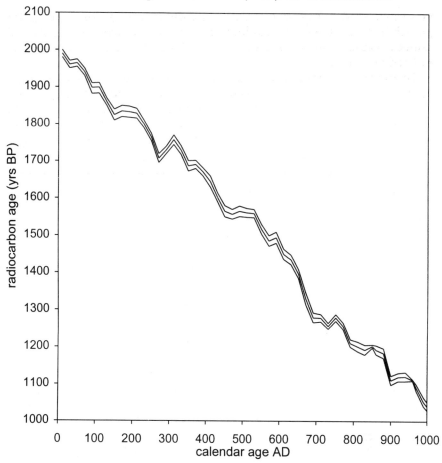

1.3: Radiocarbon calibration curve for the first millennium AD. (Data from Stuiver & Pearson 1986.)

Unfortunately, however, there are a number of problems with radiocarbon dating which mean that it can only provide an age estimate rather than a true date for an object or event. First, radiocarbon dating produces an age range, rather than a single date, because of the error term attached to every radiocarbon determination. Typically a radiocarbon laboratory would provide a date quoted in radiocarbon years BP (before present, taken as AD 1950) with an error term of, say, ±50 years (often now less, but occasionally in excess of 100 years). The error is quoted at one standard deviation, meaning that there is a 68% chance that the true radiocarbon age lies within the range given. So, if the error is 50, the range is a one hundred year span centred on the quoted date. There is, of course, a substantial likelihood that the true age lies outside this range, and it is

13

now considered necessary to work with dates at the two sigma level (95% probability). This means doubling the error term. Thus, the range of a radiocarbon date with a quoted error of ±50 years would be two hundred radiocarbon years.

To convert the radiocarbon date to calendar years, it is necessary to calibrate the whole range, not just its central point. Calibration may increase or decrease the range of the date, depending on the form of the corresponding section of the calibration curve. If the curve is steep, it will produce a narrow age range, but where there are 'wiggles' or plateaux in the curve the range of the calibrated date may be substantially larger (Figure 1.4).

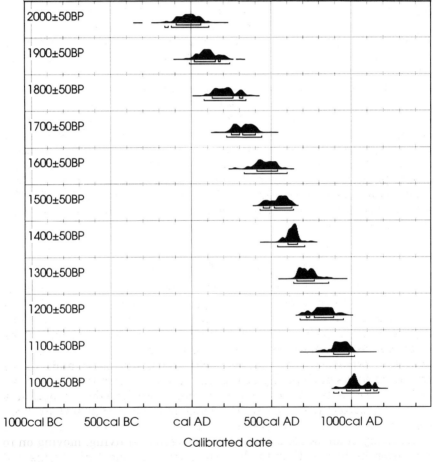

1.4: Calibration of a hypothetical series of radiocarbon dates at intervals of one hundred years throughout the first millennium AD, showing how the ranges of the probability distributions vary depending on the form of the corresponding section of the calibration curve. Drawn using OxCal (Bronk Ramsey 1995) with the datasets in Stuiver & Kra (1986).

14

1. Reconstructing environments of the first millennium AD

The nature of radiocarbon dates creates problems when we attempt to relate environmental sequences with radiocarbon chronologies to the archaeological record. Ideally one would like to establish direct chronological relationships between environmental change and well-dated historical events. For example, did the building of Hadrian's Wall in the AD 120s-30s require removal of large areas of woodland to clear its path? A pollen sequence from an adjacent peat deposit might show a decline in the frequency of tree pollen, and this horizon might then be radiocarbon dated, and produce a date of 1880±50 BP, which is centred on a calibrated date of AD 120. Even if this was the case, it would not be possible to prove, on this evidence alone, that the clearance was connected to wall construction (Dumayne *et al.* 1995). The error term attached to the date means that clearance could have occurred decades earlier or, in theory, later. This problem of the age range of radiocarbon dates for understanding human environmental impacts will remain so long as radiocarbon dating is the primary dating method.

One approach by which the age range of calibrated dates can be reduced is by the technique of Bayesian analysis (for detailed accounts of the method see, for example, Buck *et al.* 1991; Buck, Litton & Smith 1992). Where a series of radiocarbon dates from a sequence of deposits are sufficiently closely spaced for their age ranges to overlap, the method uses the fact that their order is known (i.e. moving up the sequence each date must be progressively younger) to reduce the range of the calibrated dates. Unfortunately, the expense involved in obtaining a large number of radiocarbon dates means that such an approach must, at present, be considered desirable but usually unobtainable.

Dendrochronology

Dendrochronology relies on the fact that the width of the ring of wood formed by a tree each year is related to environmental (principally climatic) conditions during that year. Because environmental conditions vary from year to year, the width of the new rings varies throughout the life of the tree. Furthermore, trees growing at the same time in different areas may experience a similar set of climatic fluctuations, and so have similar patterns of rings. By examining the wood from trees that have died at various times in the past it has been possible to obtain a complete record of tree rings for the whole of the last 10,000 years. This has been achieved by obtaining overlapping patterns of rings from successively older wood, beginning with trees still living, moving on to trees from buildings, then to older trees from archaeological sites and from peat bogs (see Baillie 1995 for a detailed account of how tree-ring chronologies are constructed).

This method has been of immense importance for dating archaeological sites where wood is preserved and has enabled some astonishingly precise dates. For example, wood from the Sweet Track in the Somerset Levels has been shown to have been cut in the winter of 3807/3806 BC (Hillam *et al.* 1990).

As mentioned above, tree-ring dating has also been of importance in enabling calibration of the radiocarbon time scale. The value of tree rings does not end there. The fact that variations in ring width are related to climate means that the rings also provide a potential means of climatic reconstruction. One area that has recently attracted much attention is so-called 'narrowest-ring events'. These are parts of a tree-ring series where the rings are exceptionally narrow, reflecting periods of unfavourable growing conditions. Remarkably, some of these events reflected in Irish tree-ring sequences have been argued to be linked to climatic cooling resulting from the gas output from major volcanic eruptions, in Iceland and even further afield (Baillie 1995). The possible climatic impacts of volcanic eruptions will be discussed further later, but the next section will deal with the value of one product of such eruptions – tephra – for dating.

Tephrochronology

Tephra, or volcanic glass, consists of microscopic particles of silica produced in vast quantities by volcanic eruptions (Figure 1.5). The particles are sent high into the atmosphere by the force of the eruption, and may be transported thousands of kilometres from their source, before being washed out of the atmosphere by rain. Many of the volcanic eruptions over recent centuries have been documented, so that their dates are known. If tephra particles from one of these historically dated eruptions occurred in a peat sequence, then it would provide a date for that part of the sequence. This, of course, relies on being able to link tephra particles to specific volcanoes. Fortunately, individual volcanoes seem to produce tephra with a specific chemical 'signature' which can be detected using the technique of electron microprobe analysis.

Before the last thousand years there are few eruptions with known historic dates. Despite this, tephra can still be of value in enabling correlation between different sites where the same tephra layers occur. In such cases a chronology is provided by radiocarbon dating of the deposits containing the tephra layer. It might seem surprising that tephrochronology could be used in a British context, but recent analysis of peat deposits in the northern half of Britain and Ireland has shown the widespread existence of thin tephra layers, and chemical analysis has linked some of these layers to Icelandic eruptions (Dugmore 1989; Pilcher & Hall 1992; Pilcher, Hall & McCormac 1996). Probably the most widely identified layer is from the Hekla 4 eruption. Multiple radiocarbon dates of the peat containing this layer give a date with a two sigma calibrated range of 2400-2270 cal BC (Pilcher, Hall & McCormac 1995, 1996).

16

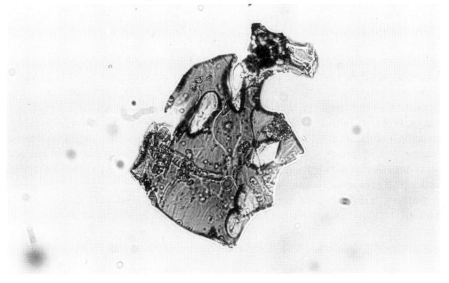

1.5: Particle of tephra from sediments in Orkney. Photographed at a magnification of x400.

Most of the tephra layers so far identified from British deposits pre-date the first millennium AD. These include a layer radiocarbon dated to *c.* 2100 BP (*c.* 170-100 cal BC) recognised from several sites in Scotland and known as the Glen Garry tephra after the site where it was first identified (Dugmore, Larsen & Newton 1995). This layer has also been recognised in peat deposits from northern England (Pilcher & Hall 1996), but has not been linked to an Icelandic source. The widespread occurrence of this layer means that it could provide a useful 'marker horizon' for comparing pollen sequences from the northern half of Britain.

From deposits of the first millennium AD a tephra layer of mixed origin, apparently representing two eruptions, has been found in Sluggan Bog, Northern Ireland. It has been dated to *c.* cal AD 770-890 by multiple radiocarbon determinations (Pilcher, Hall & McCormac 1995, 1996). This layer has been identified at two other sites in the north of Ireland, and used to correlate pollen diagrams from all three (V.A. Hall, Pilcher & McCormac 1993), illustrating the potential of tephra layers in enabling correlation of palaeoecological sequences from different sites without reliance solely on radiocarbon dating, and with greater precision than radiocarbon dating can allow. Another tephra layer from Sluggan Bog has a single radiocarbon date of 1908±21 BP (UB-3546, cal AD 20-140) (Pilcher, Hall & McCormac 1995), but its source is again apparently unknown.

17

Conventions used for dates and plant names

Uncalibrated radiocarbon dates are quoted in years before present (BP, taken as AD 1950) followed by their laboratory code number (unless this is given separately in a table) and calibrated range. Calibration has been undertaken using the program OxCal v.3.0 (Bronk Ramsey 1995), with the datasets in Stuiver and Kra (1986). The probability method has been used, and the range with the highest probability quoted in the text. Calibrated dates are quoted at two standard deviations of the determination, in the form cal AD/cal BC, rounded outwards to the nearest ten years. Historical dates and tree-ring dates are given as AD/BC.

For plant names, common names are followed by Latin names (after Stace 1991) for the first use of each plant name in each chapter.

2

Climate and sea level in the first millennium AD

In later chapters the chronological framework of archaeological periods is used in discussing environmental change, but here climate and sea level are dealt with for the first millennium AD as a whole. Long-term trends in climate and sea level then provide the background against which the role of human activity in soil and vegetation change are considered.

Climate

There are several sources of evidence for the climate of the first millennium AD, including texts from continental Europe, ice cores from the Greenland ice sheet, glacier movements in the Alps and Scandinavia, tree rings, and variations in peat growth rates from mires across Europe.

Textual sources

Textual sources inform us of human perceptions of weather and climate for the Roman and later periods, but principally refer to the Continent. Lamb (1981) has collated references to unusual weather incidents and seasonal extremes of warmth and cold in an attempt to reconstruct the pattern of climate change in the first millennium AD. He suggests that cold/wet conditions in the early Iron Age were followed, after about 150 BC, by a shift to a milder climate. By the Roman Conquest the climate may have resembled that of today, and temperatures continued to rise into the late third and fourth centuries, when they may have exceeded those of today by around 1ºC. This was accompanied by a period of relatively dry summers, but about AD 400 there was a return to colder conditions. Lamb suggests that during the eighth century the climate was more 'continental', with drier and probably warmer summers and colder winters. A similar phase seems to have occurred in the tenth century, marking the beginnning of a prolonged warm period lasting to approximately the end of the fourteenth century.

The utility of textual sources for climate reconstruction is limited by their bias towards exceptional events such as storms, floods and droughts, leaving the general character of the climate unrecorded. Scientific techniques do, however, illustrate a broadly similar pattern of climate in the first millennium AD.

Ice cores

Snowfall at the Greenland and Antarctic ice caps has accumulated over thousands of years in annual layers, identifiable by variations in texture of the snow. Measurement of the relative proportion of two isotopes of oxygen, oxygen-18 and oxygen-16, in the layers indicates the temperature at which the snow formed, providing a means of tracing long-term change in temperature (Lowe & Walker 1997). Obviously, the pattern of temperature change in Britain is unlikely to have followed that in Greenland in detail, but comparison of the most recent part of the Greenland ice-core sequence with textually-attested climate change for the last thousand years suggests similarities.

A record from north-west Greenland (Lamb 1995 after Dansgaard) shows cold conditions in the AD 400s, as suggested also by textual sources, indicating that there was a widespread climatic downturn at this time. There is some divergence between the ice core and textual sources later, however, as the ice-core data indicate a return to warmer conditions in the AD 600s, but textual sources suggest that northern Europe probably remained cold.

Some of the most recent ice-core data have come from the Greenland Ice Sheet Project 2 (GISP2) core (Stuiver, Grootes & Braziunas 1995). The implications of this for climate in the first millennium AD are currently unclear, but the start of a 'Medieval Warm Period' has been identified at *c*. AD 900, lasting until *c*. AD 1350 and peaking at *c*. AD 975.

A further aspect of the Greenland ice cores is that they provide a long-term record of global large-scale volcanic activity (back 110,000 years in GISP2), due to the deposition of aerosols from major volcanic eruptions. These aerosols increase the acidity of the ice, and this is measured by electrical conductivity or direct determination of sulphate concentrations (Hammer, Clausen & Dansgaard 1980; Zielinski *et al*. 1994, 1995; Zielinski 1995). Some of these eruptions have been argued to affect climate, including that in Britain, as will be discussed later.

Glaciers

Glaciers reflect climatic fluctuations (changes in temperature and/or snowfall) by changes in their size, leading to the advance or retreat of the front of the glacier. Long-term trends in these changes can be reconstructed by studying the deposits left behind when glaciers retreat (moraines) and the sediments of lakes that receive inwashed material from the glacial meltwater. There are problems with this type of study, however, such as determining the date at which changes occurred, and the fact that glaciers of different sizes vary in their response times to climate change (see review by Karlen 1991). Although both temperature and snowfall can affect glaciers, changes recorded from several glaciers over a wide area seem most likely to be linked to temperature. This receives some support from the fact that such changes apparently correspond to the oxygen isotope record from the Greenland ice sheet.

Studies of glacier movements in Scandinavia indicate periods of glacial advance at approximately the beginning of the first millennium AD (Karlen 1991, p. 401) and in the second half of the millennium (Karlen 1991, p. 405). The latter corresponds to other evidence for post-Roman climatic deterioration, although the former conflicts with some other data suggesting climatic warming from the late Iron Age.

Lake sediments may provide indirect evidence for glacial activity in the lake catchment because material eroded by glaciers may be transported to the lake in meltwater. Studies of annual sediment layers (varves) in lakes in the Swiss Alps (Leemann & Niessen 1994) suggest that the sediment record reflects changes in summer air temperature. The sediments appear to indicate a glacial advance (linked to cooler temperatures) from the start of the Iron Age, and then a retreat (suggesting warmer conditions) in approximately the second-third century AD. This lasted around 250 years, ending with a low stand in approximately the eighth century AD, followed by a major advance.

From studies of glacial lake sediments in southern Norway, Matthews and Karlen (1992) have constructed a curve of summer mean temperature (relative to the present) covering the last 10,000 years. During the Iron Age temperatures appear to have fluctuated to values ±0.5°C of present values. In the Roman period temperatures were apparently fractionally greater than today (estimated at just *c*. 0.1°C), followed by a minor downturn and then recovery in the second half of the first millennium AD. It cannot be assumed that the magnitude of temperature changes in Britain would have been the same, but the overall trends resemble those suggested by some other sources.

Tree rings

As discussed earlier, tree ring width is related to environmental conditions, including climate. Despite the fact that sequences of tree rings covering the last 10,000 years are now available from Ireland and Germany, their full potential for climatic reconstruction has yet to be realised. A short sequence of pine (*Pinus sylvestris*) rings from Fennoscandia, extending from AD 500 to the present, has been used to reconstruct mean summer temperature. This suggests periods of relative warmth from AD 750-780, 920-940 and 960-1000, and cool periods from AD 780-830 and 850-870 (Briffa *et al.* 1990). Lamb (1995, p. 166, after Rothlisberger) illustrates an even shorter sequence (85 years) of larch (*Larix*) tree rings from Switzerland, suggested by radiocarbon dating to cover the later Roman to early post-Roman period. These show a reduction in ring width and density of wood formed in late summer, probably suggesting cooler summer temperatures, at approximately the end of the Roman period.

Another aspect of tree rings, mentioned in Chapter 1, is that they appear to provide a record of exceptionally cold weather conditions caused by volcanic eruptions (for a fascinating account of this story see Baillie 1995). A correlation has been found between sequences of exceptionally narrow rings in oak trees (*Quercus*) preserved in Irish peat bogs, and peaks of acidity in cores from the Greenland ice sheet. The eruptions apparently responsible have been identified in some cases, with varying degrees of certainty. A particular source of controversy has surrounded the linking of the eruption of the Aegean island of Santorini to a 'narrowest-ring event' in 1628 BC (Baillie & Munro 1988; Baillie 1995; Buckland, Dugmore & Edwards 1997; Zielinski & Germani 1998).

The tree-ring and ice-core data together suggest that major volcanic eruptions, from as far afield as Iceland and the Mediterranean, may have affected the climate sufficiently to reduce the growth of oak trees on Irish peat bogs. The climatic effects are thought to result from the injection of large quantities of gases, especially sulphur, into the atmosphere. These reduced the amount of the sun's energy reaching the earth, causing the temperature to fall by a few tenths of a degree. The tree rings suggest periods of reduced growth lasting for up to ten years, but any climatic effect of an eruption is unlikely to have lasted for much more than a couple of years (Sear *et al.* 1987; Bradley 1988). A possible mechanism explaining the apparently longer-term effects of eruptions may be deposition of 'acid rain'. In areas where soils were already acid, as in many upland areas of northern and western Britain, this may have caused a 'threshold' to be crossed, reducing tree growth (Grattan & Gilbertson 1994; Grattan & Charman 1994). This may also, of course, have made at least some soils temporarily unsuitable for crops.

Effects of volcanic eruptions on climate

In seeking possible indications of the effects of volcanism on Britain's climate, tree rings provide the main source, where they can be linked with ice acidity peaks. Narrowest-ring events alone could reflect unfavourable growing conditions caused by drought, disease, insect attack etc. Conversely, not all acidity peaks in the Greenland ice sheet can be assumed to reflect volcanic eruptions that affected Britain's climate.

Textual references to unusual atmospheric phenomena, such as 'dry fogs', provide some support for the effects of major volcanic eruptions in the first millennium in Europe (Stothers & Rampino 1983a, b), but there are no records of such sightings from Britain. The most direct indication that volcanic emissions reached Britain is provided by the deposition of tephra particles in lake and peat deposits – discussed in Chapter 1 in relation to their value as chronological markers. Again, however, the fact that tephra reached an area need not imply any effect on the climate or soils.

Several studies have involved detailed pollen analysis of deposits containing tephra, with the aim of detecting vegetational responses to soil or climate change, but these have failed to provide conclusive evidence of any effect. In the context of the first millennium, pollen analyses were associated with an eighth- or ninth-century tephra layer found in several peat bogs in Northern Ireland (V.A. Hall, Pilcher & McCormac 1993). There was no evidence for any corresponding vegetational change, although at one site (Ballyscullion East) the record for cereal pollen stopped temporarily at the tephra layer. There appears to be no tree-ring evidence for a worsening of climate at this time, although the Irish Annals apparently refer to severe weather conditions and crop failures (V.A. Hall, Pilcher & McCormac 1993).

Returning to the tree-ring record, Irish tree rings show several narrowest-ring events in the latter half of the Iron Age and in the first millennium AD. Events at 207 BC and AD 540 apparently correspond to acidity peaks in the Greenland ice sheet (Hammer, Clausen & Dansgaard 1980), and have been linked by Baillie (1995, p. 81) with Chinese records of famine and 'dark skies', suggesting that they may have resulted from major volcanic eruptions that had widespread climatic effects.

Baillie (1995, pp. 84-5) points to a further dust-veil event at 44 BC, again perhaps corresponding to textually attested events in China. Etna, in Sicily, is thought on historical grounds to have erupted in 44 BC, and appears to have been the source of dry fogs and a variety of atmospheric phenomena at this time (Stothers & Rampino 1983a, b). A corresponding narrowest-ring event cannot be sought in the Irish tree-ring record because there are no timbers of this date, but oak timbers from Carlisle show very narrow rings from 40-39 BC (Baillie 1995, p. 85).

A volcanic eruption in 44 BC could be linked with the acidity peak in the Greenland (Camp Century) ice core at 50 ± 30 BC (Hammer, Clausen & Dansgaard 1980) and in the GRIP (Greenland Ice-core Project) core from Summit Greenland at 49 ± 5 BC (Johnsen *et al.* 1992). The issue is complicated, however, by recent results from the GISP2 (Greenland Ice Sheet Project 2) core (Zielinski *et al.* 1994; Zielinski 1995). This shows an extremely large signal at 53 ± 2 BC and another, much smaller, signal at 43 ± 2 BC. The former is suggested to have an Icelandic source, with the possible contribution of another high-latitude eruption, while the latter is suggested to reflect the eruption of Etna in 44 BC or an unkown northern hemisphere eruption (Zielinski 1995). Zielinski suggests that the smaller signal at 43 BC was the cause of the atmospheric phenomena discussed by Stothers and Rampino (1983a, b). Possibly this is also reflecting the event recorded in the Carlisle tree rings, mentioned above.

The major 53 BC signal (assumed to correspond to the *c.* 50 BC signal in the other cores) shows high sulphate deposition for almost three years, and Zielinski (1995) suggests that this would have had an impact on northern hemisphere climate. There is, however, no corresponding set of narrow rings in the British tree-ring sequence. It appears, then, that at least two eruptions could have impacted climate in the middle decade of the first century, yet only one affected the growth of trees in Britain.

Either of these episodes might be linked with the 'Glen Garry' tephra, referred to earlier, radiocarbon-dated to around 2100 BP. Unfortunately, calibration of the dates for this layer produces an age range of *c.* 400 cal BC-cal AD 100, so it could derive from the 53 BC, 44 BC or even the 207 BC eruption.

Returning to a more detailed consideration of the only narrowest-ring event from the first millennium AD, Irish bog oaks show reduced growth from AD 540-42 (Baillie 1994, 1995, pp. 93-107). A similar episode is recorded in oaks from Carlisle, and Whithorn in southern Scotland (A. Crone, cited in Baillie 1995, pp. 94-5). Furthermore, the reconstruction of temperature from Fennoscandian pines shows AD 536 to be among the five coldest summers of the last 1500 years (Briffa *et al.* 1990). Baillie (1994, 1995, p. 97) has combined the fifteen chronologies for the sixth century AD from England, Scotland, Ireland and Germany, demonstrating reduced growth in AD 536, recovery in AD 537-8, then a further decline in 540 and 541, followed by recovery in 546 (Figure 2.1).

Baillie (1995, p. 94) points to a number of possible links to textually attested events, in addition to the Chinese records mentioned earlier. These include references in the Irish Annals to 'failure of bread' in AD 536 and 539 (Warner 1990), and the onset of the Justinianic plague, which began in the Mediterranean in AD 542 and apparently reached Ireland by AD 544-5. Furthermore, Byzantine writers record that the sun was dim or obscured in AD 536 (Stothers & Rampino 1983b).

The tree-ring evidence for a cool period around AD 536-540 seemed to correspond to an ice acidity peak originally identified in the Greenland ice sheet (Dye 3) at AD 540±10 (Hammer, Clausen & Dansgaard 1980). Unfortunately, however, this date was later revised to AD 516±4 (Hammer 1984, p. 56). Given that historical sources appear to back up the tree-ring evidence for a major climatic event centred on AD 536, it might seem surprising if this event were absent from the ice core records (assuming that it resulted from volcanic activity). Data from other ice cores is needed to clarify the picture. The period AD 536-544 is thought to be represented in the GISP2 core, but the next seventy years are missing (Zielinski 1995). The relevant year might then be absent. A 'small to moderate' acidity peak occurs at AD 530±2 in GISP2 (Zielinski 1995), and appears also in the Dye 3 and GRIP cores (Clausen *et al.* 1997). This has been argued to be insufficient to account for the recorded atmospheric effects in the 530s (Stothers 1984; Rampino, Self & Stothers 1988), but in view of the

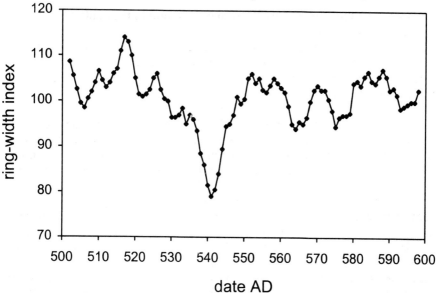

2.1: Tree-ring evidence for deterioration of climate AD 540. Mean growth indices (five-point smoothed) for fifteen European oak chronologies for the sixth century AD, showing reduced growth at AD 540. (After Baillie 1995.)

difficulty of estimating the effects of eruptions, this should presumably not rule it out.

If there is found to be no acidity peak for AD 536-540 it may be necessary to consider other possible causes of a temporary climatic downturn that apparently affected the whole of the northern hemisphere, possibly including an asteroid impact (Baillie 1994, 1995, p. 106)! The relationship of volcanic activity to the ice-core record is complex, however, and many major historically-known eruptions have no corresponding ice signal (Buckland, Dugmore & Edwards 1997).

Peat stratigraphy

Variations in the composition and degree of preservation of peat layers have for long been used in the study of climate change, forming the basis for the first division of the post-glacial period into climatic stages. Such studies also form one of the few sources of climatic information directly relating to Britain. There are some problems in interpretation, however, as peat growth in different areas varies in its response to climate change, and human activity may affect peat growth by altering the local water balance (see Chapter 1). There is also the problem of comparing sites on the basis of radiocarbon chronologies, so it is perhaps unsurprising that peat deposits from different areas may produce apparently conflicting results.

Accumulation of peat is linked to variations in ground water level, atmospheric precipitation and temperature. Raised and blanket mires form peat above the ground water table, and so are highly sensitive to changes in climate. Variations in rainfall or temperature are reflected in the types of vegetation growing on (and being incorporated into) the peat, and the state of preservation of the plant remains (humification). In cool/wet conditions plant remains are well preserved, resulting in formation of pale coloured peat, while in warm/dry conditions the plant remains decompose further and produce dark coloured peat.

The most detailed study of peat humification and plant macrofossil changes during the first millennium AD comes from Bolton Fell Moss, Cumbria (Barber 1981). Initial results suggested that a relatively wet climate in the Iron Age was followed by a shift to warmer/drier conditions in approximately the second century AD, lasting into the seventh century, followed by a return to cool/wet conditions.

Most recently a new method of macrofossil analysis has been used on the deposits from Bolton Fell Moss, to produce 'the first continuous proxy-record of climate from peat covering the last 6300 years' (Barber *et al.* 1994). This confirms the trend towards increasing dryness during the Roman period, followed by a return to wetter conditions after the Roman period. It also illustrates increasing dryness towards the end of the first millennium AD.

Similar evidence for cool/wet conditions in the Iron Age has come from several peat deposits in northern and western Britain, and from many other parts of western Europe (Dickinson 1975; Barber 1982). At Lindow Moss, Cheshire, for example, there is a major change from highly humified to unhumified peat between levels dated 2447±43 BP (UB-3240, 770-400 cal BC) and 2345±45 BP (UB-3239, 550-350 cal BC), apparently reflecting a deterioration of climate (Branch & Scaife 1995).

Support for a relatively dry climate in the Roman period comes from Burnfoothill Moss, in south-west Scotland, where a range of climatic indicators were employed (Tipping 1995a). Conversely, however, analysis of humification changes at Talla Moss, southern Scotland, suggests a 'wet shift' in the late Iron Age or early Roman period (F.M. Chambers *et al.* 1997).

The peat bog evidence for post-Roman climatic deterioration is also variable. Radiocarbon dates for a shift to less humified peat at Rusland Moss, Cumbria, suggest a wetter climate from *c.* 1500 BP – the sixth/seventh century AD (Dickinson 1975). This is supported by humification changes at blanket mires in northern England (Harold's Bog, North Yorkshire and Wood Moss in the Peak District), Wales (Brecon Beacons and Snowdonia) and Ireland (Letterfrack, Connemara) (Blackford & Chambers 1991), and macrofossil studies from Fenton Cottage, Lancashire

(Middleton, Wells & Huckerby 1995), that suggest increased wetness from c. 1400 BP – approximately the seventh century AD. At Talla Moss, however, conditions seem to have become wetter some three centuries earlier (F.M. Chambers *et al.* 1997). Another phase of wetter climate seems to be recorded towards the end of the first millennium at Burnfoothill Moss (approximately the eighth century) (Tipping 1995a) and Talla Moss (in approximately the tenth century AD) (F.M. Chambers *et al.* 1997), although this conflicts with the indications from Bolton Fell Moss of a drier climate at this time.

Summary of climate change

The different sources of evidence for climate are compared in Figure 2.2, from which it will be apparent that there is some divergence between the sources in the timing and nature of change. This is unsurprising in view of the diverse character of the evidence and its broad geographical coverage. General trends do emerge, however. Overall, the first millennium began with a change to a warmer and perhaps drier climate than that of most of the Iron Age. Temperatures may have been slightly higher than those of today in the latter half of the Roman period, but a climatic downturn followed from about the fifth century. This included a period of particularly cold conditions around AD 540, possibly linked to a volcanic

AD	TEXTS	ICE CORES (Greenland)	GLACIERS			TREE RINGS	PEAT
			glacier movements (Scandinavia)	lake sediments			
				Switzerland	Norway		
1000	⇧ increasingly warm/dry	warm peak increasing warmth				warm	
900	wetter			cooler			
800	dry/warm summers		cooler		warmer	cool warm	
700	cold winters						cool/wet
600		warmer				• NRE	
500				warmer	cooler		
400	colder dry summers T+1°C	cold				cool	warm/ dry
300	⇧				warmer		
200							
100	rising T						
0	similar to today		cooler	cooler			cool/wet

2.2: Comparison of evidence for climate change from different sources (see text). NRE = narrowest-ring event, T = temperature.

27

dust veil from a currently unknown source. Towards the end of the millennium climate seems to have become warmer and drier again, marking a trend that lasted well into the medieval period.

Sea level and coastlines

The reconstruction of former sea level and coastlines is complicated by the fact that change in the absolute height of the sea surface is only one of several factors involved. Sea level rose after the last glaciation due to the release of water from the melting ice sheets, a process termed eustatic sea-level rise. But in Britain the height of the land surface is also changing, and in different directions in different parts of the country. This is because during the last glaciation the north of Britain sank under the weight of the huge ice sheets that covered it, causing land to the south to tilt upwards. When the ice sheets melted around ten thousand years ago, northern Britain began to rise again (isostatic uplift), while the south subsided. As a result of these processes, changes in the relative positions of land and sea vary geographically. Other factors also cause local variations in the pattern of sea-level change, such as deposition of eroded sediment in estuaries and land reclamation.

Some of the most obvious indications of changes in sea level and coastal topography come from archaeological sites that would originally have occupied coastal locations, and have either eroded into the sea or now lie inland. The forts of the 'Saxon Shore' provide an example. They were originally built on or near the coast in the third and fourth centuries AD, but several have become stranded from the sea due to silting (Burnham 1989). Richborough fort in Kent is now over 3km from the coast, overlooking, and partly eroded by, the River Stour (Blagg 1989) (Figure 2.3). Other shore forts, such as Walton Castle, near Felixstowe (J.R.L. Allen *et al.* 1997, p. 125), have been eroded into the sea, however, demonstrating the variability of coastal processes. The late Roman signal stations on the Yorkshire coast provide another example of coastal erosion: the site at Scarborough has partly eroded away (Figure 2.4), and that at Filey has been almost completely lost as the cliffs beneath it have crumbled.

For the Scilly Isles, Charles Thomas (1985) has used the presence of archaeological sites and field boundaries now in the intertidal zone to reconstruct the changes in sea level that resulted in the formation of the present group of islands from a single land mass. The method relies on the assumption that settlement sites must have been above the maximum reach of the contemporary sea level. Thomas argues that most of the present islands were united until at least the end of the Roman period, and separated between the eleventh and fifteenth centuries. In this area, sea level seems to have risen by approximately four metres since the Roman period. Similarly, Waddelove and Waddelove (1990) used the presence of archaeological sites close to the sea or major rivers to produce estimates of

2.3: The Romano-British shore fort at Richborough, showing the effects of silting. (Cambridge University Collection of Air Photographs: copyright reserved.)

2.4: Scarborough late Roman signal station, showing the effects of coastal erosion. (Cambridge University Collection of Air Photographs: copyright reserved.)

sea-level rise since the Roman period. These range from 2.2m (since the late third century AD) at Caerleon, to 4.2-4.5m in the East Anglian Fens.

The variability between sites, and the limited nature of existing studies, mean that it is not possible to produce a general reconstruction of the coastline of Britain as a whole in the first millennium AD. Research has tended to focus more on long-term trends in vertical sea level, rather than on reconstructions of past coastlines (A.J. Long & Roberts 1997). J.R.L. Allen *et al.* (1997, p. 124) have recently drawn attention to the fact that 'no survey has ever been undertaken to locate the coastline of England in the Roman period', and knowledge of the Anglo-Saxon coast is similarly minimal.

Detailed studies of particular areas do make local reconstructions possible, as demonstrated by recent research in the Severn Estuary Levels and the East Anglian Fens, where a combination of archaeological and sedimentological approaches has been employed.

The Severn Estuary Levels

The estuary of the River Severn is flanked by several large areas of coastal alluvium and fen peat deposits termed 'levels'. On the English side lie the Somerset Levels, an area of intense archaeological and palaeoenvironmental research for decades (summarised in Coles & Coles 1986). More recently, attention has extended to other parts of the estuary, including the Gwent (Wentlooge and Caldicot) Levels on the Welsh side.

At an early stage of research on the Somerset Levels observations that Roman artifacts occurred below a considerable depth of alluvium led Godwin to propose a major inundation by the sea – the 'late Roman marine transgression' (Godwin 1943). Subsequently, it became apparent that the Roman material was not lying in contemporary deposits, but had been reworked into older layers by erosion from the Roman surface into creeks and inlets (Boon 1980). The principal evidence of a late Roman rise of sea level was thus removed, and subsequent research on both the Somerset and Gwent Levels has reinforced the need to abandon the concept of this marine transgression (e.g. J.R.L. Allen & Fulford 1986).

The peats of the Somerset Levels have provided the source of many pollen diagrams, illustrating vegetational change from the Neolithic to Roman periods. One of these sequences comes from Meare Heath, where shifts in deposition from raised bog to fen peat have been argued to reflect an increase in ground water level, perhaps linked to higher sea level (Hibbert 1980). Two shifts are recorded, one beginning at the start of the Iron Age and lasting into the mid-late Iron Age, and the second beginning towards the end of the Iron Age and ending in the early Roman period. Similar evidence for an early Iron Age marine incursion has been found elsewhere in the Levels (Caseldine 1986, p. 78; 1988), and radiocarbon dating of deposits from Glastonbury suggests that the estuarine clay once thought to be late Roman in origin actually belongs to this episode (Housley 1988b, pp. 79, 82). The Gwent Levels also seem to have experienced a marine transgression in the early Iron Age, leading to their almost total inundation (Rippon 1996, p. 22).

Recent research has indicated that parts of the Severn Estuary Levels, including the Wentlooge Level at Rumney Great Wharf, were reclaimed and settled in the Roman period (J.R.L. Allen & Fulford 1986; Fulford, Allen & Rippon 1994). These marshes are currently below sea level and protected by a sea wall, and their occupation during the Roman period suggests a sea level *c*. 1m lower than that of today (J.R.L. Allen & Fulford 1987). For the inner Severn Estuary, John Allen (1991) suggests that relative sea level has risen by at least 1.3m since the later Roman period.

The East Anglian Fens

The Fens consist of a large area of low-lying land around the Wash, including parts of the modern counties of Lincolnshire, Cambridge, Norfolk and Suffolk. Their low-lying position makes them highly sensitive to sea-level change, and fluctuations in the relative importance of freshwater and marine influence have resulted in a complex depositional sequence. Inputs of fresh water from the landward side of the basin result in formation of peat around its edge, while marine influences cause deposition of clay. Sea-level rise results in an increase in the area of clay/silt deposition, burying areas of peat, while falling sea levels increase the area of peat deposition. Fluctuations in sea level have, therefore, resulted in layers of interbedded organic and mineral deposits.

The Fens have long been of interest in terms of both their sedimentary record and archaeology, beginning with the work of the Fenland Research Committee in the 1930s, and culminating in the recent work of the Fenland Project (D. Hall & Coles 1994). Before the recent phase of research, the sedimentological and archaeological data from southern Fenland were interpreted by Godwin as reflecting an extension of marine influence, beginning in the Iron Age, continuing into the third and fourth centuries AD (Godwin 1978, pp. 106-7). More extensive stratigraphic work by Shennan enabled him to propose a sequence of sea-level fluctuations, including a rise in sea level throughout the Iron Age, a fall in the Roman period, and then another rise afterwards (Shennan 1986).

Most recently, synthesis of the archaeological, stratigraphic and palynological investigations by the Fenland Project have enabled construction of a series of maps showing the development of the Fenland throughout the last 10,000 years (Waller 1994a). These have confirmed the extension of marine flooding during the Iron Age and into the early Roman period, affecting the south and east Fen edges 600-800 years later than the north and west (Figure 2.5). There is also some support for a

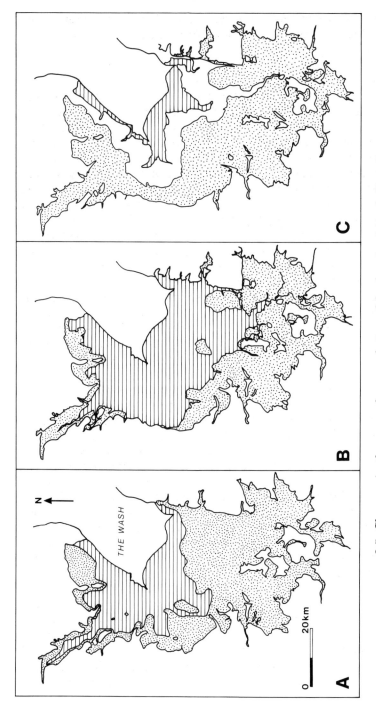

2.5: Changes in the area of accumulation of freshwater (stippled) and marine (hatched) deposits in the East Anglian Fenland. A: early Iron Age, B: early Roman, C: post-Roman. (Based on Waller 1994.)

regional fall in sea level in the Roman period, followed by an extension of the area of peat deposits (Waller 1994a, p. 79).

Summary of sea-level change and coastlines

It is likely that little of Britain's existing coastline is identical to that of any stage of the first millennium AD, but identification of past coastlines is problematic. The processes of uplift, erosion, silting and reclamation have varied around the coast to such an extent that no general reconstruction is possible. Most research has concentrated on trends in vertical sea level rather than on reconstructing coastal topography, and detailed maps of former coastlines are currently available only from the East Anglian Fens. Despite the limitations of the existing data, they at least alert us to the dynamic nature of the coastal zone and urge caution in interpreting the archaeological record of settlement in relation to current topography.

3

The Iron Age context

Introduction

By the end of the Iron Age much of Britain was densely settled by
communities principally involved in agriculture (Fowler 1983) (Figure
3.1). The density of this settlement itself suggests that large areas of the
landscape had been cleared of their original woodland cover. Field systems
of probable Iron Age date remain visible today in many parts of Britain,
again attesting to the extent of agricultural activity (Fowler 1983; Fleming
1987). Unfortunately, these fields are unlikely to be a representative
selection of what was originally present. Prehistoric field systems tend to
survive mainly in areas that later become marginal for cultivation, so that
their boundaries escaped damage by subsequent ploughing. For example,
Dartmoor was cleared of its original woodland and divided into a system

3.1: Reconstruction of an Iron Age farm at Butser, Hampshire.

of boundaries (reaves) in the Bronze Age, apparently for stock rearing (Fleming 1988). It is unclear how common such systems were elsewhere, but similar land divisions do occur on Bodmin Moor (Johnson & Rose 1994).

Structures and artefacts used in agriculture occur commonly on Iron Age sites (Fowler 1983; Rees 1979). These include grain storage pits and groups of post-holes thought to reflect the presence of timber granaries, remains of ploughs (ards), tools for harvesting, and implements for crop-processing such as quernstones. Structural evidence for animal husbandry is less obvious, as byres are difficult to distinguish on most sites, but some artefacts do seem to be associated with stock-herding, such as the metal points known as ox goads.

Remains of the plant and animal products of these agricultural systems also occur widely on archaeological sites. Animal bones are common where calcareous soil conditions favour their preservation – principally in central southern England (see reviews by Maltby 1981, 1996; Noddle 1984) – and suggest that cattle, sheep and pigs were the main animals exploited for food. The limited distribution of the data means that regional variations in animal husbandry are unclear. It appears, however, that sheep were kept mainly on well-drained downland areas, in preference to low-lying sites prone to flooding, probably because they are susceptible to infection by liver fluke (*Fasciola hepatica*) (Grant 1984). Cattle are less suited to downland sites as they need an abundant water supply, and so tended to be kept predominantly in lower-lying areas.

Horses are commonly represented in Iron Age bone assemblages, and were probably mainly used as pack animals and for transport. Horse-meat seems not to have been a major part of the human diet, although butchery marks have been found on the horse bones from some sites, such as the hillfort of Danebury, in Hampshire (Grant 1991). Dogs were also common-place in the Iron Age, and again sometimes show signs of butchery, although they were probably mainly kept for herding. Domestic fowl (*Gallus gallus*) had been introduced to Britain by the late Iron Age, and have been recorded at several sites, including Danebury (Coy 1984; Serjeantson 1991), Ashville, Abingdon (Bramwell 1978), and Gussage All Saints, Dorset (Harcourt 1979). A presumably accidental introduction during the Iron Age was the house mouse (*Mus musculus*), which has also been recorded at Gussage All Saints (Harcourt 1979) and Danebury (Coy 1984), as well as at Maiden Castle, Dorset (Armour-Chelu 1991). Access to stored grain and other foodstuffs presumably made human proximity attractive to the house mouse, although the presence of domestic cats must have made this lifestyle hazardous!

Remains of crops are usually found only where they have been charred, and until recently such evidence also came predominantly from the south of England (see reviews by M. Jones 1981, 1996; Greig 1991). This is due partly to the fact that pits apparently used for grain storage have been found at several sites in southern England, as at Danebury (Cunliffe 1984). After each period of use the pits were cleared of any mouldy or germinated grain by burning, before another harvest was stored (P.J. Reynolds 1981). The resulting charred cereal remains have provided an important source of evidence for Iron Age agriculture. In the north and west crops seem instead to have been stored in raised timber granaries, where they were unlikely to become charred unless the granary caught fire. Crop remains could, however, be exposed to fire at various stages before storage. Some cereals need to be exposed to heat ('parched') before they are threshed, and could easily become charred. In recent years there has been an increasing trend towards sampling a wide range of archaeological deposits for charred plant remains, in addition to the obvious storage features. Analysis of such deposits from sites in northern and western Britain (e.g. van der Veen 1992) is providing evidence for cereal cultivation in many areas generally assumed to have practised predominantly pastoral agriculture.

The main cereals grown in Britain in the Iron Age were spelt wheat (*Triticum spelta*) and hulled six-row barley (*Hordeum vulgare*) (M. Jones 1981, 1996; Greig 1991). Both can grow on a variety of soils. Spelt rarely seems to have been grown before the Iron Age, and barley, although in use from the Neolithic period, was now predominantly of the 'hulled' form. There was also some cultivation of emmer wheat (*Triticum dicoccum*), the principal wheat grown during the Neolithic and Bronze Age, and bread/club wheat (*Triticum aestivum / compactum*). Bread and club wheat are usually grouped together because they are rarely sufficiently well preserved in archaeological material to enable them to be identified separately. This type had been a minor crop since the Neolithic, but seems to have been used to a greater extent at some sites in the Iron Age.

Oats (*Avena*) also appear in assemblages from Iron Age sites, although in many cases the wild form (*Avena fatua*) may be represented. Rye (*Secale cereale*), a crop suited to a wide range of soils, occurs sparsely on some Iron Age sites and has, until recently, been considered to be an Iron Age or Roman introduction. Occurrences of rye pollen in off-site deposits of Bronze Age date, and a few records of rye grain from late Bronze Age archaeological sites, suggest an earlier presence, although not necessarily deliberate cultivation as a crop (F.M. Chambers & Jones 1984; F.M. Chambers 1989).

There are few indications that other crops were widely grown, although peas (*Pisum sativum*), 'Celtic bean' (*Vicia faba* var. *minor*) and flax (*Linum usitatissimum*) have been found in late Iron Age contexts at some sites. Flax provides a source of fibre and linseed oil, although it is uncertain how it was used in the Iron Age. Doubtless other plants were used, but they may not be preserved in archaeological contexts because of their method of preparation. Plant foods exposed directly to fire during processing or preparation are likely to be charred and so preserved, whereas foods prepared by boiling (such as leaf and root vegetables) are unlikely to be preserved.

Cereal cultivation seems to have been widespread in Iron Age Britain and was apparently, in at least some areas, highly productive. Experimental cultivation of crops at Butser Ancient Farm, Hampshire, clearly indicates that Iron Age crops and cultivation methods were capable of producing a substantial surplus (Figure 3.2). The yields of emmer and spelt, for example, were comparable to modern yields achieved prior to the use of chemicals (Reynolds 1981, 1995, p. 183).

3.2: Spelt wheat growing at the reconstruction of an Iron Age farm at Butser.

3. The Iron Age context

There are hints of changes in cultivation regime during the Iron Age. Martin Jones (1981, 1984) has argued that the replacement of emmer by spelt was linked to the expansion of arable into previously marginal areas, such as heavy or damp soils or in areas prone to frost. Conversely, the use of bread/club wheat may have been favoured by more intensive farming methods on the most favourable soils. Such methods, including deep ploughing, weeding, and the application of fertiliser, seem increasingly to have been used in the late Iron Age in some areas. By the end of the Iron Age there may, therefore, have been two contrasting cropping systems, one based on spelt and barley in shallow-ploughed fields infested with weeds, and the other based on bread/club wheat, rye, oats and beans in deep-ploughed and relatively weed-free fields (M. Jones 1991, 1996).

In an attempt to shed further light on changes in cereal cultivation in the Iron Age, van der Veen and Palmer (1997) planted experimental plots of emmer, spelt and club wheat at sites across Britain. Spelt produced higher yields than emmer in most areas, except for parts of the south. This increased yield would seem to provide an obvious incentive to grow spelt, but the results appear not to explain the changes in wheat cultivation in prehistoric Britain because the shift to spelt is first recorded in the south, where it seems to grow least well. Where there was a change from intensive to extensive cultivation regimes, spelt would have been favoured, however, as it competes better under such conditions (van der Veen 1992; van der Veen & O'Connor 1998).

Assemblages of cereal remains often include seeds of various weeds, apparently accidentally harvested with the crop. These weeds provide information on the type of land cultivated, time of sowing, and harvesting methods (Hillman 1981; Charles, Jones & Hodgson 1997). Many of these weeds were native plants, but some may have been introduced in the late Iron Age, such as the corn marigold (*Chrysanthemum segetum*) and cornflower (*Centaurea cyanus*).

Weed assemblages suggest that some of the soils cultivated in the Iron Age would today be considered marginal for agriculture. For example, the late Iron Age and early Roman settlement at Thorpe Thewles, near Durham, produced a large assemblage of weeds, especially heath-grass (*Danthonia decumbens*), accompanied by some grain and chaff, predominantly of spelt and barley (van der Veen 1987, 1992). Similar assemblages came from late Iron Age sites at Stanwick and Rock Castle, North Yorkshire (van der Veen 1992), and from Cefn Graeanog, north Wales (Hillman 1981). Heath-grass today is a plant of damp acid soils, and the abundance of this and other perennial weeds could reflect the use of former damp pasture for arable (Hillman 1981, p. 147; van der Veen 1992, pp. 137-8).

Similarly, weed remains from several sites in southern England indicate expansion of cultivation onto very damp soils. At the Upper Thames Valley sites of Farmoor (Lambrick & Robinson 1979) and Ashville (M. Jones 1978), for example, remains of the common spike-rush (*Eleocharis palustris*) – a plant of damp or waterlogged soils – were common amongst the cereal remains. This suggests that the rush was a weed of arable fields. Occasional records of stinking mayweed (*Anthemis cotula*) from Iron Age sites may indicate cultivation of heavy clay soils. At Ashville, finds of this plant were associated with evidence for artifical field drainage (M. Jones 1978, p. 109).

Clearly, Iron Age agriculture was by no means limited to the most favourable soils, perhaps suggesting that pressure on the land was considerable in some areas. The results of intensive land-use may also be indicated by an increasing frequency of weedy legumes in some late Iron Age crop assemblages. Legumes can grow in soils low in nitrogen, and their presence as weeds in crop assemblages may indicate the cultivation of nutrient-poor soils. This is also illustrated by sites in the Upper Thames Valley: at Ashville legume frequencies increased gradually from the mid-first millennium BC, while legume seeds were abundant in deposits of the late Iron Age/early Roman period at Mount Farm, Gravelly Guy and Claydon Pike (Lambrick 1992).

By the end of the Iron Age crops were being traded, perhaps over considerable distances. No certain link can therefore be made between the crop assemblage from a site and its local environment. For example, at least some of the cereals found at the hill-fort at Danebury may have been grown several kilometres from the site (M. Jones 1984).

An alternative approach to reconstructing the extent of arable land is to seek cereal pollen in off-site deposits. Such deposits are likely to reflect local cereal cultivation because cereal pollen is dispersed only short distances from the parent plant. Using pollen analysis the extent of potential agricultural land can also be reconstructed from the relative abundance of woodland and open land. Variations in this ratio may then provide evidence for fluctuations in land use over time.

Archaeological evidence suggests the possibility of a major phase of agricultural innovation in the late Iron Age (M. Jones 1981). If this involved an expansion in the area under cultivation, then it would be something we can look for in the pollen record.

Vegetation change in the first millennium BC

There are two main ways of approaching off-site pollen sequences in relation to the archaeological record of human activity. One is to examine individual pollen sequences, often covering several cultural phases, on a site-by-site basis. This gives a long-term perspective on environmental history around each site, but may lack chronological precision for specific parts of the sequence. The second is to focus on parts of the pollen record in relation to specific archaeological periods, and to compare as many pollen diagrams as possible over a large area to look for regional patterns.

3. The Iron Age context

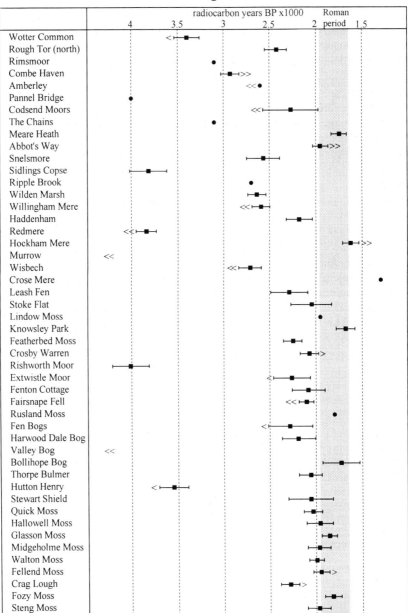

3.3a: Timing of the first extensive woodland clearance in England: date at which tree/shrub pollen percentages first fall below 50% (for at least two consecutive samples) at sites discussed in the text, arranged from south to north. Radiocarbon dates indicated by squares, with error bars at two standard deviations of the determination; interpolated dates indicated by circles; < immediately before, << before, > immediately after, >> after.

40

3. The Iron Age context

This approach requires particularly close chronological control, to enable accurate identification of the relevant part of each pollen sequence.

The first part of this section will look at the evidence for human impacts on the environment in the Iron Age on a regional basis, concentrating on the timing of the first major woodland clearance at sites where this event has been radiocarbon dated. The emphasis is on the off-site pollen record, but some on-site pollen assemblages are also discussed where they complement the off-site record. Later discussion will focus more closely on those pollen sequences that are sufficiently well dated to enable a reconstruction of the environment in the late Iron Age, on the eve of the Roman Conquest. In the following, it should be noted that interpretation of the sequences may not necessarily correspond with that of the original authors.

In Figure 3.3 the date at which extensive woodland clearance first occurred is plotted for selected sites for which the published pollen data and radiocarbon dates enable this point to be identified with reasonable confidence. Extensive clearance is here defined as the point at which tree/shrub pollen frequencies first fall to values at or below 50% of the total count of pollen and spores of vascular plants (excluding obligate aquatics). Obviously, clearance will usually have begun at an earlier date, a point which must be remembered when comparing Figure 3.3 with the pattern of clearance described in the text. As several different pollen sums have been used by the original authors of the sequences, some of the original

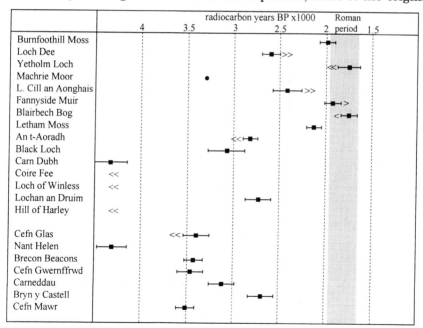

3.3b: Timing of the first extensive woodland clearance in Scotland and Wales. For details see Figure 3.3a.

41

data have had to be recalculated. Analysts of peat sequences often exclude from the sum plants that may have grown on the bog surface, especially ferns and members of the heather family (Ericaceae). These plants may, however, also have grown on dry land. The approach adopted here is to use a standard basis for calculation of tree and shrub pollen frequencies at all sites. It should be noted that, in this calculation, heathers are excluded from the shrub category (some analysts include them as shrubs). Where over-representation of local herb-dominated vegetation may have had a significant impact on peat sequences, this is discussed in the text. Locations of sites in Figure 3.3, and of other sites mentioned in this chapter, are shown in Figure 3.4.

A clear trend seems to emerge from Figure 3.3 of a wide spread of dates for extensive clearance in the southern half of England, mainly in the

3.4: Locations of sites discussed in relation to vegetational reconstruction for the Iron Age.

1. Hill of Harley/
   Freswick Links
2. Loch of Winless
3. Lochan an Druim
4. Loch Cleat
5. Loch Ashik
6. Loch Meodal
7. Loch Davan
8. Braeroddach Loch
9. Coire Fee
10. Carn Dubh
11. Black Loch
12. Letham Moss
13. Fannyside Muir
14. Blairbech Bog
15. An t-Aoradh
16. Loch Cill an Aonghais
17. Machrie Moor
18. Cranley Moss
19. Dogden Moss
20. Yetholm Loch
21. The Dod
22. Loch Dee
23. Ellergower Moss
24. Carsegowan Moss
25. Burnfoothill Moss
26. Glasson Moss
27. Bolton Fell Moss
28. Walton Moss
29. Midgeholme Moss
30. Fellend Moss
31. Crag Lough

32. Fozy Moss
33. Steng Moss
34. Quick Moss
35. Stewart Shield
    Meadow
36. Bollihope Bog
37. Valley Bog
38. Hallowell Moss
39. Hutton Henry
40. Thorpe Bulmer
41. Harwood Dale Bog
42. Fen Bogs
43. Willow Garth
44. Rusland Moss
45. Fairsnape Fell
46. Fenton Cottage
47. Extwistle Moor
48. Rishworth Moor
49. Featherbed Moss
50. Lindow Moss
51. Knowsley Park
52. Crosby Warren/
    Dragonby
53. Stoke Flat
54. Leash Fen
55. Cefn Mawr
56. Bryn y Castell
57. Crose Mere
58. Fenemere
59. The Breiddin
60. Carneddau
61. Tregaron Bog

62. Cefn Gwernffrwd
63. Brecon Beacons
64. Nant Helen
65. Cefn Glas
66. Wilden Marsh
67. Ripple Brook
68. Sidlings Copse
69. Port Meadow
70. Farmoor
71. Mingies Ditch
72. Snelsmore
73. Murrow
74. Wisbech
75. Hockham Mere
76. Redmere
77. Haddenham
78. Willingham Mere
79. Robertsbridge
80. Sharpsbridge
81. Stream Farm
82. Combe Haven Valley
83. Pannel Bridge
84. Amberley
85. Rimsmoor
86. Glastonbury
87. Meare
88. Meare Heath
89. Abbot's Way
90. Codsend Moors
91. The Chains
92. Rough Tor
93. Wotter Common

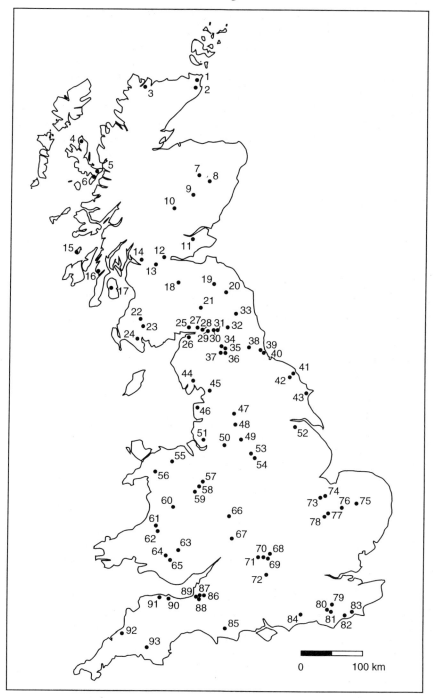

Bronze Age and early Iron Age. There is a trend towards later clearance moving north, where much of the landscape remained predominantly wooded until at least the mid-late Iron Age. The southern half of Scotland seems to continue this trend of late clearance, but in the far north some areas never developed dense woodland due to climatic constraints on tree growth. In Wales there are fewer sites, mostly from upland areas, but these suggest substantial clearance from the Bronze Age. These and other sites are now considered in more detail in regional groups, in an attempt to highlight patterns in clearance histories prior to the first millennium AD.

Regional patterns in Iron Age and earlier vegetational history

South-east England

From south-east England most of the radiocarbon-dated pollen sequences spanning the Iron Age come from peat and alluvial deposits in Sussex. One of the most detailed sequences is from peat deposits at Pannel Bridge, on the south coast (Waller 1993). This shows woodland disturbance from the early Bronze Age, continuing through to the Iron Age, when the area seems to have been almost entirely open. Unfortunately, the chronology of subsequent environmental change is uncertain, as there are no radiocarbon dates after the early Iron Age.

Later developments are illustrated by the sequence from Amberley, further west. Here, major woodland clearance apparently began in the Bronze Age, followed by woodland regeneration in the late Bronze Age or early Iron Age (Waton 1982, 1983). Clearance continued, with a further interruption, throughout the Iron Age, and by the late Iron Age or early Roman period the landscape must have been almost entirely open.

A further insight into the history of clearance in this area is provided by the study of alluvial valley fills. The Combe Haven valley, in the Weald of east Sussex, contains organic deposits overlain by mineral-rich material, apparently derived from erosion of the local hill-slopes (Smyth & Jennings 1988). Pollen analysis suggested that creation of the minerogenic floodplain was linked with a major decline in the extent of catchment woodland in the late Bronze Age, implying a similar history of clearance to that at Amberley.

Analysis of valley fills elsewhere in Sussex, including the Ouse valley at Sharpsbridge, the Cuckmere valley at Stream Farm, and the Rother valley at Robertsbridge, has prompted the suggestion that alluviation occurred from at least the Neolithic period (Scaife & Burrin 1983, 1985, 1987). Doubt must be cast on this interpretation, however, as these sequences lack radiocarbon dates, and much of the pollen in the alluvium is likely to be reworked from earlier deposits.

3. The Iron Age context

Further west, a pollen sequence from Snelsmore, on the Berkshire Downs, shows that significant clearance of local woodland began at approximately the end of the Bronze Age or in the early Iron Age, at 2570±90 BP (HAR-4241, 900-410 cal BC) (Waton 1982, 1983). This clearance was apparently closely followed by a minor phase of woodland regeneration – perhaps comparable to the regeneration episode at Amberley. After this, clearance continued throughout the Iron Age and into the early Roman period, although much woodland remained.

Evidence for major Bronze Age clearance in the Oxford region comes from a valley mire at Sidlings Copse (Day 1991, 1993) (Figure 3.5), where much of the original woodland on dry land was cleared in the first half of the Bronze Age. A period of woodland regeneration followed at the end of the Bronze Age and probably into the early Iron Age, but the landscape still remained predominantly open. The secondary woodland began to be removed again from a level dated 2350±70 BP (OxA-2048, 800-200 cal BC), and this process continued throughout the Iron Age.

The course of woodland removal at Sidlings Copse can be compared with the pattern of environmental change in the Upper Thames Valley overall provided by deposits of alluvium. Archaeological sites stratified within alluvium have enabled an assessment of the timing of water-table fluctuations and periods of soil erosion. These indicate a rise of the water table in the floodplain between the mid-late Bronze Age and the mid-Iron Age (M. Robinson & Lambrick 1984). By the mid-late Iron Age flooding had begun on some sites, and alluviation began in the late Iron Age or Roman period. These changes appear to reflect a response to human activity rather than climate change. The rise of water table presumably reflects the loss of woodland cover which, accompanied by agricultural activity, increased movement of sediment into water courses.

The rising water table preserved a range of biological remains on archaeological sites on the floodplain, and these remains provide an indication of the nature of the local environment. The enclosure ditches around an Iron Age settlement at Mingies Ditch contained pollen assemblages suggesting that the site lay in an area of damp grassland with willows (*Salix*) (M. Robinson 1981; Lambrick & Robinson 1988). Analysis of beetles and macroscopic plant remains confirmed the local presence of grassland. Similar results came from the Iron Age settlements at Port Meadow and Farmoor (M. Robinson 1981; Lambrick & Robinson 1988).

Conclusion. In south-east England major woodland clearance occurred during the course of the Bronze Age. Several sites indicate a period of woodland regeneration towards the end of the Bronze Age or in the early Iron Age, suggesting a reduction in the extent of agricultural activity. This was followed by a major increase of clearance, and by the end of the Iron Age most of the landscape seems to have been devoid of woodland. Cereal cultivation was apparently widespread, and the loss of woodland cover,

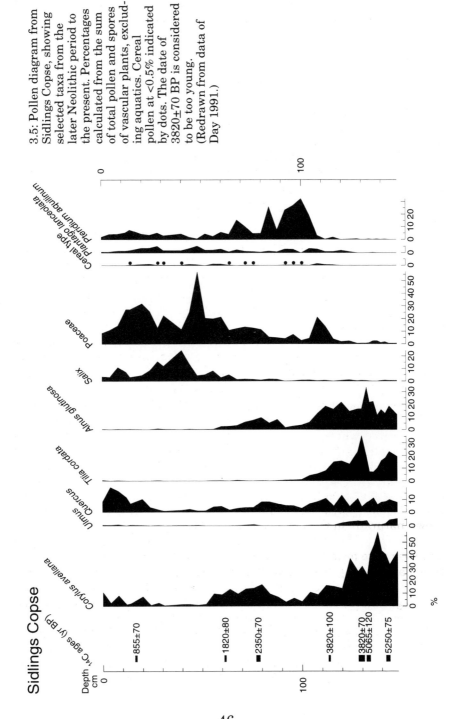

3.5: Pollen diagram from Sidlings Copse, showing selected taxa from the later Neolithic period to the present. Percentages calculated from the sum of total pollen and spores of vascular plants, excluding aquatics. Cereal pollen at <0.5% indicated by dots. The date of 3820±70 BP is considered to be too young. (Redrawn from data of Day 1991.)

combined with agricultural activity, seems to have resulted in major soil erosion and the onset of alluviation in at least some river valleys.

East Anglia

East Anglia provides a major source of pollen sequences for reconstructing the Iron Age environment, both from the peat deposits of the Fens and the widespread lakes (meres). In particular, the Fenland Project has provided a large body of information relating to sea-level change, environmental history, and human settlement for the area around the Wash (D. Hall & Coles 1994). Reconstructing the vegetational history of this area is complicated by the fact that the effects of human land-use are superimposed on the natural variations in local vegetation caused by sea-level changes and flooding (see Chapter 2). Rising water levels during the Iron Age resulted in inundation of much of the area closest to the Wash, although the southern Fens seem to have escaped marine incursions (Waller 1994a).

One of the most detailed pollen sequences from the area comes from Redmere, a former lake in the south-eastern part of the Fens. Woodland seems already to have been sparse by the Iron Age, and apparently disappeared entirely at the end of the Iron Age or start of the Roman period – just below a level dated 1850±50 BP (Q-2593, cal AD 50-260), at which time cereals may have been cultivated locally (Waller 1994b).

Willingham Mere is another former lake, in the south-central Fens (Waller 1994c). The site seems to have been largely deforested, and perhaps cultivated, when rising water levels caused accumulation of organic deposits to begin in the late Bronze Age or early Iron Age. At the end of the Iron Age or in the early Roman period (1910±60 BP, Q-2582, 60 cal BC-cal AD 240) the area seems to have become drier and local fen woodland developed, although some areas probably still supported both arable and pastoral agriculture. A record of 'Cannabis type' pollen immediately above the dated horizon could reflect local cultivation or processing of hemp (*Cannabis sativa*) for fibre. There are no Iron Age macroscopic remains of hemp recorded from Britain, however, and it is perhaps more likely that this pollen comes from hop (*Humulus lupulus*), which may have grown naturally in the fen environment (see Chapter 1).

Just 1km to the north-east, at Haddenham an organic deposit overlying clays began to form at the end of the Bronze Age and accumulated until a level dated 2180±70 BP (CAR-771, 400-80 cal BC), after which deposition of silty deposits suggests flooding (Cloutman 1994). Willow and alder (*Alnus glutinosa*) carr occurred here during the Iron Age, although there were some open areas and cereals may have been cultivated locally.

Further Iron Age peat deposits sandwiched between silty clays occurred at Murrow and Wisbech, in the central area of the Fens. At Murrow, peat accumulation spanned virtually the whole of the Iron Age until 2130±50 BP (Q-2590, 270-40 cal BC), when the site again appears to have undergone marine flooding (Waller 1994d). During the first half of the Iron Age conditions seem to have been open, but there was increasing development of woodland in the latter half of the period. At Wisbech analysis of organic deposits spanning most of the Iron Age indicated substantial areas of fen carr woodland before marine inundation in the late Iron Age (Alderton & Waller 1994a, b).

Away from the Fens, a rather different perspective on the East Anglian landscape is provided by Hockham Mere, a former lake on the edge of the Breckland in Norfolk. Two radiocarbon-dated pollen diagrams have been produced from the site (Sims 1978; K.D. Bennett 1983) and there are discrepancies between the timing of human environmental impacts suggested by each: the radiocarbon dates from Sims' sequence are consistently older than those obtained by Bennett. The former sequence may have been affected by inwash of older organic material, so Bennett's chronology is followed here. Woodland clearance appears to have begun rather later than elsewhere in the south, in the first half of the Iron Age. The spread of heathland began in the late Iron Age or early Roman period, immediately below a level dated 1980±50 BP (Q-2224, 110 cal BC-cal AD 120). Cereals, including rye, were cultivated locally in the Iron Age, but the landscape remained predominantly wooded.

Conclusion. Most of the pollen evidence for the Iron Age environment of East Anglia comes from the Fenland area, which seems to have undergone major clearance in the Bronze Age. There was a further reduction in the extent of the little remaining woodland in the Iron Age, accompanied by evidence for cereal cultivation. Several areas developed fen carr woodland towards the end of the Iron Age, before marine inundation. In contrast, the Breckland landscape remained substantially wooded up to and throughout most of the Iron Age, with the spread of heathland beginning in the late Iron Age or early Roman period.

South-west England

The vegetational history of an area peripheral to the Dorset chalklands is illustrated by a pollen diagram from organic deposits in a solution hollow at Rimsmoor (Waton 1982, 1983). Woodland clearance began in the Bronze Age, but was interrupted by regeneration in approximately the early Iron Age – a similar pattern to that seen at many of the sites in the south-east. This was followed by renewed clearance which peaked at a level dated 2080±80 BP (HAR-3923, 270 cal BC-cal AD 70), and then further regeneration. Pollen grains of rye and 'Cannabis type' (probably hop) occur in part of the sequence dated approximately to the late Iron Age or early Roman period.

Further west, the wetlands of the Somerset Levels have yielded an abundance of evidence for environmental change, associated with the discovery of prehistoric wooden trackways and settlements (Coles & Coles

1986) (Figure 3.6). The Meare Heath trackway is of Bronze Age date, and the pollen sequence from the site indicates a decline of hazel (*Corylus avellana*) pollen shortly before construction of the track. Much of the landscape on dry land areas apparently remained wooded until well after this phase, however, and there was no major increase of clearance until the latter half of the Iron Age, at a level dated 2062±45 BP (SRR-912, 200 cal BC-cal AD 30) (Beckett & Hibbert 1979). Cereals seem to have been cultivated locally from this date, but much woodland remained.

3.6: Reconstruction of the landscape of the Somerset Levels. (Painting by John Pearson, © The British Museum.)

3.7: Rough Tor, Bodmin Moor. Remains of settlements and field systems, probably of Bronze Age date.

The Abbot's Way pollen sequence, 3km to the south-east, was associated with a late Neolithic trackway. The sequence unfortunately ends just after a level dated 1954±40 BP (SRR-1011, 60 cal BC-cal AD 130), so the final Iron Age deposits may be missing. Woodland clearance began in approximately the mid-Iron Age, at a level dated 2322±45 BP (SRR-1013, 550-200 cal BC), and was probably accompanied by cereal cultivation (Beckett & Hibbert 1979).

Also in the Levels, the late Iron Age 'lake villages' of Glastonbury and Meare (Bulleid & Gray 1911, 1917, 1948, 1953; Coles 1987; Coles & Minnitt 1995) have provided a focus for palaeoenvironmental research. Pollen sequences from the vicinity of these sites illustrate an increase of clearance and cereal cultivation on adjacent dry land areas from the late Bronze Age (Caseldine 1986, 1988; Housley 1988a, b), coinciding with a regional trend towards increasingly wetter conditions (Caseldine 1988; Housley 1988a, and see Chapter 2).

Moving west to the uplands of Exmoor, pollen analysis of blanket peat deposits from a plateau site known as The Chains indicated that the site was predominantly open by the mid-Bronze Age (Merryfield & Moore 1974; Moore, Merryfield & Price 1984). Local clearance, accompanied by cereal cultivation, increased from approximately the mid-Iron Age – between levels dated 2335±260 (UB-819, 1100 cal BC-cal AD 300) and 2215±90 BP (UB-817, 420-10 cal BC) – and continued into the Roman period. Shallower peat deposits from Codsend Moors apparently began to accumulate in the Iron Age – although the large error term for the basal date of 2270±150 BP (I-16,087, 800 cal BC-cal AD 0) leaves room for doubt. By this time the landscape had a mixture of wooded and open areas (Francis & Slater 1992).

Pollen analysis has also been undertaken on peat deposits from Dartmoor (Caseldine & Maguire 1981; Caseldine & Hatton 1996), partly in association with the excavations of Bronze Age reaves mentioned earlier (Fleming 1988). Unfortunately, most of these sequences have acceptable radiocarbon dates only for pre-Iron Age deposits. The Wotter Common sequence on Shaugh Moor is of interest, however, in indicating a substantially open landscape from the mid-Bronze Age, before the reave system was laid out (K. Smith et al. 1981). There is only a single record for cereal pollen until well after a level dated 2520±80 BP (HAR-3816, 810-410 cal BC), suggesting that initial clearance, at least, was predominantly to provide pasture. On other parts of the moor clearance seems to have begun later, and may have been more closely linked to construction of the reave system (Balaam, Smith & Wainwright 1982).

On Bodmin Moor, Cornwall, archaeological research has suggested a similar peak of activity in the Bronze Age, including settlements and field systems (Johnson & Rose 1994). Pollen analysis has been undertaken on peat deposits from Rough Tor, on the northern edge of the moor (Gearey & Charman 1996) (Figure 3.7), close to a hill-top enclosure of possible Neolithic date. The date for the onset of major clearance in the Rough Tor South sequence is uncertain as the corresponding radiocarbon date appears to be anomalous, but extrapolation from the rest of the dates suggests much removal of woodland from the Neolithic period. Some woodland regeneration seems to have occurred after this, but renewed clearance from the mid-late Bronze Age resulted in a landscape almost devoid of woodland. A return of woodland commenced below a level dated 1675±45 BP (OxA-6007, 230-450 cal AD), but the pollen diagram is insufficiently detailed to enable the date of onset of this regeneration to be estimated. At Rough Tor north (monolith C), c. 1.5km away, peat deposition apparently did not begin until perhaps the late Bronze Age, at which time the local landscape seems to have remained substantially wooded. The sequence records the creation of a largely open landscape in the Iron Age, at 2430±60 BP (Beta-78542, 770-400 cal BC). This late clearance is apparently in conflict with the archaeological evidence from the moor, which has been interpreted as suggesting abandonment of some areas in the Iron Age (Todd 1987). Unfortunately, problems of dating the pollen sequences, and their poor chronological resolution, mean that further research will be needed to resolve this issue.

Conclusion. Rimsmoor in Dorset records a pattern of vegetational changes similar to those further east, with a period of woodland regeneration in the early Iron Age, following clearance from the Bronze Age. From the wetlands of the Somerset Levels clearance began at dates ranging from the mid-Bronze Age to late Iron Age. Here more woodland survived than elsewhere in southern England, presumably because the damp soils were less suitable for agricultural purposes. The uplands of Dartmoor, Exmoor and Bodmin Moor were extensively cleared in the mid-Bronze Age, and apparently earlier in some areas.

The Midlands

The Midlands, and especially the centre of the region, present a major void in the distribution of pollen sequences spanning the Iron Age, and indeed earlier and later periods. This is largely due to a scarcity of suitable pollen-bearing deposits from the area.

The available pollen sequences are concentrated in the northern part of the region, in the Peak District. At Leash Fen minor disturbances throughout the Bronze Age were followed by major clearance, affecting predominantly hazel, dated 2290±100 BP (GaK-2288, 800-100 cal BC) (Hicks 1971). This was followed by a period of woodland regeneration immediately above a level dated 2090±100 BP (GaK-2289, 390 cal BC-cal AD 80). Unfortunately the latter date is questionable, in view of a result of 2110±100 BP (GaK-2290, 390 cal BC-cal AD 70) from *c.* 1m further up the sequence. In fact, the date centred on 2290 BP may also be problematic, as both deviate markedly from the pattern of accumulation suggested by the radiocarbon dates from the rest of the sequence. At 1910±100 BP (GaK-2291, 200 cal BC-cal AD 350) a new phase of clearance began, associated with pollen evidence for cereal cultivation.

At Stoke Flat, just 5km north-west of Leash Fen, pollen analysis was undertaken on peat deposits associated with a prehistoric field system, providing a rare opportunity to investigate the period and type of use of the fields (D.J. Long, Chambers & Barnatt 1998). The fields were probably laid out in the second millennium BC and continued in use, apparently for cereal cultivation, into the first millennium BC. Much woodland survived in the area, despite the arable activity. From the pollen sequence a date in the Iron Age or early Roman period – 2050±110 BP (Beta-52534, 400-cal AD 200) – was obtained for a major decline of alder and increase of grasses, apparently post-dating the arable use of the fields. The changes in the pollen record were attributed to a switch towards pastoralism and abandonment of woodland management, with woodland areas being lost due to unrestricted browsing by livestock.

At Featherbed Moss, 20km north of Stoke Flat, woodland clearance and cereal cultivation began in the mid-Iron Age, dated 2251±50 BP (Q-854, 400-190 cal BC) (Tallis & Switsur 1973). This is similar to the results from Leash Fen, suggesting that much of the Peak District first experienced major woodland clearance in the mid-late Iron Age, despite a prolonged earlier history of cereal cultivation.

To the south-west, Crose Mere in Shropshire shows an earlier episode of clearance, in the early Bronze Age, but this was followed by woodland recovery in the first half of the Iron Age (Beales 1980). Renewed clearance and cereal cultivation began just below a level dated 2086±75 BP (Q-1232, 260 cal BC-cal AD 70), but the landscape seems to have remained well wooded in the Iron Age (Figure 3.8). A single record of 'Cannabaceae' pollen in the early-mid Iron Age deposits probably represents hop at this early date.

Also in Shropshire is the site of Fenemere, a small lake approximately 1.5km south-east of the hill-fort known as The Berth of Baschurch. The four radiocarbon dates from the pollen sequence suggest deposition from the latter half of the Bronze Age into the post-Roman period, but two dates from the lower half of the sequence, separated by half a metre of deposit, are effectively identical, while the two upper dates, separated by only 10cm, differ by over a thousand years (Barber & Twigger 1987; Twigger & Haslam 1997). Twigger suggests that some of the dates may have been affected by inwash of older organic material due to disturbance in the catchment, but there is a problem in identifying which of the dates may have been affected in this way. Tentatively, it appears that woodland clearance and sporadic cereal cultivation began in the latter half of the Bronze Age. Clearance peaked at a level dated 2940±60 BP (SRR-2921, 1320-990 cal BC), suggested by the Twigger to be too old. Woodland regeneration followed at a level dated 1890±50 BP (SRR-2920, cal AD 0-240), but the uncertainty over other dates in the sequence casts doubt on this one also.

To the south, study of floodplain deposits of the Ripple Brook, a tributary of the River Severn, provides another perspective on landscape change (A.G. Brown & Barber 1985). A major increase of sediment deposition occurred in the late Bronze Age and early Iron Age, apparently reflecting soil erosion due to deforestation and agriculture. Pollen analysis of the deposits indicated a major decline in the extent of woodland in this period, followed by removal of all remaining woodland from the catchment between 2570±50 BP (SRR-1908, 730-520 cal BC) and 2350±50 BP (SRR-1907, 800-350 cal BC).

A similar sequence of events is recorded at Wilden Marsh, on the River Stour (A.G. Brown 1988). Here almost total deforestation occurred towards the end of the Bronze Age, at a level dated 2640±50 BP (SRR-2827, 920-760 cal BC), again apparently linked with agricultural activity.

To the east, in Lincolnshire, archaeological excavations at the Iron Age and Roman settlement of Dragonby (May 1996) provided the impetus for

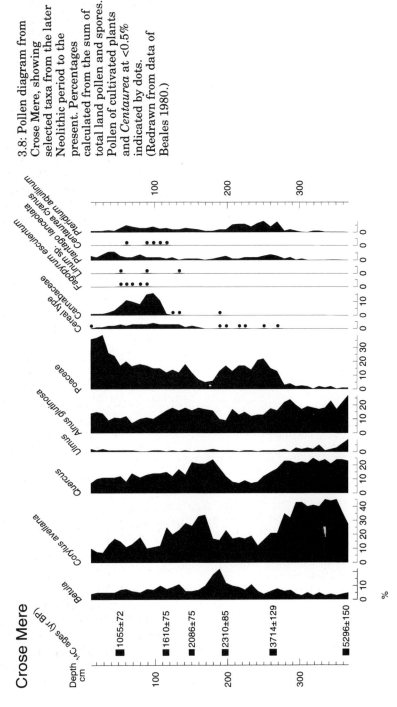

3.8: Pollen diagram from Crose Mere, showing selected taxa from the later Neolithic period to the present. Percentages calculated from the sum of total land pollen and spores. Pollen of cultivated plants and *Centaurea* at <0.5% indicated by dots. (Redrawn from data of Beales 1980.)

54

production of several short pollen sequences from peat deposits buried below sand at Crosby Warren, 1km to the south-east. One of the organic sequences had a basal date of 2285±70 BP (UB-860, 550-100 cal BC), coinciding with a decline of elm (*Ulmus*) and lime (*Tilia*), and minor increase of grasses, in an environment dominated by woodland of oak (*Quercus*), alder and hazel (Halland 1996). Major clearance began later (20cm higher up the sequence), although the date is uncertain. A radiocarbon date of 1640±435 BP (UB-862, 800 cal BC-cal AD 1300) from deposits 60cm above the onset of this clearance is obviously of little help due to its large range. A second pollen profile suggests local cereal cultivation, in a landscape of mixed woodland and open land, by a level dated 2070±50 BP (UB-859, 210 cal BC-cal AD 30).

Pollen analysis was also undertaken on the ditches of the Iron Age settlement at Dragonby. These assemblages were dominated by tree pollen, especially of alder. Macroscopic remains of trees and shrubs were also abundant (Hayes 1996). This suggests that woodland remained a conspicuous element of the local landscape during occupation of the settlement, a picture not inconsistent with that from Crosby Warren.

Conclusion. The Midlands sites form a rather disparate group, fringing the area while leaving the centre as a void. For several of the sequences there are uncertainties over the chronology, and a range of dates for the onset of major clearance occurs, ranging from the early Bronze Age to the mid-Iron Age.

North-west England

North-west England has been the focus of intensive palaeoecological survey in recent years, largely as a result of the work of the North West Wetlands Survey. This has led to the production of several new pollen sequences, of which the most detailed are from Fenton Cottage, in the lowlands around Over Wyre, Lancashire (Middleton, Wells & Huckerby 1995; Wells, Huckerby & Hall 1997) and Knowsley Park, Merseyside (Cowell & Innes 1994). At Fenton Cottage major clearance apparently began at a level dated 2080±90 BP (GU-5159, 370 cal BC-cal AD 80) and peaked at 1810±90 (GU-5157, cal AD 10-420), at which point cereals may have been grown locally (Figure 3.9). At Knowsley Park clearance apparently began at a similar date, in the late Iron Age or early Roman period, but the landscape remained substantially wooded and there is no indication of cereal cultivation.

Pollen analysis of upland peat deposits on Extwistle Moor, Lancashire, revealed that much of the landscape had already been cleared of woodland when the peat began to accumulate in the late Bronze Age (Bartley & Chambers 1992). A major decline in the extent of remaining woodland dated 2260±100 BP (Birm-689, 800-50 cal BC) was followed by regenera-

Fenton Cottage

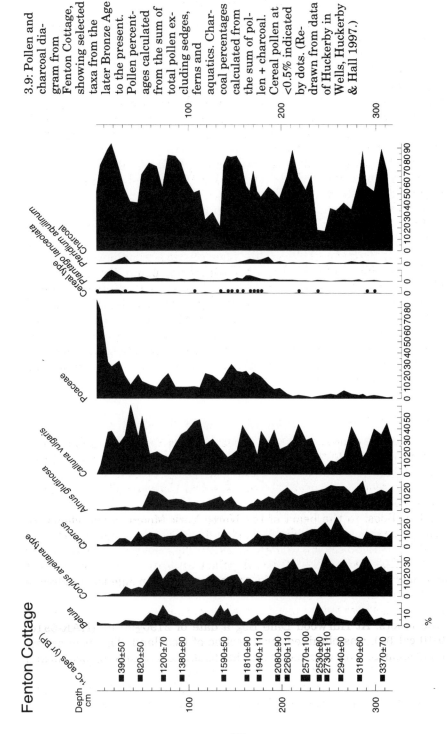

3.9: Pollen and charcoal diagram from Fenton Cottage, showing selected taxa from the later Bronze Age to the present. Pollen percentages calculated from the sum of total pollen excluding sedges, ferns and aquatics. Charcoal percentages calculated from the sum of pollen + charcoal. Cereal pollen at <0.5% indicated by dots. (Redrawn from data of Huckerby in Wells, Huckerby & Hall 1997.)

tion, and then a later further decline of woodland in the late Roman or post-Roman periods.

A particularly detailed pollen diagram has been produced from Fairsnape Fell in the Forest of Bowland, central Pennines (Mackay & Tallis 1994). Here blanket peat formation began in approximately the mid-Iron Age, by which time much woodland had already been cleared, and cereals were grown locally. Further clearance occurred in the late Iron Age or at the start of the Roman period, from a level dated 2025±40 BP (SRR-4506, 120 cal BC-cal AD 70).

Lindow Moss in Cheshire is well known for the discovery in 1984 of 'Lindow Man', part of a late Iron Age or early Roman body preserved in the peat (Stead, Bourke & Brothwell 1986). Other human remains have also come from the site, including another near-complete body known as Lindow III (R. Turner & Scaife 1995). Pollen analysis of deposits close to the site of discovery of these remains showed limited woodland clearance from a level dated 2345±45 BP (UB-3239, 550-350 cal BC), with indications of cereal cultivation later in the Iron Age (Branch & Scaife 1995).

Conclusion. Pollen sequences from north-west England suggest major clearance of upland areas in the Bronze Age and early-mid Iron Age. In the lowlands clearance appears to have occurred later, from the second half of the Iron Age. Unfortunately, however, more pollen sequences are needed to establish whether this apparent difference reflects a real divergence between upland and lowland areas in terms of their vegetational history, or if local site factors are involved.

North-east England

Many pollen sequences have been produced from Yorkshire, and particularly from the North York Moors, but the focus of attention has been on the Mesolithic and Neolithic periods (summarized by I.G. Simmons *et al.* 1993). Few sequences cover the Iron Age and later periods, and most of these are poorly dated.

At Fen Bogs, in the heart of the North York Moors, major clearance probably began in the Iron Age, immediately below a level dated 2280±120 BP (T-1085, 800-50 cal BC) (Atherden 1976). This clearance corresponded with the first occurrence of cereal pollen and an increase of ribwort plantain (*Plantago lanceolata*). By the end of the Iron Age the landscape had little remaining woodland.

An Iron Age date for the onset of major clearance is apparent elsewhere on the Moors. At Harwood Dale Bog a date of 2190±90 BP (HAR-5916, 410-10 cal BC), was obtained for a decline of woodland. This was apparently associated with a spread of heather (*Calluna vulgaris*) moorland and local cereal cultivation (I.G. Simmons *et al.* 1993).

A contrasting environment is provided by Willow Garth on the Yorkshire Wolds (Bush & Flenley 1987; Bush 1993). Here a shallow organic deposit spans the whole of the last two millennia, but later Mesolithic to Iron Age deposits seem to be at least partly missing. It has been claimed that the sequence demonstrates the continuous presence of chalk grassland around the site since the end of the last glacial, but the breaks in the sequence mean that this interpretation is doubtful (see discussions by K.D. Thomas 1989, and Day 1996). Deposits of the late, but apparently not earlier, Iron Age do seem to be represented. In the late Iron Age there was almost no local woodland, and cereals may have been cultivated locally.

To the west, in the Pennines, a pollen sequence from blanket peat on Rishworth Moor (Bartley 1975) shows rather open conditions since at least the Neolithic period. Some of the remaining woodland was removed in the early Bronze Age, followed by another clearance phase in the first half of the Iron Age. This continued through to a peak in the late Iron Age or early Roman period, at 1920±80 BP (GaK-2825, 110 cal BC-cal AD 260). Heather, grasses, ribwort plantain and bracken (*Pteridium aquilinum*) all increased, and cereals were probably cultivated locally in the mid-Iron Age. Woodland seems to have been sparse at this time, but immediately above the dated level major woodland regeneration began, suggesting an abandonment of substantial areas of agricultural land.

Conclusion. In north-east England the Iron Age seems to have seen the onset of major woodland clearance, associated in upland areas with a spread of heather moorland. Cereals seem to have been widely cultivated, at upland and lowland sites.

Northern England

Northern England has the densest coverage of pollen sequences spanning the Iron Age and later periods from any part of Britain. There is a particular concentration of sites within 20km of Hadrian's Wall (Figure 4.9), and research has focused on the effects of Roman occupation of the area, and the extent to which woodland was cleared before the Roman period. This issue was first addressed by Judith Turner in the late 1970s (J. Turner 1979), on the basis of nine radiocarbon-dated pollen sequences from the eastern part of the region. She argued that the landscape remained densely wooded up to, and during most of, the Iron Age, but that major clearance occurred in the late Iron Age.

Since the 1970s much new research has been undertaken on the environmental history of the area, and the issues of the purpose and timing of woodland clearance have remained controversial. It may have been part of a general agricultural expansion by native farmers (Hanson 1996; Tipping 1997), or could have been undertaken by the Roman military who arrived in the area in the AD 70s-80s and built Hadrian's Wall in the AD 120s-130s (Dumayne 1993, 1994; Dumayne & Barber 1994). The reliance on radiocarbon dating means that the chronological control of pollen sequences is usually insufficiently precise to enable separation of latest Iron Age from early Roman clearance activity (Dumayne *et al.* 1995). Here, discussion will concentrate on aspects of environmental change most likely to have occurred in the Iron Age, but there will inevitably be some overlap with possible Roman-period events (discussed in Chapter 4).

Several pollen sequences have been produced from sites within 500m of the line that was to become the Roman frontier. From east to west these are Fozy Moss, Crag Lough, Fellend Moss, Midgeholme Moss and Glasson Moss. The pollen record suggests that much of the landscape remained substantially wooded until the mid-Iron Age, but with some areas of cereal cultivation. Dates for the onset of major clearance episodes range from immediately after 2280±50 BP (AA-28173, 410-190 cal BC) at Crag Lough (P. Dark forthcoming), 2215±45 BP (SRR-4534, 400-180 cal BC) at Glasson Moss (Dumayne & Barber 1994), just before 2100±60 BP (GU-5082, 260 cal BC-cal AD 20) at Midgeholme Moss (Wiltshire 1997), to just above a level dated 1948±45 BP (SRR-876, 90 cal BC-cal AD 140) at Fellend Moss (Davies & Turner 1979). At Midgeholme the initial clearance was immediately followed by a minor episode of regeneration (mainly of alder), then a further increase of clearance dated 1970±60 BP (GU-5081, 120 cal BC-cal AD 150) (Wiltshire 1997).

At Fozy Moss there appears to have been no major clearance until the Roman period, beginning at 1820±45 BP (SRR-4539, cal AD 80-260) (Dumayne & Barber 1994) (Figure 4.11). Crag Lough is only 6km west of Fozy Moss, and the difference in the timing of clearance at these sites may reflect local variation in land-use due to soil conditions. Crag Lough was surrounded by well-drained soils suitable for cultivation, and indeed the pollen sequence suggests that cereals were grown locally throughout the Iron Age (Figures 3.10 and 4.12). The wetter soils around Fozy Moss seem to have been cleared only when it was necessary for establishment of the Roman frontier, as cereal pollen occurs only sporadically in the pre-Roman deposits (see Chapter 4).

At Fellend Moss the clearance could be either late Iron or Roman in date. It involved substantial increases of grasses, ribwort plantain and heather, followed by the first record of cereal pollen. This sequence might reflect the creation of new areas of pasture by native farmers, or clearance of the military zone before construction of Hadrian's Wall, immediately next to the site.

Moving further from the area of the later Hadrianic frontier there is a similar variability in the dates for woodland clearance. At Walton Moss clearance began in approximately the mid-late Iron Age and peaked in the late Iron Age or early Roman period, immediately above a level dated 2000±40 BP (SRR-4531, 110 cal BC-cal AD 80) (Dumayne & Barber 1994). This was followed by woodland regeneration and a decline in the extent of open land by 1925±40 BP (SRR-4530, 40 cal BC-cal AD 150). Just to the north, at Bolton Fell Moss clearance seems to have begun later in the Iron Age and peaked at 1860±60 BP (Hv-3085, cal AD 10-260), at the end of the

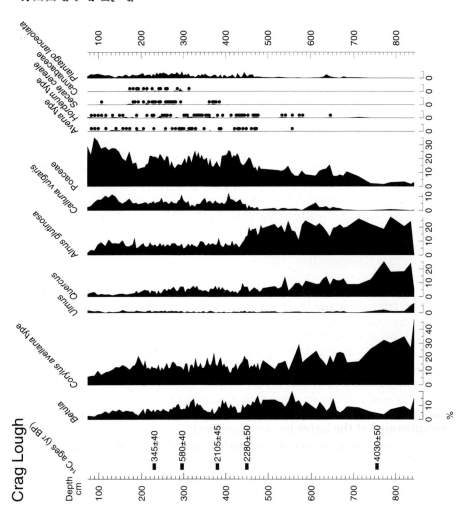

Crag Lough

3.10: Pollen diagram from Crag Lough, showing selected taxa only. Percentages calculated from the sum of total pollen and spores of vascular plants, excluding aquatics. Pollen of cultivated plants at <0.5% indicated by dots. The date of 2105±45 BP may be slightly too old.

Iron Age or in the Roman period (Barber 1981; Dumayne-Peaty & Barber 1998).

At Steng Moss, to the north-east, sustained clearance began in approximately the early Iron Age, and cereal pollen occurs sporadically throughout the Iron Age deposits (Davies & Turner 1979). A further major increase of clearance occurred in the late Iron Age or early Roman period, dated 1970±60 BP (Q-1520, 120 cal BC-cal AD 150). This was accompanied by increases of cereals, grasses, and ribwort plantain, suggesting the creation of both pasture and arable land.

A cluster of pollen sequences has been produced from the Durham area, most of which were discussed in Turner's synthesis, referred to earlier (J. Turner 1979). Some of these have radiocarbon dates with very large error terms. For example, the radiocarbon date of 2060±120 BP (GaK-3033) for the onset of clearance at Stewart Shield Meadow (Roberts, Turner & Ward 1973) produces a two sigma calibrated range of 400 cal BC-cal AD 200. Similar problems apply to the sequence from Bollihope Bog (Roberts, Turner & Ward 1973), where major clearance began at a level dated 1730±100 BP (GaK-3031, cal AD 80-540).

Turning to the more securely dated sequences from this area, at Hallowell Moss major clearance began in the late Iron Age or early Roman period, at 1956±70 BP (SRR-415, 120 cal BC-cal AD 230), apparently accompanied by cereal cultivation (Donaldson & Turner 1977). At Hutton Henry clearance began much earlier, in the Bronze Age, but there was a further major reduction of woodland in the late Iron Age or Roman period, at 1842±70 BP (SRR-600, cal AD 0-350) (Bartley, Chambers & Hart-Jones 1976). Records of cereal pollen from this site are sporadic from the Bronze Age to the late Iron Age/early Roman period, after which they cease to occur.

At Thorpe Bulmer extensive clearance and cereal cultivation apparently began at 2064±60 BP (SRR-404, 210 cal BC-cal AD 80), although part of the Bronze Age and Iron Age sequence may be missing (Bartley, Chambers & Hart-Jones 1976). Pollen specifically identified as hemp appears from the same level, suggesting the possibility of cultivation of the plant in the late Iron Age. Hemp pollen percentages later peaked at a level dated 1730±120 BP (GaK-3713, cal AD 0-600), however, and it is possible that the pollen in the Iron Age deposits has somehow moved down the profile from this later phase.

In the northern Pennines, pollen sequences from Quick Moss and Valley Bog show a sustained episode of woodland clearance beginning in approximately the mid-Iron Age (Rowell & Turner 1985; C. Chambers 1978), accompanied at the latter by cereal cultivation. At Valley Bog this episode followed a prolonged history of rather open conditions, with sporadic records of cereal pollen form the latter half of the Neolithic period.

To the south-west, in Cumbria, few of the pollen sequences from lakes in the area have radiocarbon dates for Iron Age deposits (see Pennington

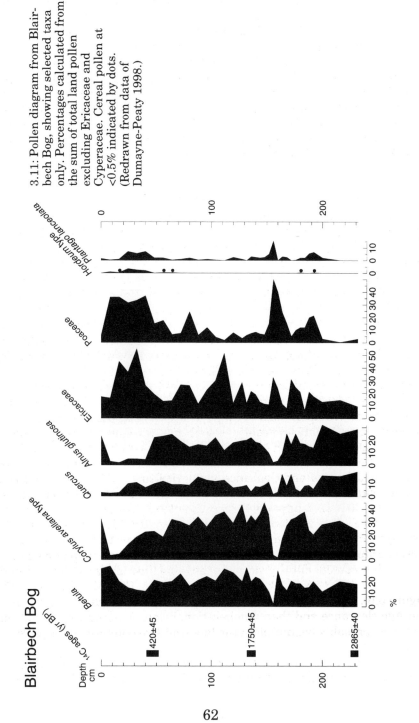

3.11: Pollen diagram from Blairbech Bog, showing selected taxa only. Percentages calculated from the sum of total land pollen excluding Ericaceae and Cyperaceae. Cereal pollen at <0.5% indicated by dots. (Redrawn from data of Dumayne-Peaty 1998.)

1970 for a summary). Pollen analysis of peat deposits at Rusland Moss shows only minor disturbance during the Iron Age (Dickinson 1975).

Conclusion. The pollen evidence from northern England overall suggests that much of the area remained substantially wooded until the middle of the Iron Age. Extensive clearance began in most areas in the latter half of the Iron Age, but at some sites not until the early Roman period. Unsurprisingly, woodland seems to have survived longest in areas least well suited to agriculture, especially on soils prone to waterlogging. Clearly, Iron Age peoples were responsible for removing much woodland prior to Roman occupation of the area, and this pattern occurred across northern England, not just in the later frontier zone.

Scotland

Pollen evidence for environmental history in Scotland has recently been reviewed by Tipping (1994) and Edwards and Whittington (1997). Tipping (1994) identifies a widespread period of clearance or agricultural intensification in the early Bronze Age (*c.* 2000-1800 BC), followed in southern Scotland (and to a lesser extent in other areas) by further intensification of agriculture after 500 BC. Tipping concludes that much of Scotland had been deforested by the end of the Iron Age, although in central and north-central Scotland some woodland seems to have survived throughout the prehistoric period. Human activity was probably instrumental in woodland removal in most areas, but in the extreme north of Scotland and the Northern and Western Isles climate change may also have been involved, leading to soil deterioration and the spread of blanket peat.

There are remarkably few pollen sequences with well-dated Iron Age deposits from Scotland, considering the widespread occurrence of lakes and peat deposits. Most recent research has concentrated on southern Scotland, between Hadrian's Wall and the Antonine Wall (Dumayne 1993; Dumayne *et al.* 1995; Dumayne-Peaty 1998), in an assessment of the extent to which woodland clearance and agricultural activity preceded the Roman occupation. At Letham Moss, by the River Forth, major clearance and cereal cultivation apparently began quite rapidly in the latter half of the Iron Age, at a level dated 2125±40 BP (SRR-4543, 260-50 cal BC) (Dumayne *et al.* 1995; Dumayne-Peaty 1998) (Figure 4.14). To the southwest, at Fannyside Muir major clearance seems to have begun at a similar date, but occurred more gradually, peaking just above a level dated 1925±45 BP (SRR-4617, 40 cal BC-cal AD 210) (Dumayne-Peaty 1998) (Figure 5.5). At Blairbech Bog, in the west, there are indications of early Iron Age clearance and then regeneration, before a temporary episode of clearance, probably beginning in the late Iron Age (Dumayne-Peaty 1998) (Figure 3.11).

Pollen sequences from sites further south – Cranley Moss, Dogden Moss, Ellergower Moss and Carsegowan Moss – suggest a variable pattern of pre-Roman land use (Dumayne 1993). At Dogden there seems to have been substantial clearance prior to the Roman period, while at the other sites the landscape remained substantially wooded until, or just before, the Roman occupation.

Other pollen sequences from southern Scotland have come from Burnfoothill Moss, Yetholm Loch, and Loch Dee. At Burnfoothill Moss major woodland clearance, affecting especially alder and birch (*Betula*), began in the late Iron Age or early Roman period. The radiocarbon date for this event was obtained on two different components of the peat: the 'humic' fraction gave a result of 2015±45 BP (SRR-3752, 120 cal BC-cal AD 80) and the 'humin' fraction 1965±45 BP (90 cal BC-cal AD 120) (Tipping 1995a, b). Corresponding increases of grasses and ribwort plantain suggest the spread of grassland, and there are possible records of cereal pollen immediately below and above this level. At Yetholm Loch, in the Cheviot Hills, a substantial mineral inwash layer was deposited in approximately the late Iron Age. In the pollen sequence this was followed, just below a level dated 1750±60 BP (GU-2514, cal AD 130-410), by a major decline of trees and increase of grasses and plantain, implying almost total clearance (Tipping 1992). Tipping suggests that the apparent decline of woodland after the erosion event, rather than coinciding with it, reflects the inwash of secondary pollen from the previously wooded soils.

Signs of earlier clearance come from blanket peat deposits from Loch Dee, in the Galloway hills. Here woodland disturbance and possibly cereal cultivation began towards the end of the Bronze Age, at 2600±50 BP (GrN-13131, 900-750 cal BC) (Edwards, Hirons & Newell 1991). This was also accompanied by deposition of a mineral layer, presumably reflecting soil destabilisation as a result of human activity.

The Dod, a late Iron Age hill-fort in the Borders, provides a source of on-site pollen data to compliment the off-site sequences discussed so far (Innes & Shennan 1991). Pollen analyses of deposits from the ditch and below the bank illustrate the environment in which it was built. A series of colluvial layers was preserved below the bank, presumably reflecting phases of woodland clearance and soil erosion. The final layer was a major hillwash deposit, perhaps derived from erosion of a plough-soil uphill from the site, which seems to have accumulated shortly before its construction. The ditch sequence had a basal date of 1905±50 BP (GU-1269, 30 cal BC-cal AD 230), providing an indication of when the embankment and ditch may have fallen into disuse. The pollen spectra were dominated by grasses, suggesting an open environment locally, with few trees.

Moving to western Scotland, a pollen sequence from Loch Cill an Aonghais suggests that significant woodland clearance did not occur until after a level dated 2420±80 BP (Q-1410, 790-390 cal BC) (Birks 1993c). On the Island of Arran a pollen sequence from Machrie Moor shows intense human activity in the late Bronze Age, followed by a decline in the Iron

Age (D.E. Robinson & Dickson 1988). Cereals (cf *Hordeum*) appear to have been cultivated locally in the Bronze Age, but this apparently ceased in the Iron Age, perhaps associated with soil deterioration and/or a shift toward pastoralism. Two records of '*Cannabis/Humulus* type' pollen occur in the early-mid Iron Age deposits, probably from wild hops growing locally.

On the island of Oronsay, a pollen sequence from An t-Aoradh also suggests clearance from the late Bronze Age, although the absence of most of the earlier deposits means that this may not reflect the start of disturbance. By the late Iron Age the landscape was almost entirely treeless (Beck & Gilbertson 1987).

In eastern Scotland, a pollen diagram from Black Loch, Fife, again indicates major woodland clearance from the late Bronze Age (Figure 4.15). Local cereal cultivation may have begun at this time, with sporadic records for '*Hordeum* type' pollen. Ribwort plantain pollen is especially frequent in the Iron Age deposits, but the end of the Iron Age is marked by a major episode of woodland regeneration (Whittington, Edwards & Cundill 1991; Whittington & Edwards 1993).

Further north, pollen sequences from Loch Davan and Braeroddach Loch almost certainly span the late Iron Age, but there are dating problems. At Loch Davan clearance again appears to have begun towards the end of the Bronze Age, and '*Hordeum* type' pollen is recorded from approximately the middle of the Iron Age (Whittington & Edwards 1993). Clearance seems to have peaked at a level dated 1980±105 BP (250 cal BC-cal AD 300), followed by woodland regeneration at a level dated 1865±105 BP (100 cal BC-cal AD 400). The large ranges for these dates mean that comparison with the Black Loch sequence must be tentative, but it is tempting to assign the regeneration phases apparent in both phases to the same event. At the nearby site of Braeroddach Loch the date sequence shows a reversal from the mid-Bronze Age, apparently caused by inwash of older organic material from soils (Edwards & Rowntree 1980; Whittington & Edwards 1993). The pollen sequence appears to show a similar pattern of regeneration to that at Black Loch and Loch Davan, but again a correlation cannot be proven. Whittington and Edwards (1993) assign the regeneration phases in these three sequences to disruption of agricultural systems by the Roman army, but this interpretation is open to question due to the poor chronological control for the sequences.

At Carn Dubh, Perthshire, pollen analysis of upland peat deposits indicates major woodland clearance from the early Bronze Age (Tipping 1995c), with a further decline in the Iron Age, at 2310±60 BP (GU-3377, 550-150 cal BC). At Coire Fee, to the north-east, the woodland had always been open in structure, and its extent was reduced at a level dated 2605±75 BP (Q-1419, 950-500 cal BC) (B. Huntley 1981).

In the far north, at Loch of Winless, Caithness, woodland cover was never extensive, and seems to have disappeared at a level dated 2210±50 BP (Q-1329, 400-160 cal BC) (Peglar 1979). The local vegetation was dominated by heather, but cereals and ribwort plantain both appear at this date, suggesting local agricultural activity. A pollen sequence from blanket peat on Hill of Harley, also in Caithness, shows similarly open moorland conditions, although the sporadic records of '*Hordeum* type' pollen suggest local agricultural activity (J.P. Huntley 1995).

In the extreme north-west, at Lochan an Druim a major phase of woodland clearance, affecting especially alder, occurred at 2730±70 BP (SRR-779, 1050-790 cal BC) (Birks 1980, 1993a). Grassland increased, accompanied by evidence for cereal cultivation and a limited increase of heathland. At 2280±60 BP (SRR-778, 520-180 cal BC), however, regeneration of alder and birch suggests a return to conditions similar to the pre-Iron Age landscape.

Moving to the Hebrides, on the Isle of Skye a pollen sequence from Loch Ashik records the spread of blanket bog and moorland from the late Bronze Age or early Iron Age, while at nearby Loch Meodal clearance began in the Neolithic period (Birks 1993b). At Loch Cleat, also on Skye, a major episode of woodland clearance with increases of grasses, heather, ribwort plantain and cereal pollen, occurred immediately below a level dated 2530±70 BP (SRR-933, 820-460 cal BC), again following clearance from the Neolithic (Birks 1993b).

Conclusion. Sites in Scotland show a variable date for the onset of extensive woodland clearance, ranging from the Neolithic period to late Iron Age. Moving from south to north clearance seems to have occurred progressively earlier, suggesting an interaction between climate and human activity. Further north, woodland was probably less likely to regenerate after clearance than to the south, as a wetter climate would have encouraged the spread of peat. While the emphasis of farming was probably pastoral, cereals were cultivated in some areas, including in the extreme north of Scotland.

Wales

There are very few pollen sequences from Wales with well-dated deposits spanning the Iron Age, but some of the most detailed from north Wales come from an area of wetland close to the late Iron Age/Roman-period hill-fort of Bryn y Castell, in the uplands of Snowdonia (Mighall & Chambers 1995, 1997). Analysis of multiple profiles indicated that much of the local woodland was removed in the late Bronze Age, and the landscape then remained substantially open throughout the Iron Age. Cereal-type pollen occurs sporadically throughout the Bronze Age and Iron Age parts of the sequence. Iron-working at the hill-fort in the late Iron Age and Roman period may have led to some further reduction of woodland, especially of birch and alder, but the effect was minor. It is possible that the fuel requirements for iron-working were not sufficiently great to have much effect on local woodland resources. There would, however, have been many other demands on wood, such as for building roundhouses and domestic hearths, and it is possible that the small amount of woodland remaining in the Iron Age was managed as an important resource rather than destroyed.

Further east, peat deposits at Cefn Mawr illustrate a substantial decline in the extent of woodland in the mid-Bronze Age (Jenkins, Lacelles & Williams 1995). The woodland seems to have been replaced by grassland and there is an increase in the presence of charcoal particles, possibly reflecting domestic hearths. A further decline of woodland began in the late Bronze Age, after which the landscape remained fairly open throughout the Iron Age.

On the Welsh border near Shrewsbury, excavations of the Breiddin hill-fort were accompanied by pollen analysis of a natural pool in the interior. The hill-fort was constructed in the late Bronze Age and re-occupied in the Iron Age and Roman period (Musson 1991), while the pool revealed a sequence spanning the whole of the post-glacial up to the late Iron Age (A.G. Smith *et al.* 1991). Woodland clearance began in the latter half of the Bronze Age, and continued throughout the early Iron Age. Later deposits had unfortunately been disturbed or removed, probably in connection with construction of a cistern in the Iron Age.

From the uplands of mid-Wales, five pollen diagrams have been produced from peat deposits at Carneddau, close to the site of a Bronze Age cairn (Walker 1993). There appears to have been a decline of alder, and to a lesser extent hazel and oak, in the mid-Bronze Age, accompanied in one of the sequences by the appearance of cereal pollen. Extensive clearance of woodland on well-drained soils did not occur until the late Iron Age or Roman period, however: from three of the sequences there are radiocarbon dates for a major increase of grasses at 1790±70 BP (Carneddau 1, CAR-1244, cal AD 70-400), 1880±70 (Carneddau 3, CAR-1238, 50 cal BC-cal AD 260) and 1960±70 BP (Carneddau 5, CAR-1242, 120 cal BC-cal AD 220).

The most detailed pollen sequence from south Wales is from a peat-covered plateau at Cefn Gwernffrwd, close to the site of a Bronze Age stone circle and ring cairn (F.M. Chambers 1983a). Blanket peat formation began in the early Bronze Age, probably as a result of a rise in water table caused by woodland clearance. Pollen analysis of the peat showed that by the latter half of the Bronze Age most local woodland had disappeared, but this was followed by a return of some woodland at the end of the Bronze Age and into the early Iron Age. The overall extent of woodland remained stable throughout the Iron Age, although some areas of birch seem to have been replaced by hazel. Renewed clearance began from a level dated 1900±45 BP (CAR-74, cal AD 0-230).

Comparison may be made with the well-known site of Tregaron Bog, 15km to the north-west (J. Turner 1964). Here it seems that major clearance occurred much later than at Cefn Gwernffrwd, beginning only towards the latter half of the Iron Age.

From a small upland valley bog at Cefn Glas three pollen diagrams have been produced from sites only a few tens of metres apart (A.G. Smith & Green 1995). Peat formation began in the Bronze Age, perhaps again as a result of woodland clearance, and the resulting open landscape persisted throughout the Iron Age.

20km to the north-west, a high altitude blanket peat deposit in the Brecon Beacons shows clearance and sporadic cereal cultivation from the mid-Bronze Age, with woodland regeneration in the Iron Age (F.M. Chambers 1982). This was followed by renewed clearance from a level dated 2065±70 BP (CAR-57, 250 cal BC-cal AD 80), resulting in a very open landscape with extensive blanket peat which persisted into the Roman period.

At Nant Helen, Mynydd y Drum, analysis of another blanket peat again showed clearance from at least the Bronze Age (F.M. Chambers, Lageard & Elliot 1990). The resulting mixture of woodland and open land persisted from the Bronze Age into the Roman period, interrupted by an episode of hazel regeneration in approximately the early Iron Age.

Conclusion. Most sites in Wales began to be cleared of their woodland in the Bronze Age, accompanied in some areas by cereal cultivation. In the south there was an increase in the extent of woodland in the Iron Age, perhaps similar to that in southern England, suggesting a widespread decline in agricultural activity at this time. Renewed clearance followed in the late Iron Age or Roman period, apparently reflecting increased demand for farmland, especially pasture.

Reconstructing the extent of woodland and cereal cultivation in the late Iron Age

Discussion so far has focussed on the long-term history of clearance and agricultural activity but attention is now directed specifically at the nature of the environment at the end of the Iron Age, as a prelude to consideration of the environmental consequences of the Roman Conquest. The emphasis here is on pollen sequences from which deposits of the late Iron Age (here taken to have begun at 100 BC = 2070 BP and ended at AD 43 = 1960 BP) are well dated. As discussed in Chapter 1, even where deposits have radiocarbon dates centred on the late Iron Age, the calibrated range of the date is likely in many cases to extend into the mid-Iron Age or early Roman period. The purpose here is to provide an indication of the general character of the vegetation at a period centred approximately on the late Iron Age.

Site selection

As we have seen, the main way in which pollen sequences reflect the character of the landscape is in terms of the relative amounts of woodland (indicated by tree and shrub pollen) and open land (indicated by an abundance of pollen of herbaceous plants). Consequently, mapping the distribution of pollen sequences and indicating the frequency of tree and shrub pollen in the late Iron Age deposits from each site can provide an indication of the overall extent of woodland, which is inversely proportional to the extent of open land. The presence of cereal pollen is also indicative of the extent of arable, although the low production and poor dispersal of cereal pollen means that nothing can be deduced from its absence.

The first stage is to locate pollen sequences with sufficient chronological control to enable identification of deposits of the late Iron Age with reasonable confidence. As discussed in Chapter 1, most pollen sequences from lakes and mires span several thousand years, and a chronology is based on a series of radiocarbon dates from the deposits. Typically, there would only be approximately one radiocarbon date for every thousand years, so that even where the sequence spans the Iron Age, deposits of this period may not be dated directly.

Pollen sequences are used here only if there is at least one radiocarbon date with a calibrated range lying at least partially in the late Iron Age, and this date must form part of a series of supporting dates (to allow for the possibility of anomalous dates). In a few instances sites where late Iron deposits are closely bracketed by radiocarbon determinations have been included (as at Glasson Moss). Sites where the relevant dates have particularly large error terms (>±80) are excluded. The sites included are listed in Table 3.1, where the dates are given with their calibrated ranges.

For present purposes it is necessary to attempt to identify the total span of the late Iron Age deposits in each sequence. This has been achieved by interpolation between the late Iron Age date(s) and the dates for the rest of the sequence, assuming a constant accumulation rate where the nature of the stratification seemed to warrant this. Lake muds and peats often appear to have accumulated at a remarkably constant rate in the past, and any changes are often identifiable because they are linked to a change in the character of the deposit.

Another key aspect is the temporal resolution of the sequence – the time interval between samples. Even when a sequence spans the late Iron Age, there may be few or no pollen samples from the corresponding deposits. Only sequences with at least two pollen samples for the late Iron Age are mapped. Obviously, this provides insufficient detail to illustrate any vegetational changes that occurred during the period, but it does provide a general idea of the extent of woodland for the purposes of mapping.

Turning to representation of the pollen data, for each site percentages of tree and shrub pollen have been calculated from published pollen diagrams as an average figure for the late Iron Age. Comparison between sites is complicated by the fact that different workers have based their calculations on different pollen sums, as discussed earlier in this chapter. The standard sum used for calculations is total pollen and spores of vascular plants, excluding obligate aquatics. Members of the heather family are excluded from the shrub category. The results are plotted in one of four percentage ranges (Figure 3.12).

Percentages of tree and shrub pollen provide an indication of the amount of woodland, but land that was not wooded may, of course, have been occupied by various types of vegetation, including grassland, arable land, heath and moor. The nature of these open land communities is not easily reconstructed from the pollen evidence. This is especially the case where grasses were dominant, because different species of grasses from a wide variety of vegetation types have similar pollen grains.

Obviously, pollen of crops provides clues to the presence of arable land, although few crops have pollen sufficiently distinctive to be separable from non-cultivated members of the same family. The only types that occur in the late Iron Age sequences are cereals and possibly hemp (*Cannabis sativa*), and there are problems with the identification of these also. In many early pollen diagrams cereal pollen is not distinguished at all, and even sequences analyzed over the last decade may not separate the different types. Here, cereals are usually treated together, but where rye has been separately identified this is indicated. Because cereals are under-represented in the pollen record they have been mapped only by presence (Figure 3.13).

In relation to pollen resembling that of hemp, analysts have sometimes used the category 'Cannabis type' or identified the pollen to family level, Cannabaceae, to allow for the uncertainty in separating it from hop (*Humulus lupulus*). Occasionally, however, a specific identification is made. Because of the uncertainties attached to the identification of hemp pollen, possible records for its presence in late Iron Age deposits are discussed in the text but not mapped.

As already stressed, the problems of chronology mean that the mapped distribution of tree and shrub pollen percentages and cereal pollen must be considered an approximation of the amount of woodland and extent of cereal cultivation at a period centred on the late Iron Age. In reality, the

3.12: Woodland in the late Iron Age: percentages of tree and shrub pollen in radiocarbon-dated sequences spanning the period.

1. Hill of Harley	12. Steng Moss	23. Crose Mere
2. Black Loch	13. Quick Moss	24. Carneddau
3. Letham Moss	14. Valley Bog	25. Cefn Gwernffrwd
4. An t-Aoradh	15. Hallowell Moss	26. Brecon Beacons
5. Machrie Moor	16. Hutton Henry	27. Abbot's Way
6. Burnfoothill Moss	17. Thorpe Bulmer	28. Meare Heath
7. Glasson Moss	18. Rusland Moss	29. Rimsmoor
8. Walton Moss	19. Fairsnape Fell	30. Murrow
9. Midgeholme Moss	20. Willow Garth	31. Wisbech
10. Fellend Moss	21. Rishworth Moor	32. Willingham Mere
11. Fozy Moss	22. Featherbed Moss	

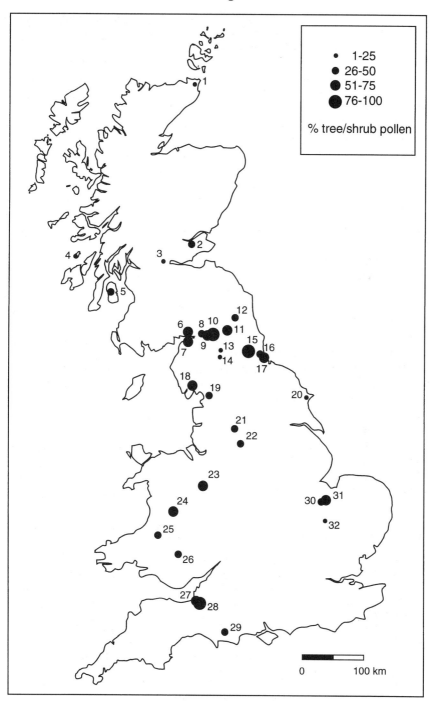

3.13: Cereal cultivation in the late Iron Age: presence of cereal pollen in radiocarbon-dated sequences spanning the period. For key to sites see Figure 3.12.

environment during this period was far from static, as will be obvious from the previous discussion.

Table 3.1. Pollen sequences with radiocarbon dates and at least two pollen samples from the late Iron Age deposits

Note that these results may differ from the calibration (if any) given by the original analysts, due to the use of different calibration curves.

Site	Radiocarbon date (BP)	Lab code	Cal range (95.4% confidence)	Reference
England				
Abbot's Way	1954±40	SRR-1011	60 BC-AD 130	Beckett & Hibbert
	2090±45	SRR-1012	210 BC-AD 20 (90.9%)	1979
			360-310 BC (4.5%)	
Crose Mere	2086±75	Q-1232	260 BC-AD 70 (82.8%)	Beales 1980
			370-280 BC (12.6%)	
Fairsnape Fell	2025±40	SRR-4506	120 BC-AD 70 (92.8%)	Mackay & Tallis
			160-140 BC (2.6%)	1994
	2105±40	SRR-4507	250-10 BC (88.4%)	
			360-300 BC (7.0%)	
Featherbed Moss	2028±50	Q-853	170 BC-AD 70	Tallis & Switsur
				1973
Fellend Moss	1948±45	SRR-876	90 BC-AD 140	Davies & Turner
				1979
Fozy Moss	1820±45	SRR-4539	AD 80-260 (87.5%)	Dumayne & Barber
			AD 280-330 (7.9%)	1994
Glasson Moss	1860±40	SRR-4533	AD 60-250	Dumayne & Barber
	2215±45	SRR-4534	400-180 BC	1994
Hallowell Moss	1956±70	SRR-415	120 BC-AD 230	Donaldson &
				Turner 1977
Hutton Henry	1842±70	SRR-600	AD 0-350	Bartley *et al.* 1976
Meare Heath	2062±45	SRR-912	200 BC-AD 30	Beckett & Hibbert
				1979
Midgeholme Moss	1970±60	GU-5081	120 BC-AD 150 (94.4%)	
			160-140 BC (1.0%)	
	2100±60	GU-5082	260 BC-AD 20 (82.4%)	Wiltshire 1997
			370-280 BC (13.0%)	
Murrow	2130±50	Q-2590	270-40 BC (72.8%)	Waller 1994d
			370-280 BC (22.6%)	
Quick Moss	2035±50		180 BC-AD 70	Rowell & Turner
				1985

3. The Iron Age context

Site	Radiocarbon date (BP)	Lab code	Cal range (95.4% confidence)	Reference
Rimsmoor	2080±80	HAR-3923	270 BC-AD 70 (83.3%) 370-280 BC (12.1%)	Waton 1982, 1983
Rishworth Moor	1920±80	GaK-2825	110 BC-AD 260 (94.4%) AD 300-320 (1.0%)	Bartley 1975
Rusland Moss	1963±50	SRR-126	100 BC-AD 130	Dickinson 1975
Steng Moss	1970±60	Q-1520	120 BC-AD 150 (94.4%) 160-140 BC (1.0%)	Davies & Turner 1979
Thorpe Bulmer	2064±60	SRR-404	210 BC-AD 80 (91.7%) 360-310 BC (3.7%)	Bartley et al. 1976
Valley Bog	2212±55	SRR-88	400-160 BC (94.1%) 140-120 BC (1.3%)	C. Chambers 1978
	2175±55	SRR-89	390-110 BC	
Walton Moss	1925±40	SRR-4530	40 BC-AD 150 (92.9%) AD 160-200 (2.5%)	Dumayne & Barber 1994
	2000±40	SRR-4531	110 BC-AD 80	
Willingham Mere	1910±60	Q-2582	60 BC-AD 240	Waller 1994c
Wisbech (Railway Crossing)	2100±50	Q-2511	250 BC-AD 10 (86.1%) 360-290 BC (9.3%)	Alderton & Waller 1994a
	2130±50	Q-2512	270-40 BC (72.8%) 370-280 BC (22.6%)	
Wisbech (New Bridge Rd)	2010±50	Q-2508	170 BC-AD 90	Alderton & Waller 1994b
	2120±50	Q-2509	260-30 BC (77.2%) 370-280 BC (18.2%)	
Willow Garth	2120±50	SRR-2669	260-30 BC (77.2%) 370-280 BC (18.2%)	Bush & Flenley 1987

Scotland

Site	Radiocarbon date (BP)	Lab code	Cal range (95.4% confidence)	Reference
An t-Aoradh	2100±40	Q-2440	210 BC-AD 0 (90.1%) 360-310 BC (5.3%)	Beck & Gilbertson 1987
Black Loch	1885±75	UB-2294	60 BC-AD 270 (91.6%) AD 280-330 (3.8%)	Whittington et al. 1991
	2015±75	UB-2295	210 BC-AD 140 (94.0%) 350-310 BC (1.4%)	
	2235±75	UB-2296	420-90 BC	
Burnfoothill Moss (paired dates)	2015±45	SRR-3752	120 BC-AD 80 (93.0%) 170-140 BC (2.4%)	Tipping 1995a, b
	1965±45		90 BC-AD 120	
Hill of Harley	2120±60	GU-2076	370 BC-AD 0	J.P. Huntley 1995

3. The Iron Age context

Site	Radiocarbon date (BP)	Lab code	Cal range (95.4% confidence)	Reference
Letham Moss	2125±40	SRR-4543	260-50 BC (78.8%)	Dumayne-Peaty
			360-280 BC (16.6%)	1998
Machrie Moor	2115±55	GU-1422	260 BC-AD 0 (78.3%)	D.E. Robinson &
			370-280 BC (17.1%)	Dickson 1988
Wales				
Brecon Beacons	2065±70	CAR-57	250 BC-AD 80 (89.0%)	F.M. Chambers 1982
			360-290 BC (6.4%)	
Carneddau (3)	1880±70	CAR-1238	50 BC-AD 260 (92.0%)	Walker 1993
			AD 280-330 (3.4%)	
Cefn Gwernffrwd	1900±45	CAR-74	AD 0-230	F.M. Chambers
	2030±45	CAR-73	170 BC-AD 70	1983a

Results and interpretation

There are thirty-two sites with pollen sequences from which deposits of the late Iron Age can be identified with reasonable certainty, but there are unfortunately large areas of Britain with no data. This bias is largely a reflection of the fact that lakes and peat deposits are abundant in the north and west, and in the East Anglian Fens, in contrast to the south and Midlands where suitable deposits are rare.

Of these sites, thirteen have tree/shrub pollen percentages greater than 50%, and seven have tree/shrub percentages of 25% or less. In the light of the factors discussed in Chapter 1, this suggests that much of the landscape probably consisted of a mixture of woodland and open land in the late Iron Age, but in a few areas woodland was already scarce.

Turning to the pollen evidence for agriculture, cereal pollen is recorded in late Iron Age deposits from eighteen of the sequences, stretching from Dorset to Caithness and from East Anglia to south-east Wales. Of these, rye is specifically identified only at Rimsmoor in Dorset (Waton 1983), although an early Roman date for this record is possible. Because cereal pollen is under-represented in the pollen record, this distribution is likely to provide a major underestimate of the true extent of cereal cultivation in the late Iron Age.

Pollen of hemp or hop is recorded in probable Iron Age deposits from Willingham Mere (Waller 1994c), Rimsmoor (Waton 1983), Thorpe Bulmer (Bartley et al. 1976), and Machrie Moor on Arran (D.E. Robinson & Dickson 1988). In view of the lack of macrofossil records for hemp from Iron Age archaeological sites, and the uncertainty over the chronology of some of the pollen records, it would be unwise to argue that they provide evidence for hemp cultivation in the Iron Age.

3. The Iron Age context

Management of natural resources

Pollen sequences are of considerable value in indicating the general character and distribution of different vegetation types, and providing an indication of the extent of cereal cultivation. Unfortunately, however, they provide less information about the ways in which human groups exploited the different plant communities around them. Many of the vegetation types that existed in the Iron Age are likely to have owed both their creation and continued survival to human intervention, either directly or indirectly. In lowland areas grassland, for example, quickly reverts to woodland unless colonisation by shrubs and trees is prevented by grazing or mowing. Evidence for deliberate management is difficult to detect from pollen sequences, because different types of management practice tend to be reflected in the species composition of plant communities, and this can rarely be reconstructed from pollen evidence alone. Macroscopic plant remains enable closer identification, but assemblages from off-site contexts tend to be strongly biassed towards *in situ* vegetation, growing on the peat surface or in lake-side communities. Plant remains from archaeological sites more often provide indications of management, of which the most 'visible' is woodland management.

Woodland management

Management of woodland can take a variety of forms, designed to increase the production of specific types of wood and timber (O. Rackham 1980, 1990). The most common management practice in the past was probably coppicing. This involves cutting trees down virtually to ground level, and then allowing regrowth for a few years (around ten) before the resulting poles are cut again (Figure 3.14). Many species of trees can be coppiced, including hazel, elm, ash and lime. The resulting poles are of fairly uniform size, and can be used for wattle-work for walls, fences and doors (Figure 3.15).

It has been suggested that coppicing can be detected in pollen sequences by an increase in the abundance of hazel (e.g. J. Turner 1965; Coles & Orme 1977). This is because hazel shoots flower rapidly after cutting – from their second year (O. Rackham 1990, p. 71) – while most other trees take several years to flower. So, if an area of woodland is cut on a short rotation, flowering of most trees may be prevented, while hazel not only still manages to flower, but benefits from the reduced shade and produces more pollen. Hazel pollen may increase in abundance for a variety of reasons, however, not least as a result of an increase in the extent of hazel woodland! One way to detect coppicing might be to look for the cycle of pollen production introduced by the cutting regime. This would require sampling with an annual scale of resolution, but most pollen sequences have a sampling interval of decades or even centuries. Alternatively, it

3.14: Woodland management by coppicing: well-grown coppice being cut in Waresley Wood, Cambridgeshire.

3.15: Use of wattle-work for fencing in the reconstruction of an Iron Age Farm at Butser.

might be possible to detect managed woodland by the presence of assemblages of plants characteristic of such woodland today (cf Stevenson & Harrison 1992). Unfortunately, however, many plant species associated with managed woodland in Britain produce little pollen, and/or pollen that is not closely identifiable (Day 1993).

From archaeological assemblages of wood, coppicing may be suggested by the occurrence of large numbers of even-sized poles, as long straight poles tend not to occur abundantly in natural unmanaged woodland (O. Rackham 1977). Further evidence for coppice management may come from a concentration in the ages of stems from a large sample of poles (Morgan 1983), or by the presence of morphological features associated with growth from a coppice stool or subsequent cutting. These include the 'heel' of wood produced by tearing an incompletely cut stem from the stool (O. Rackham 1977). There is archaeological evidence for coppicing from as early as the Neolithic period from the the wooden trackways of the Somerset Levels, referred to earlier.

In the Iron Age it is likely that large areas of woodland were managed, a point reinforced by the abundant use of wood for building roundhouses and other structures (D.M. Reynolds 1982; P.J. Reynolds 1982, 1995). Archaeological evidence for the use of wood from coppicing comes predominantly from waterlogged, or partially waterlogged, sites where wood has been preserved. For example, the late Iron Age Glastonbury 'lake village' produced extensive remains of wattle-work hurdles, walling and fencing (Bulleid & Gray 1911, 1917; Coles & Minnitt 1995). At least some of the panels consisted of alder rods interlaced between oak uprights. Excavations at the nearby site of Meare (Bulleid & Gray 1948, 1953; Orme, Coles & Sturdy 1979) produced less wood, although the remains of hurdles were found from some of the mounds, again mostly consisting of oak and alder uprights with alder rods. There also appears to have been a preference for the use of coppiced alder at the early Iron Age enclosures on Sutton Common, South Yorkshire (Parker Pearson & Sydes 1997). As most evidence for coppicing comes from waterlogged wood, the frequent bias towards alder is perhaps unsurprising as this tree grows predominantly on damper soils. At other sites different species were used, as at Dragonby, in Lincolnshire, where Iron Age pits (probably wells) were lined with wattle-work of oak stakes interwoven with horizontal hazel branches (May 1996, pp. 59, 67).

Caution must be exercised in the assumption that wattle-work necessarily comes from coppiced woodland. For example, rectangular Iron Age buildings from the Severn Estuary at Goldcliff had alder wattle walls, but the wood seems to have been cut at a range of ages, and need not have come from managed woodland (Bell 1992a, b; Bell & Neumann 1997).

Conclusion

The Iron Age was a period of major change in the environment of Britain, especially in terms of the extent of woodland clearance and agriculture. While in parts of southern Britain extensive woodland clearance had already brought about a major landscape transformation in the Bronze Age, further north much of this process of woodland removal began in the Iron Age. In upland areas of the north and west human activity may have triggered formation of peat deposits in raised and blanket mires, a process ongoing since the later Mesolithic period. Most of Britain at the end of the Iron Age probably remained more wooded than today, but a few parts of southern England may already have been as open as the modern landscape. In such areas there would have been little potential for further expansion of farmland because most suitable land was already exploited. Cereal cultivation and pastoral agriculture were widespread, and cereals were grown on a much wider range of soils than would be considered productive today.

Martin Jones has suggested, on the basis of assemblages of cereal remains from archaeological sites, that there was a major phase of agricultural innovation in the late Iron Age, with changes in the crop repertoire and more extensive farming. It is notable that many pollen sequences do show increased woodland clearance at this time, either representing the initial inroads into previously untouched forest, or following woodland regeneration after earlier clearance.

Clearly, then, much of the shaping of our modern landscape, in terms of removal of woodland and creation of agricultural land, seems to have happened in the first millennium BC. This argument should not pushed too far, however, as it adopts too static a view of vegetational change. We should not think simply in terms of a continuing process of woodland removal, until only essential amounts remain. Even in prehistory there were periods of abandonment of agricultural land and woodland regeneration, so that some of the woodland cleared in the first millennium AD would have been secondary. Particularly striking is the period of widespread woodland regeneration in the late Bronze Age-early Iron Age in parts of Wales and southern England. This presumably reflects a relaxation of land use, possibly due to climatic deterioration. No comparable phase appears in northern England and Scotland, as most sites in these areas remained predominantly wooded well into the Iron Age.

The dynamic nature of vegetational change means that we cannot see the essentially agricultural landscape of much of Iron Age Britain as approaching the finishing point in the creation of an agricultural landscape from wilderness. Much of this hard-won agricultural land would rapidly revert to woodland without constant human intervention. In the following chapters we shall see the extent to which the legacy of prehistoric environmental manipulation lasted into the first millennium AD.

4

The Roman period

Introduction

During the Roman occupation of Britain, AD 43-410, much of England underwent major changes in terms of the character of human settlement, while settlement in the south-west and north of England, Wales and Scotland continued largely along pre-Roman lines (see K. Dark & Dark 1997). Roman villas, most of which seem to have operated as agricultural estate centres, became widespread in central, southern and eastern England (Figure 4.1). These villas would almost certainly have been surrounded by extensive field systems, as illustrated by recent excavations at

4.1: Reconstruction of a Romano-British villa. (Painting of the villa at Chignall St James, Essex, by Frank Gardiner, © Essex County Council.)

Roughground Farm, Gloucestershire. Here a villa built in the early second century was surrounded by a series of rectangular enclosures (perhaps paddocks), and larger open fields covering at least 15ha (T.G. Allen *et al.* 1993). On downland areas some prehistoric field systems seem to have been re-used in the Roman period, as at Chalton in Hampshire (Cunliffe 1977). In other cases the Roman period saw a reorganisation of the landscape, as on the Berkshire Downs, where excavations suggest that there was little re-use of prehistoric field boundaries (Bowden, Ford & Mees 1993). The Roman period also saw the foundation of many towns, again mainly in England, providing new markets for agricultural produce, and creating a new 'urban environment'.

In northern and western Britain agriculture remained based on the type of farmsteads occupied in the Iron Age. Probably the main impact of the Roman Conquest on the landscape of these areas was Roman military occupation, with the founding of a series of forts, roads and of course, the Hadrianic and Antonine Walls. These required not only land, but also resources for their construction and agricultural produce to feed the army.

In some parts of Roman Britain pressure on the land was sufficiently intense to prompt major land drainage, as in the Severn Estuary Levels (J.R.L. Allen & Fulford 1986, 1992; Fulford, Allen & Rippon 1994) and the East Anglian Fens (B.B. Simmons 1979). At Rumney Great Wharf, on the Wentlooge Level of the Severn, this took the form of drainage ditches cut into the alluvium, presumably protected by some form of sea defence. Finds of lamb, calf and horse bones suggest the possibility that the area was reclaimed to provide pasture (Fulford, Allen & Rippon 1994).

Drainage seems also increasingly to have been used at individual farms, usually to increase the amount of land available for agriculture. On the gravels of the Upper Thames Valley later Iron Age and Romano-British settlements were constructed with ditched enclosures and fields. At Ashville, Abingdon, evidence that these ditches did indeed lower the local water table is provided by a decline in the frequency of the spike-rush (*Eleocharis palustris*) in the assemblages of plant remains from the site (M. Jones 1978).

In addition to using drainage to increase the extent of agricultural land, there appear to have been attempts at improving the nutrient status of soils by addition of manure and household refuse. The widespread pottery scatters found in Roman and earlier field systems are usually assumed to reflect the spread of midden material on fields (Gaffney & Tingle 1989, pp. 210, 224-5). Crop rotation may also have been employed to reduce soil exhaustion and prevent the build-up of pests and disease. Rotation involving legumes would have been especially beneficial because of the ability of such plants to 'fix' atmospheric nitrogen. Hints of crop rotation come from finds of non-cereal crops mixed in with cereal assemblages from archaeological sites, suggesting survival of the previous year's crop. For example, flax (*Linum usitatissimum*) and 'Celtic bean' (*Vicia faba*) have been found together with cereal remains in a corndrier at Barton Court Farm, Oxford-shire – a group of plants which is highly unlikely to have been grown together deliberately (M. Jones 1981, p. 113).

As for the Iron Age, finds of structures and implements connected with crop production and processing are widespread from Roman Britain (Rees 1979) (Figure 4.2). There were large granaries in many Roman forts and towns, suggesting mobilisation of a substantial agricultural surplus (Figure 4.3). In some cases there are hints that cereals were not only brought to these sites from the surrounding countryside, but were imported from considerable distances, perhaps even from the Continent. For example, excavation of a military warehouse in York revealed a mixture of spelt wheat (*Triticum spelta*), barley (*Hordeum vulgare*) and rye (*Secale cereale*), with several weeds with current distributions well to the south of Yorkshire. While the presence of such weeds might partly be explained by the warmer climate of a least the later Roman period, the occurrence of larkspur (*Delphinium* sp.), a plant not native to Britain (Williams 1979), suggests a continental source. Similarly, the range of insect pests infesting the grain suggests transport from some distance away (Kenward 1979).

Evidence that cereal production and processing may have been large-scale operations comes also from the occurrence of watermills, identified at Chesters, Willowford and Haltwhistle on Hadrian's Wall (Spain 1984). Another feature associated with crop processing that occurs commonly on Roman sites is the corndrier. There is some debate over the function of these structures, but the fact that they frequently contain charred grain has led to the assumption that they were used to dry the crop before

4.2: Quernstones at Corbridge, near Hadrian's Wall.

4.3: Roman granaries at Corbridge, near Hadrian's Wall.

storage. Experiments at Butser Ancient Farm, however (see Chapter 3), suggested that the structures could not perform such a function efficiently (Reynolds & Langley 1980). Germinated barley has been found in corn-driers at several sites, and it seems that at least some were used to roast germinated grain for malt production (van der Veen 1989).

In terms of plough technology, the light wooden ard of the Iron Age continued in use into the Roman period, but the later Roman period saw the introduction of heavier ploughs able to penetrate the soil more deeply. From the third or fourth centuries this was aided by the introduction of the coulter, which ran through the soil in front of the share (Rees 1979, pp. 59-61), and also the assymetric share, of a type that would be expected from a mouldboard plough. Such a plough both cuts and turns the soil, enabling greater weed control and cultivation of heavier soils.

Another type of artefact that suggests changes in land utilisation in the Roman period is the scythe. Scythes have not been found in pre-Roman contexts from Britain, and first occur at first-century military sites, such as the fort at Newstead in southern Scotland (Rees 1979, p. 474). Possibly they were used to cut hay for horse fodder. Scythes appear later at non-military sites, such as Farmoor in Oxfordshire and Great Chesterford in Essex, and were much larger than the earlier type (Rees 1979, pp. 475-7). Such scythes may have been of use for cutting both hay and cereals.

Independent indications of the presence of hay meadows in Roman Britain come from assemblages of waterlogged plant remains from archae-ological sites. For example, excavations at Farmoor produced not only the scythe mentioned above, but also a second-century well containing cut hay, including seeds of such characteristic meadow plants as ox-eye daisy (*Leucanthemum vulgare*), yellow rattle (*Rhinanthus* sp.) and knapweed (*Centaurea nigra*) (M. Robinson 1979). Evidence for hay has also come from wells from several other sites (Greig 1988), including an example from Lancaster, where horse droppings were found containing seeds of fairy flax (*Linum catharticum*), clovers (*Trifolium* spp.) and knapweed.

Charred and waterlogged crop remains have also been found at several Roman-period sites. Unfortunately, however, the problem of long-distance transport and trade of crops – mentioned already in relation to assemblages from granaries – means that it is often impossible to link them to the local environment. Plant remains from a variety of sites suggest that the main crops grown in Britain continued, as in the Iron Age, to be spelt wheat and barley, but with increasing use of bread wheat (*Triticum aestivum*), rye and oats (*Avena sativa*) (M. Jones 1981; Greig 1991). Bread wheat is especially suited to fertile clay and silt soils, and its greater use may reflect a further expansion in the exploitation of such soils for arable, when they might previously have been left to grass. Oats and rye are tolerant of a much wider range of soil conditions, and could have been grown on soils that were becoming depleted after prolonged cultivation. Martin Jones (1989, p. 133) has suggested that the parallel increase of these crops in the Roman period may reflect an increasing economic disparity between wealthy farmers intensively cultivating fertile loams, and poorer farmers working increasingly nutrient-depleted soils.

Evidence for the cultivation of bread wheat is patchy, however, and it is unclear when it became the dominant crop. In the south it may already have become significant in the late Iron Age at some sites, as at Barton Court Farm, Oxfordshire (M. Jones & Robinson 1986 fiche ch. 9), but the earliest record from northern England is from a terminal Iron Age context at Rock Castle, near Stanwick, North Yorkshire (van der Veen 1992, p. 45). In other areas bread wheat seems to have remained a minor crop until the Anglo-Saxon period (M. Jones 1981, p. 107).

In a few cases it has been possible to examine the impact of romanisation on crop production at sites that were occupied in both the Iron Age and Roman periods. The two Upper Thames Valley sites of Ashville and Barton Court Farm provide an example. The settlement at Ashville produced a rich assemblage of plant remains from a series of pits, ditches, post-holes and wells (M. Jones 1978). Spelt wheat and barley were predominant, with a little emmer (*Triticum dicoccum*) and club wheat (*Triticum compactum*). The range of cereals grown does not seem to have changed significantly during the period of use of the site, although as mentioned above, there are indications of attempts to improve drainage in the late Iron Age by digging ditches. At Barton Court Farm, late Iron Age and early Roman enclosed settlements were succeeded by a villa towards the end of the third century. Plant remains were recovered from corn-driers, pits and a well (M. Jones & Robinson 1986). The range of crops grown in the Roman period was more diverse than that at Ashville, and included spelt, bread wheat, emmer, barley, flax and Celtic bean. This package presumably reflects the greater degree of romanisation of the Barton Court Farm villa, with a shift from the cereal-based arable economy characteristic of the Iron Age to a wider range of products.

In addition to cereals, flax, Celtic bean and peas (*Pisum sativum*) a variety of other useful plants were cultivated in Roman Britain. There are occasional records for remains of hemp (*Cannabis sativa*), including fruits from Roman York, although such finds may represent imports for oil production (A.R. Hall, Kenward & Williams 1980, p. 143; A.R. Hall & Kenward 1990, p. 302). Hemp may also have been grown for fibre, and some of the pollen records from lake deposits could derive from processing the plant during fibre production. This involved soaking the stems in water to soften the tissues, and lakes would have provided an obvious place for this process.

Culinary herbs such as dill (*Anethum graveolens*) and coriander (*Coriandrum sativum*) (M. Jones 1981, p. 97; Greig 1991, p. 312) may have been grown in gardens, of which a particularly elaborate example has been excavated at the villa at Fishbourne (Cunliffe 1971, pp. 123-8). The gardens at Fishbourne also illustrate the use of plants for purely aesthetic reasons: a series of planting trenches arranged in decorative patterns probably contained ornamental hedges, possibly of box (*Buxus sempervirens*) (Cunliffe 1971, p. 128) (Figure 4.4). Remains of box, perhaps from hedge-clipping, have been found at several Roman-period sites, including the towns of London (Armitage, Locker & Straker 1987, p. 273), York (A.R. Hall, Kenward & Williams 1980, pp. 143-4; A.R. Hall & Kenward 1990, p. 359) and Silchester (Reid 1903, p. 426), and also from Farmoor (Lambrick & Robinson 1979, p. 127).

There has been some debate over whether or not grapes (*Vitis vinifera*) were grown in Britain in the Roman period (Williams 1977). This issue has been difficult to resolve because, until recently, evidence for grapes from Roman-period contexts consisted entirely of pips. Grape pips are quite commonly found in Roman towns, as at London (Willcox 1978; Tyers 1988, p. 448; Pearson & Giorgi 1992, p. 165), Silchester (Reid 1903, p. 427), and York (Greig 1976; A.R. Hall & Kenward 1990, p. 407), and occasionally from villas, such as Gorhambury, near St Albans (Wainwright 1990, p. 218). In such situations they are usually accompanied by a range of exotic food plants, suggesting that the pips arrived in imported raisins. Grape pollen can provide better evidence of cultivation because it suggests the presence of grape vines, rather than merely the fruit. Until recently there was no pollen evidence for grapes from Roman Britain, but the discovery of grape pollen in a series of planting trenches at Wollaston, Northamptonshire, offers convincing evidence for the existence of a vineyard (Meadows 1996) (Figure 4.5).

In addition to changes in plant cultivation, animal husbandry also

4.4: Reconstruction of the formal garden at Fishbourne Romano-British villa: box (*Buxus sempervirens*) hedges have been planted in the original bedding trenches, revealed during excavation.

underwent some changes during the Roman period. The main animals providing food continued to be cattle, sheep and pigs, as in the Iron Age (for reviews see King 1978, 1984, 1991; Maltby 1981; Luff 1982; Noddle 1984), but there was an increase in the number of cattle relative to sheep (Grant 1989). This trend was apparently initiated in the late Iron, perhaps reflecting the need for larger or more intensively cultivated areas of arable land – cattle would have been used to pull ploughs, in addition to providing a source of food, and raw materials, such as leather and horn (Grant 1989). Another factor in this shift may have been a Roman dietary preference for beef (King 1978).

Horse bones are commonly recovered from sites of the Roman period, and the occasional presence of butchery marks suggest that horse meat may have formed a minor part of the diet (e.g. Dobney, Jaques & Irving nd, p. 46). Domestic fowl also occur widely on Roman-period sites (Maltby 1979), but it is again uncertain to what extent they contributed to the diet.

Bones of red deer (*Cervus elaphus*) and roe deer (*Capreolus capreolus*)

4.5: Planting trench for vines – part of a complex of similar trenches covering several hectares – excavated in a Pioneer Aggregates quarry at Wollaston, Northamptonshire. (Photograph provided by Ian Meadows, © Northamptonshire County Council.)

are frequent in later Roman contexts, perhaps reflecting an interest in hunting (King 1978). Hunting may also be the origin of the bones of wild boar (*Sus scrofa*) occasionally recovered from Romano-British sites, such as the villas at Fishbourne (Grant 1971) and Bignor (Armitage, Rudling & Parfitt 1995) in Sussex.

Domestic pig bones also seem to become more abundant at later Roman sites, and it has been suggested that this, and the increase of red deer remains, may reflect exploitation of woodland areas. Neither species requires woodland, however. Pigs have traditionally been linked with woodland because of the medieval practice of pannage, in which pigs were released into oak or beech woods to feed on acorns or beech-mast. Pigs could have been fed in other ways, however, such as on the waste products of cereal processing (Biddick 1984).

Roman dietary preferences may have led to the introduction to Britain of the garden dormouse (*Eliomys quercinus*), remains of which have been recovered from York (Hall & Kenward 1990) and a Roman warehouse at South Shields (Younger 1994). The latter context suggests the possibility of accidental introduction in imported grain, however. Other additions to the British fauna that seem to date from this period are the common garden snail (*Helix aspersa*) and the Roman or edible snail (*Helix pomatia*), both of which can also be used for food (Kerney 1966).

Having briefly considered the nature of agriculture in Roman Britain, we turn now to an examination of the vegetation. This begins with a reconstruction of the character of the landscape in terms of the relative abundance of woodland and open land, followed by a consideration of regional trends in land-use change in the course of the Roman period.

Vegetation in the Roman period: the pollen evidence

Here pollen evidence for the Roman period overall is assembled to provide a generalised reconstruction of the extent of woodland, and of crop cultivation, following the approach adopted for the late Iron Age (Chapter 3). Ideally one would divide the data for the Roman period into shorter 'time slices' to see the effects of the initial conquest, consolidation within the Empire, and then Roman withdrawal. Unfortunately, however, the reliance on radiocarbon chronologies and poor temporal resolution of most pollen sequences mean that such an approach is impossible. Instead, for the purpose of mapping, the pollen data have had to be averaged over the whole of the Roman period. There will obviously be some overlap with the late Iron Age and early post-Roman periods, but this is unavoidable. All that can be achieved is an indication of the general character of the vegetation at a period centred approximately on the Roman period. The questions of the impact of the Roman Conquest and withdrawal are discussed separately later, using the most detailed and well-dated pollen sequences.

4. The Roman period

Site selection

Sites have been selected for the maps following the method described in detail in Chapter 3: pollen sequences are used only if there is at least one radiocarbon date with a calibrated range lying at least partially in the Roman period. Sites where the relevant dates have particularly large error terms (>±80) are excluded. Furthermore, at least two pollen samples must come from the Roman-period deposits. The relevant sites and dates are listed in Table 4.1 (see p. 94). Tree and shrub pollen percentages have been calculated as an average figure for the Roman period, and the results plotted in one of four percentage ranges (Figure 4.6).

The main crops represented in the Roman-period pollen sequences are cereals and hemp (*Cannabis sativa*) and/or hop (*Humulus lupulus*). Cereals are mapped together because most do not have sufficiently distinctive pollen to enable their separate identification, although the few specific records of rye pollen are indicated (Figure 4.7). Pollen of hemp is similar to that of hop, so most analysts do not separate the two. It should, therefore, be remembered that 'hemp type' or Cannabaceae pollen could belong to either plant (Figure 4.8). As crops are generally under-represented in the pollen record, they are mapped only by presence.

Results and interpretation

There are forty-eight pollen sequences that fit the criteria adopted here as reflecting the vegetation of the Roman period. Their distribution is patchy, leaving most of south-east England and the Midlands, and mainland

4.6: Woodland in the Roman period: percentages of tree and shrub pollen in radiocarbon-dated sequences spanning the period.

1. Dallican Water	18. Hallowell Moss	35. Cefn Glas
2. Sheshader	19. Hutton Henry	36. Nant Helen
3. Loch Meodal	20. Thorpe Bulmer	37. Sidlings Copse
4. An t-Aoradh	21. Rusland Moss	38. Swineshead
5. Machrie Moor	22. Fairsnape Fell	39. Wiggenhall St
6. Blairbech Bog	23. Fenton Cottage	Germans
7. Fannyside Muir	24. Rishworth Moor	40. Hockham Mere
8. Letham Moss	25. Featherbed Moss	41. Redmere
9. Black Loch	26. Lindow Moss	42. Willingham Mere
10. Burnfoothill Moss	27. Knowsley Park	43. Meare Heath
11. Glasson Moss	28. Crose Mere	44. Abbot's Way
12. Walton Moss	29. Llyn Cororion	45. Rimsmoor
13. Midgeholme Moss	30. Bryn y Castell	46. Aller Farm
14. Fellend Moss	31. Crawcwellt	47. Hoar Moor
15. Fozy Moss	32. Moel y Gerddi	48. Rough Tor
16. Steng Moss	33. Cefn Gwernffrwd	
17. Quick Moss	34. Brecon Beacons	

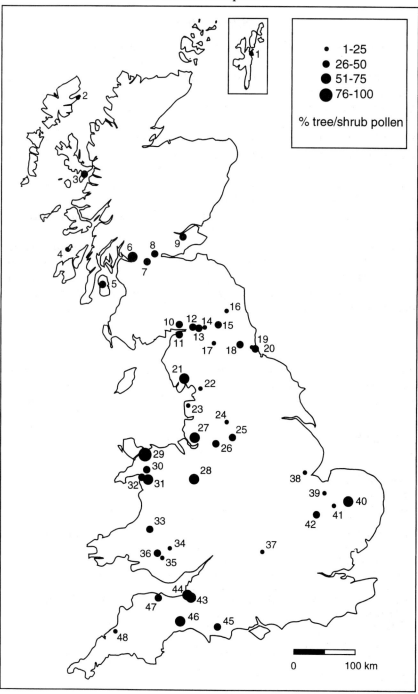

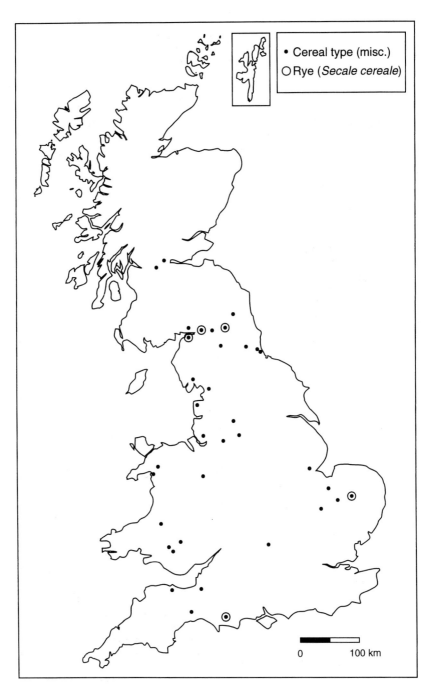

4.7: Cereal cultivation in the Roman period: presence of cereal pollen in radiocarbon-dated sequences spanning the period. For key to sites see Figure 4.6.

4.8: Cultivation of hemp/hop in the Roman period: presence of Cannabaceae pollen in radiocarbon-dated sequences spanning the period. For key to sites see Figure 4.6.

4. The Roman period

Table 4.1. Pollen sequences with radiocarbon dates and at least two pollen samples from the Roman-period deposits

*detailed sequences – 7 or more relevant samples

Site	Radiocarbon date (BP)	Lab code	Cal range (95.4% confidence)	Reference
England				
Abbot's Way	1954±40	SRR-1011	60 BC-AD 130	Beckett & Hibbert 1979
Aller Farm	1790±50	GU-2710	AD 110-350 (94.0%)	Hatton & Caseldine
			AD 360-380 (1.4%)	1992
Crose Mere	1610±75	Q-1231	AD 250-610	Beales 1980
	2086±75	Q-1232	260 BC-AD 70 (82.8%)	
			370-280 BC (12.6%)	
*Fairsnape Fell	1595±45	SRR-4504	AD 340-570	Mackay & Tallis
	1735±45	SRR-4505	AD 190-420 (93.2%)	1994
			AD 140-170 (2.2%)	
	2025±40	SRR-4506	120 BC-AD 70 (92.8%)	
			160-140 BC (2.6%)	
Featherbed Moss	2028±50	Q-853	170 BC-AD 70	Tallis & Switsur 1973
Fellend Moss	1948±45	SRR-876	90 BC-AD 140	Davies & Turner 1979
*Fenton Cottage	1590±50	GU-5144	AD 340-600	Middleton et al. 1995;
	1810±90	GU-5157	AD 10-420	Wells et al. 1997
	1940±110	GU-5158	250 BC-AD 350	
	2080±90	GU-5159	370 BC-AD 80	
*Fozy Moss	1820±45	SRR-4539	AD 80-260 (87.5%)	Dumayne & Barber
			AD 280-330 (7.9%)	1994
*Glasson Moss	1860±40	SRR-4533	AD 60-250	Dumayne & Barber 1994
Hallowell Moss	1782±60	SRR-414	AD 110-400	Donaldson & Turner
	1956±70	SRR-415	120 BC-AD 230	1977
Hoar Moor	1760±80	I-15,548	AD 70-340	Francis & Slater 1990
Hockham Mere	1625±45	Q-2225	AD 330-550 (92.1%)	K.D. Bennett 1983
			AD 260-290 (3.3%)	
	1980±50	Q-2224	110 BC-AD 120	
Hutton Henry	1842±70	SRR-600	AD 0-350	Bartley et al. 1976
Knowsley Park	1680±50	Birm-1177	AD 220-460 (94.3%)	Cowell & Innes 1994
			AD 480-530 (1.1%)	

4. The Roman period

Site	Radiocarbon date (BP)	Lab code	Cal range (95.4% confidence)	Reference
*Lindow Moss	1764±48	UB-3238	AD 130-390	Branch & Scaife 1995
Meare Heath	1746±45	SRR-911	AD 180-400 (91.4%) AD 140-170 (4.0%)	Beckett & Hibbert 1979
	2062±45	SRR-912	200 BC-AD 30	
*Midgeholme Moss	1740±90	GU-5179	AD 70-460	Wiltshire 1997
	1970±60	GU-5081	120 BC-AD 150 (94.4%) 160-140 BC (1.0%)	
Quick Moss	2035±50		180 BC-AD 70	Rowell & Turner 1985
*Redmere	1850±50	Q-2593	AD 50-260 (92.6%) AD 290-330 (2.8%)	Waller 1994b
Rimsmoor	2080±80	HAR-3923	270 BC-AD 70 (83.3%) 370-280 BC (12.1%)	Waton 1982, 1983
Rishworth	1920±80	GaK-2825	110 BC-AD 260 (94.4%) AD 300-320 (1.0%)	Bartley 1975
Rough Tor (N C)	1840±70	Beta-78541	AD 10-350	Gearey & Charman 1996
*Rusland Moss	1963±50	SRR-126	100 BC-AD 130	Dickinson 1975
Sidlings Copse	1820±80	OxA-2047	AD 20-400	Day 1991
*Steng Moss	1970±60	Q-1520	120 BC-AD 150 (94.4%) 160-140 BC (1.0%)	Davies & Turner 1979
Swineshead	1590±60	Q-2558	AD 330-610	Waller & Alderton 1994
	1740±60	Q-2557	AD 130-420	
Thorpe Bulmer	2064±60	SRR-404	210 BC-AD 80 (91.7%) 360-310 BC (3.7%)	Bartley et al. 1976
*Walton Moss	1925±40	SRR-4530	40 BC-AD 150 (92.9%) AD 160-200 (2.5%)	Dumayne & Barber 1994
	2000±40	SRR-4531	110 BC-AD 80	
Wiggenhall St Germans	1820±50	Q-2587	AD 70-270 (85.1%) AD 280-340 (10.3%)	Waller 1994e
Willingham Mere	1910±60	Q-2582	60 BC-AD 240	Waller 1994c

Scotland

An t-Aoradh	1700±40	Q-2439	AD 240-420	Beck & Gilbertson 1987
*Black Loch	1885±75	UB-2294	60 BC-AD 270 (91.6%) AD 280-330 (3.8%)	Whittington et al. 1991

Site	Radiocarbon date (BP)	Lab code	Cal range (95.4% confidence)	Reference
	2015±75	UB-2295	210 BC-AD 140 (94.0%)	
			350-310 BC (1.4%)	
*Blairbech Bog	1750±45	SRR-4619	AD 140-400	Dumayne-Peaty 1998
*Burnfoothill Moss (paired dates)	2015±45	SRR-3752	120 BC-AD 80 (93.0%)	Tipping 1995 a, b
			170-140 BC (2.4%)	
	1965±45		90 BC-AD 120	
Dallican Water	1565±65	Q-2760	AD 340-630	K.D. Bennett *et al.* 1992
*Fannyside Muir	1925±45	SRR-4617	40 BC-AD 210	Dumayne-Peaty 1998
*Letham Moss	1715±40	SRR-4542	AD 230-420	Dumayne-Peaty 1998
Loch Meodal	1930±50	Q-1310	50 BC-AD 220	Birks 1993b
Machrie Moor	1615±55	GU-1349	AD 320-570 (91.0%)	D.E. Robinson & Dickson 1988
			AD 250-300 (4.4%)	
Sheshader	1840±60	GU-1455	AD 20-270 (87.4%)	Newell 1988
			AD 280-340 (8.0%)	

Wales

Site	Radiocarbon date (BP)	Lab code	Cal range (95.4% confidence)	Reference
Brecon Beacons	1855±80	CAR-58	40 BC-AD 350	F.M. Chambers 1982
	2065±70	CAR-57	250 BC-AD 80 (89.0%)	
			360-290 BC (6.4%)	
*Bryn y Castell	1655±50	GrN-17582	AD 250-540	Mighall & Chambers 1995
Cefn Glas	1700±70	CAR-415	AD 140-460 (91.9%)	A.G.Smith & Green 1995
			AD 480-530 (3.5%)	
*Cefn Gwernffrwd	1900±45	CAR-74	AD 0-230	F.M. Chambers 1983a
	2030±45	CAR-73	170 BC-AD 70	
Crawcwellt	1780±35	GrN-18405	AD 130-340	F.M. Chambers & Lageard 1993
Llyn Cororion	1585±65	SRR-3468	AD 330-610 (93.9%)	Watkins 1990
			AD 260-290 (1.5%)	
Moel y Gerddi	1665±60	CAR-660	AD 240-540	F.M. Chambers & Price 1988
Nant Helen	1820±70	CAR-1150	AD 50-390	F.M. Chambers *et al.* 1990

Scotland north of the Antonine Wall, lacking any relevant data. Of these sites, only ten have tree and shrub pollen frequencies greater than 50%, and seventeen have tree and shrub pollen frequencies of 25% or less. This suggests that much of the landscape was rather open in the Roman period.

Cereal pollen is recorded in thirty-six of the sequences, stretching from Dorset to southern Scotland and from west Wales to East Anglia. Rye is specifically identified from five of these: Rimsmoor in Dorset (Waton 1983), Hockham Mere in Norfolk (K.D. Bennett 1983), and three sites in Northumberland: Fozy Moss, Glasson Moss and Walton Moss (Dumayne & Barber 1994) (although an Iron Age date for some of these records is possible, as discussed earlier). Pollen evidence for cereal cultivation north of the Antonine Wall is lacking, however, and this, combined with the rarity of macroscopic remains of cereals from archaeological sites in the area (Boyd 1988), suggests that agricultural activity was principally pastoral. Pollen of hemp or hop is similarly sparse in Scotland, with a single record from Machrie Moor on Arran (D.E. Robinson & Dickson 1988). There are scattered records for hemp/hop from sites in England, and a single record from Wales – Moel y Gerddi (F.M. Chambers & Price 1988).

Regional patterns of vegetation in the Roman period

The vegetation of the Roman period is here discussed on a regional basis, following the approach adopted for the late Iron Age. Obviously there has to be some overlap between vegetational changes described here and in the previous chapter, in view of the uncertainties imposed by radiocarbon dating. Note that laboratory codes for radiocarbon dates are given only for sites not listed in Table 4.1.

South-east England

The only pollen sequence with directly dated Roman-period deposits from central southern or south-eastern England is from Sidlings Copse in Oxfordshire (Day 1991, 1993) (Figure 3.5). This site lay next to a Roman villa, Headington Wick (Jewitt 1851), and was within the area of production of Oxfordshire ware pottery (Young 1977, see later). Here little local woodland remained by the beginning of the Roman period, and alder (*Alnus glutinosa*) seems to have disappeared entirely immediately above a level dated 1820±80 BP (cal AD 20-400). Willow (*Salix*) replaced the local alder stands on soils prone to waterlogging and, along with the limited amount of oak (*Quercus*) and hazel (*Corylus avellana*) woodland on drier land, may have provided fuel for the local kilns. Cereals were also cultivated locally, and loss-on-ignition analysis of the deposits indicates substantial inputs of mineral soil material, presumably derived from ploughing the surrounding soils (Day 1991). In a broader context, archaeological evidence suggests that alluviation in the Upper Thames Valley began in the late Iron Age or Roman period (M. Robinson & Lambrick 1984), probably also reflecting widespread soil erosion due to agricultural activity.

East Anglia

From East Anglia most of the pollen sequences are from sites peripheral to the Fenland basin, and show a predominantly open landscape, with some areas of fen woodland (Waller 1994a). Cereal cultivation seems to have been widespread, and from Willingham Mere there is a record of '*Cannabis* type' pollen immediately above a level dated 1910±60 BP (60 cal BC-cal AD 240) (Waller 1994c). This record could derive from wild hops growing in the fenland, rather than reflecting hemp cultivation. Further inland, the pollen sequence from Hockham Mere, at the edge of the Breckland, suggests an extension of heathland from just before a level dated 1980±50 BP (110 cal BC-cal AD 120), although much local woodland persisted throughout the Roman period (K.D. Bennett 1983). Cereals, including rye, were cultivated locally.

South-west England

At Rimsmoor in Dorset a peak of woodland clearance, associated with cultivation of rye and possibly hemp, at 2080±80 BP (270 cal BC-cal AD 70) was followed by woodland regeneration (Waton 1982, 1983). This suggests some abandonment of agricultural land in the Roman period, a pattern recorded at very few other sites in the southern half of Britain.

At Aller Farm, Devon, peat accumulation began at a level dated 1790±50 BP (cal AD 110-350) in an environment dominated by alder carr (Hatton & Caseldine 1992). The pollen record probably reflects only very local vegetation, and shows little change during the Roman period, although there is evidence for local cereal cultivation.

On the Somerset Levels pollen sequences associated with the prehistoric Meare Heath and Abbot's Way trackways indicate a mixture of woodland and open land in the Roman period, with cereal cultivation on dry land areas (Beckett & Hibbert 1979). Further west, on the uplands of Exmoor, a pollen sequence from Hoar Moor suggests that the local landscape remained predominantly wooded until the Roman period (Francis & Slater 1990). The extent of woodland then declined markedly at a level dated 1760±80 BP (cal AD 70-430), perhaps associated with an expansion of local cereal cultivation. Clearance began in the Iron Age elsewhere on the moors (Chapter 3), so there was evidently regional variation in the pattern of land-use. At Rough Tor, on Bodmin, the landscape had been cleared of most of its woodland by the end of the Iron Age (Gearey & Charman 1996), and this open landscape persisted throughout the Roman period.

4. The Roman period

The Midlands

The only pollen sequences with well-dated Roman-period deposits from the Midlands are from Crose Mere in Shropshire and Featherbed Moss in Derbyshire. Around Crose Mere the landscape remained quite wooded in the Roman period, with little sign of renewed clearance following that of the late Iron Age (Beales 1980) (Figure 3.8). Cereal cultivation seems to have expanded locally, however, perhaps accompanied by hemp – pollen identified as 'Cannabaceae' becomes abundant immediately above a level dated 1610±75 BP (cal AD 250-610). The age range of this date spans the late Roman and post-Roman periods, however, so it is possible that the sparse record of Cannabaceae pollen in the presumed Roman-period deposits represents contamination with pollen from a later phase of hemp cultivation or processing.

At Featherbed Moss there was some extension of clearance in the Roman period, with increases of bracken (*Pteridium aquilinum*), grasses and plantain (*Plantago*) (Tallis & Switsur 1973). Much of the landscape probably consisted of a mixture of open land and woodland, and the sporadic records for cereal pollen suggest at least some local arable.

North-west England

At Lindow Moss, Cheshire, a pollen sequence was obtained from peat deposits close to the site of discovery of the Lindow III 'bog body' (see Chapter 3). The sequence suggests that the landscape at the start of the Roman period remained substantially wooded (Branch & Scaife 1995). Some cereal cultivation occurred locally in the early Roman period, and there was a major decline of oak and hazel in approximately the mid-Roman period. Tree and shrub pollen frequencies fall to a minimum at 1764±48 BP (cal AD 130-390), accompanied by an increase of grasses and then heather (*Calluna vulgaris*). This might reflect the spread of heather onto depleted soils previously used for agriculture, although colonisation of drier areas of the peat surface is also possible. There was some recovery of woodland towards the end of the Roman period, a trend that continued into the post-Roman period.

At Knowsley Park Moss, Merseyside, the Roman-period environment was again predominantly wooded (Cowell & Innes 1994), although oak declines and herbs (especially ribwort plantain, *Plantago lanceolata*) and heather begin to increase immediately above a level dated 1680±50 BP (cal AD 220-460). The cleared areas probably consisted of a patchwork of moorland, pasture and arable areas. A record of '*Cannabis*-type' pollen at the same point suggests the possibility of hemp cultivation, although the range of the radiocarbon date means that this could reflect post-Roman cultivation.

Further north the landscape seems to have been less wooded in the

Roman period. The pollen sequence from Fenton Cottage suggests removal of most of the local woodland at the end of the Iron Age or in the Roman period, by a level dated 1810±90 BP (cal AD 10-420) (Middleton *et al.* 1995; Wells *et al.* 1997) (Figure 3.9). This was associated with a peak of heather, suggesting woodland was replaced largely by moorland, although there are signs of cereal cultivation from the pollen record also. Towards the end of the Roman period (or in the immediate post-Roman period) there was some regeneration of local woodland, until it was probably of similar extent to that in the late Iron Age.

A decline of heather in the latter half of the Roman period at Fenton Cottage corresponds with a period of abundant charcoal deposition, suggesting the possibility that moorland areas were regularly burned. This may have been a deliberate form of management, designed to improve the grazing potential of the area (see Gimingham 1972, pp. 186-205). Burning encourages the growth of young heather shoots, but if it is frequent and/or followed by intensive grazing it may lead to replacement of heather by grasses. An alternative possibility is that natural fires may have become more frequent due to a change in climate. The macroscopic plant remains from the site suggest that there was a drier phase at this time, and this would itself have encouraged the spread of fire, whatever its source of ignition.

A predominantly open landscape is also indicated at Fairsnape Fell in the central Pennines, 30km north-east of Fenton Cottage. Here the landscape seems to have been dominated by moorland throughout the Roman period (Mackay & Tallis 1994). An increase of grasses in the latter half of the period could reflect grazing of animals on the mire surface, leading to a decline of heather, or increased woodland clearance. Cereal pollen occurs throughout the Roman-period deposits, suggesting crops were grown nearby.

North-east England

Much of Yorkshire is devoid of Roman-period pollen evidence, and only the sequence from Rishworth Moor has radiocarbon-dated deposits for the period. Here a date of 1920±80 BP (110 cal BC-cal AD 260) marks a reduction in the extent of woodland and peaks of grasses, ribwort plantain and bracken (Bartley 1975), perhaps reflecting an increase in the extent of grazing. This was followed by a sharp drop in frequency of herbs and bracken, and woodland regeneration, suggesting abandonment of local agricultural land towards the end of the Roman period.

Northern England

Further north, the concentration of pollen sequences within 20km of Hadrian's Wall provides an opportunity for a more detailed reconstruction

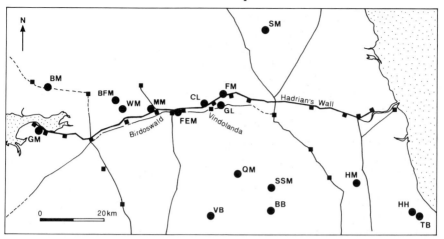

4.9: The Hadrian's Wall area, showing the wall, roads and forts (squares), and locations of off-site pollen sequences (circles): BB - Bollihope Bog, BFM – Bolton Fell Moss, BM – Burnfoothill Moss, CL – Crag Lough, FEM – Fellend Moss, FM – Fozy Moss, GL – Grindon Lough, GM – Glasson Moss, HH – Hutton Henry, HM – Hallowell Moss, MM – Midgeholme Moss, QM – Quick Moss, SM – Steng Moss, SSM – Stewart Shield Meadow, TB – Thorpe Bulmer, VB – Valley Bog, WM – Walton Moss. (Forts and roads after S. Johnson 1989.)

of Roman-period vegetation change than from any other part of Britain (Figure 4.9). All of the sequences from this area have tree/shrub pollen frequencies of 50% or less for the Roman period, and four have frequencies less than 25%, indicating a substantially open environment. Cereal pollen occurs in Roman-period deposits from most of these sites, with records for rye at three.

Much research has focused on the effects of the Roman occupation on woodland and agriculture in this area, and the extent to which the Roman military were responsible for the first extensive clearance. Roman occupation of the area began in the AD 70s-80s, with construction of the Stanegate road from Corbridge to Carlisle. This was associated with a line of forts, including Vindolanda and Corbridge. Hadrian's Wall was built later, in the AD 120s to 130s, along a near-parallel route running from the estuary of the Tyne to the Solway Firth (Breeze & Dobson 1987) (Figure 4.10).

In terms of the environmental implications of Hadrian's Wall, attention has focused especially on the need for timber and fuel for construction of the wall and its forts, and also on the possibility of agricultural expansion to supply the Roman forces (e.g. Dumayne 1993, 1994; Dumayne & Barber 1994). Problems of a reliance on a radiocarbon chronology mean that in several cases the date of vegetational changes cannot be pinpointed closely enough to tell whether the Roman military or native peoples were in-

4.10: Hadrian's Wall at Sycamore Gap.

volved. Nevertheless, at some sites extensive clearance and cereal cultivation evidently began in the late Iron Age or before (see Chapter 3).

Several pollen sequences have come from sites within a few hundred metres of the wall, providing the opportunity to examine variations in the pattern of vegetation change along the frontier. These sequences are from various types of deposit, including mires (Fellend Moss, Fozy Moss, Glasson Moss and Midgeholme Moss), lakes (Crag Lough and Grindon Lough), and on-site deposits from forts along the line of the wall (Vindolanda and Birdoswald).

Fellend Moss lies adjacent to the vallum – a large ditch flanked by banks running to the south of the wall. Here the first significant woodland clearance began just above a level dated 1948±45 BP (90 cal BC-cal AD 140) (Davies & Turner 1979). The reduction of woodland was accompanied by substantial increases of grasses, ribwort plantain and heather, and a single record of cereal pollen. This sequence might reflect either clearance of woodland by native farmers, or clearance of the military zone before construction of the vallum and wall.

Fozy Moss lies just 200m north of the central sector of the wall, and the pollen sequence indicates a major, and apparently rapid, reduction in the extent of woodland beginning at a level dated 1820±45 BP (cal AD 80-260) (Dumayne & Barber 1994). Pollen of rye appears for the first time at the same level. Clearance seems to have continued throughout the Roman period, culminating in an almost totally cleared landscape (Figure 4.11). Here, then, it is possible that the onset of major clearance may well have been connected with construction of the wall. Obviously, the range of the date means that such a link can only be tentative, but given the proximity of the site to the wall, it is very unlikely that major woodland clearance would have been left until after the local section of the wall was built. The pollen of rye and other cereals suggests that some arable land was created, perhaps reflecting an increased need for agricultural produce to supply the army. There is also a record for '*Cannabis* type' pollen from deposits likely to be either late Roman or early post-Roman in date, suggesting the possibility of local hemp cultivation.

At Glasson Moss, just 500m south of the western end of the wall, sustained clearance began in approximately the mid-Iron Age, although substantial areas of woodland remained throughout the Iron Age (Dumayne & Barber 1994) (Figure 4.11). Further clearance, affecting particularly oak, occurred at 1860±40 BP (cal AD 60-250). At this point a single record of rye pollen occurs, after which cereal pollen is absent from the Roman-period deposits. Here, then, it seems that establishment of the military zone may have put some agricultural land out of use.

These sites illustrate the problems of linking the palaeoecological record with a well-dated archaeological sequence. It is not usually possible to go beyond identifying an approximate coincidence between woodland

4.11: Pollen curves of grasses from Fozy Moss, Glasson Moss and Walton Moss, near Hadrian's Wall, showing variable patterns of clearance. Percentages based on the sum of non-mire pollen. (Redrawn from data of Dumayne in Dumayne & Barber 1994.)

4.12: Crag Lough, lying immediately below Hadrian's Wall where it runs along Highshield Crags.

clearance at some sites and construction of Hadrian's Wall. In reality, clearance could have occurred decades earlier or, in theory, later.

A recent attempt to provide a more detailed linkage between the archaeological and palaeoenvironmental records from Hadrian's Wall has sought 'markers' from construction of the wall (including particles of building materials and charcoal) in the sediments of an adjacent lake, Crag Lough (Fig. 3.10, 4.12) (P. Dark in prep.). This approach seeks to establish a direct stratigraphic link between the pollen sequence and construction of the adjacent section of wall, avoiding the imprecision of radiocarbon dating. The results indicate that the wall was built in a landscape that was already fairly open, following the onset of major clearance immediately after a level dated 2280 ± 50 BP (AA-28173, 410-190 cal BC). Construction of the wall appears to have involved only limited further clearance, and did not coincide with any major transformation in the character of the local environment.

A similar approach has been adopted to providing a landscape context for the Stanegate road. Analysis of a sediment sequence from Grindon Lough, immediately north of the Stanegate, suggests that construction of the road led to a major episode of clay inwash (P. Dark in prep). This, again, provides a 'marker' for detailed correlation of Roman activity and local environmental change, indicating that the line of the road was already substantially clear of woodland before the Roman occupation. Thus, both sequences indicate that construction of the frontier was able to take advantage of clearance undertaken before the Roman occupation, at least along much of its route.

A picture of the local vegetation at specific points along the frontier is provided by deposits directly associated with some of the forts. However, such evidence usually provides only a 'snapshot' view, covering a short period. For example, pollen assemblages from the ditches of the first fort at Vindolanda shed light on the nature of the environment soon after it was built, *c.* AD 85 (Manning, Birley & Tipping 1997). Pollen of grasses is abundant, and the authors argue that this reflects a largely open landscape. Over half of the samples have frequencies of tree and shrub pollen greater than 50%, however, and in several samples up to 80%. The significance of these assemblages is uncertain, as preservation was poor (most samples contained over 40% deteriorated pollen), and much of the pollen could have been reworked from erosion of the ditch sides. Given the fact that the location of the pollen in the ditches means that it must post-date initial construction of the fort, and that some open land must have been created to lay out the site, it is hardly surprising that there are indications of clearance in the pollen spectra. Unfortunately, however, the pollen assemblages shed no new light on the nature of the landscape before the arrival of the Roman military, because, obviously, they post-date that event. It is notable, however, that the use of turf in the fort ramparts indicates that at least some local grassland must have been present.

Further on-site pollen spectra from the Hadrianic frontier come from the fort at Birdoswald (Wilmott 1997), located at a point where the wall was originally built of turf. Here pollen samples were analysed from the buried surface beneath the Turf Wall (Wiltshire 1997), which was partially demolished when the stone fort was built. The pollen assemblages suggest that the site was wooded immediately before the wall was built in the AD 120s, so here clearance seems directly related to wall construction. In contrast, pollen analysis of a buried land surface below the Turf Wall at Appletree, just 2km west of Birdoswald, indicated an open moorland environment before construction (Wiltshire 1997).

Peat deposits from Midgeholme Moss, just north of Birdoswald, provide a longer chronological context for the local vegetational sequence (Wiltshire 1997). Local clearance apparently began just before a level dated 2100±60 BP (GU-5082, 260 cal BC–cal AD 20), but was followed immediately by a minor episode of woodland regeneration (mainly of alder), before a further increase of clearance dated 1970±60 BP (120 cal BC–cal AD 150). Despite this clearance, much woodland remained. Once again, the radiocarbon date is insufficiently precise to be certain that the clearance recorded at Midgeholme is the same as the phase that obviously accompanied construction of the Turf Wall, but this seems the most obvious explanation. It is interesting to note that, despite the pollen evidence that much of the local landscape was well-wooded, there was evidently enough turf for construction of the local section of wall.

4. The Roman period

Overall, the pollen sequences from Hadrian's Wall suggest that the extent of woodland remaining in the early Roman period was variable. Where local soils were prone to waterlogging, the landscape seem to have been predominantly wooded, as around Fozy Moss and at Birdoswald. But where soils were more favourable for agriculture much woodland had already been cleared in the Iron Age, as in the central sector around Crag Lough. Some pollen sequences, notably that from Fozy Moss, suggest that local woodland clearance was directly connected with establishment of the Roman frontier. Where the line of the wall remained wooded, some of this clearance can obviously be attributed simply to clearance of its projected route. Provision of structural timber and fuel requirements (including lime-burning for mortar) would also have had an effect on local woodland resources, although it is likely that at least some areas of woodland were managed rather than destroyed (see later).

Further evidence that much of the line of Hadrian's Wall was cleared before the wall was built comes from plough marks sealed below the wall and its forts (Topping 1989a, b; Higham 1991; Bidwell & Watson 1996). These marks are mostly of uncertain date, and need not necessarily indicate normal ploughing. Some could have resulted from the initial attempt to break up the soil after woodland clearance or conversion of grassland to arable, as suggested for the marks from Turret 10A at Throckley (J. Bennett 1983). Alternatively, some of the marks may reflect attempts to level the ground before building works.

Turning to pollen sequences from sites further from Hadrian's Wall, at Walton Moss, 3km to the north, clearance from the mid-late Iron Age was followed by woodland regeneration and a decline in the extent of open land by a level dated 1925±40 BP (40 cal BC-cal AD 150) (Dumayne & Barber 1994). Possibly this reflects land abandonment as the local tribe, the Brigantes, resisted the Roman occupation. Renewed clearance followed, probably in the mid-late Roman period, resulting in a very open landscape of grassland and moorland with some cereal cultivation (Figure 4.11). At nearby Bolton Fell Moss clearance peaked at 1860±60 BP (Hv-3085, cal AD 10-260) (Barber 1981). Here a Roman-period regeneration phase is less obvious than at Walton Moss, despite the close proximity of the sites, perhaps because the Bolton Fell Moss sequence is less detailed than that from Walton Moss (Dumayne-Peaty & Barber 1998).

Another detailed sequence comes from Steng Moss to the north-east. Here a major increase of clearance at a level dated 1970±60 BP (120 cal BC-cal AD 150) included an expansion of cereal cultivation, increases of grasses, sorrel (*Rumex*) and ribwort plantain, and massive rise in frequency of heather pollen (Davies & Turner 1979). This suggests an expansion of moorland, as well as pasture and arable land, at the end of the Iron Age or in the early Roman period.

A cluster of pollen sequences has been produced from the Durham area, forming the basis for Turner's analysis of vegetation in the Roman period

4. The Roman period

(J. Turner 1979). As discussed in Chapter 3, some of these sequences are excluded from the present analysis due to the large age ranges for the radiocarbon dates. Of the more securely dated sequences, that from Hallowell Moss shows the onset of major clearance in the late Iron Age or early Roman period, at a level dated 1956±70 BP (120 cal BC-cal AD 230) (Donaldson & Turner 1977). Local cereal cultivation apparently began at this time, but there were also increases of grasses, ribwort plantain and bracken, perhaps suggesting pasture. Clearance peaked at 1782±60 BP (cal AD 110-400), followed by woodland regeneration. At Hutton Henry there was an increase of clearance at 1842±70 BP (cal AD 0-350) (Bartley, Chambers & Hart-Jones 1976), while at Thorpe Bulmer extensive clearance and cereal cultivation seem to have begun at 2064±60 BP (210 cal BC-cal AD 80). Pollen of hemp appears at this point in the Thorpe Bulmer sequence, and peaks at 1730±120 BP (GaK-3713, cal AD 0-600) (Bartley *et al.* 1976). The range of the date, however, means that this cannot be taken as certain evidence of hemp cultivation in the Roman period.

Further south, in Cumbria, at Rusland Moss there appears to have been a period of woodland regeneration at the end of the Iron Age or start of the Roman period, dated 1963±50 BP (100 cal BC-cal AD 130) (Dickinson 1975). Later in the Roman period there was a phase of clearance and the onset of local cereal cultivation, although much of the landscape probably remained wooded. A pollen sequence from nearby Devoke Water shows a major increase of grasses and heather, and the first record of cereal pollen, at 1750±130 BP (NPL-117, 50 cal BC-cal AD 600) (Pennington 1964, 1970), although the large age range for the date means that this could have happened at any time from the Iron Age to post-Roman period.

Pollen evidence from the north of England overall suggests that some areas had already undergone extensive woodland clearance by the end of the Iron Age, but that there was a major new episode of activity across most of the region in the late Iron Age or early Roman period. At some sites near Hadrian's Wall clearance may have been directly related to construction of the frontier – to clear its route – or indirectly to create new farmland to meet increased demands for agricultural produce from the Roman army. It is notable that clearance occurred at a similar date at many sites several kilometres from Hadrian's Wall, however, suggesting a general agricultural expansion in the late Iron Age/early Roman period. A few pollen diagrams show a period of woodland regeneration at approximately the start of the Roman period, possibly reflecting temporary land abandonment at the time of the Conquest.

Scotland

As was the case for the Iron Age, there are remarkably few well-dated pollen sequences with Roman-period deposits from Scotland. Most relevant sequences are from the islands, or the region around the Antonine

Wall. For the latter group, the focus of attention has, as with the Hadrianic frontier, concentrated on whether woodland clearance was connected with the Roman military presence, or occurred earlier for agricultural purposes (Dumayne 1993; Dumayne *et al.* 1995; Dumayne-Peaty 1998). The Antonine Wall consisted of a turf and timber boundary constructed across the Forth-Clyde isthmus in the AD 140s. It seems to have been abandoned briefly in the 150s, and then reoccupied until the mid-160s, after which it fell into disuse (Hanson & Maxwell 1986).

Three pollen sequences are available from mires within 10km of the wall, from Blairbech Bog, Fannyside Muir and Letham Moss (Dumayne-Peaty 1998), but unfortunately none are immediately adjacent to it (Figure 4.13). At Letham Moss, to the north, local clearance and cereal cultivation apparently began in the late Iron Age, resulting in a fairly open landscape with some woodland (Figure 4.14). The extent of woodland then remained approximately constant into the Roman period, although there seems to have been some increase of alder and hazel in the mid-Roman period, and again towards the end of the Roman period, at which time local cereal cultivation apparently ceased. At Fannyside Muir, south of the central sector of the wall, clearance again began in the late Iron Age, but appears to have occurred more gradually than at Letham, and continued into the Roman period (Figure 4.14, 5.5). The extent of open land peaked in approximately the mid-Roman period, just above a level dated 1925±45 BP (40 cal BC-cal AD 210), but substantial areas of local woodland remained. Towards the end of the Roman period there was some increase in the extent of woodland, but the presence of '*Hordeum* type' pollen suggests local cereal cultivation.

At Blairbech Bog, north of the western end of the Antonine Wall,

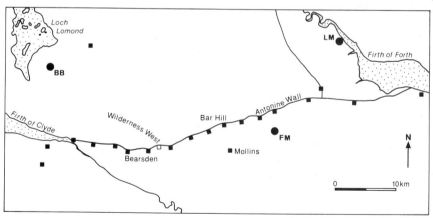

4.13: The Antonine Wall area, showing the wall, road and forts (squares), and locations of off-site pollen sequences (circles): BB – Blairbech Bog, FM – Fannyside Muir, LM – Letham Moss. (Forts and road after Frere, Rivet & Sitwell 1987.)

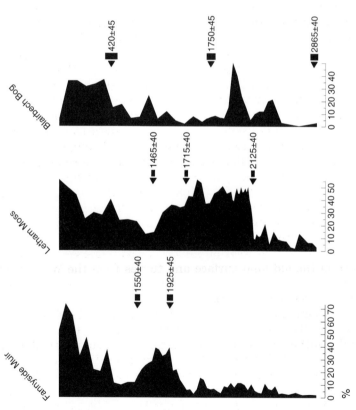

4.14: Pollen curves of grasses from Fannyside Muir, Letham Moss and Blairbech Bog, near the Antonine Wall, showing variable patterns of clearance. Percentages based on the sum of total land pollen excluding Ericaceae and Cyperaceae. (Redrawn from data of Dumayne-Peaty 1998.)

clearance had begun earlier in the Iron Age, with a period of regeneration before almost total removal of local woodland at the end of the Iron Age or the start of the Roman period (Figure 3.11, 4.14). There are no indications of local cereal cultivation contemporary with this clearance from the pollen record, and an apparently rapid recovery of woodland followed. Some of the fluctuations in the extent of woodland and cereal cultivation at these sites may well relate to periods of occupation and abandonment of the area by the Roman military, but the radiocarbon chronologies are insufficiently precise to enable a detailed correlation to such events.

As was the case for Hadrian's Wall, it appears that parts of the area around the Antonine Wall were cleared of woodland prior to the Roman period. It is unfortunate that the closest off-site pollen sequence is 3km from the wall, but the on-site pollen evidence from some of the Roman forts and enclosures on or close to the Antonine Wall provides a more detailed picture of the environment of their immediate surroundings. Such information is, however, severely limited by problems of poor dating control, poor pollen preservation, and very local pollen source areas. An example is provided by the marching camp at Mollins, 4km south of the Antonine Wall. The camp was probably built, and then deliberately demolished, in approximately the AD 80s. The ditches were backfilled with soil and blocks of turf – possibly the same material originally dug from them (Boyd 1984, 1985a, b). Assuming that these blocks did come from the original cutting of the ditch, their surface pollen spectra would reflect the vegetation at the time the fort was constructed. Obviously, the presence of turf itself suggests locally open conditions. One of the turves had a pollen spectrum dominated by grasses with heather, ribwort plantain and some trees. The other showed a substantially greater woodland component. Given the probable local source of pollen to these turves, the difference between them need not suggest that they were cut from widely different areas, simply that one of the turves came from close to the edge of an area of woodland.

Similar results have been obtained elsewhere in the area. Ditches underlying the Antonine fort at Bar Hill, constructed around AD 142, have yielded turves with surface pollen spectra indicative of a substantially open landscape with grasses and heather (Boyd 1984). Similarly, pollen spectra from the old land surface and turves from the Wilderness West enclosure on the Antonine Wall suggest construction in open heathland with some birch (Newell 1983).

A pollen sequence through ditch deposits from the fort at Bearsden suggests that the landscape around the site consisted of a mixture of woodland, heather and grassland, possibly with some cereal cultivation (Knights *et al.* 1983). Interpretation of pollen from ditch fills is problematic because secondary pollen from soils may be washed into the deposits from the ditch sides, mixing with the contemporary pollen from local vegetation. It is, therefore, possible that the abundance of trees suggested by the

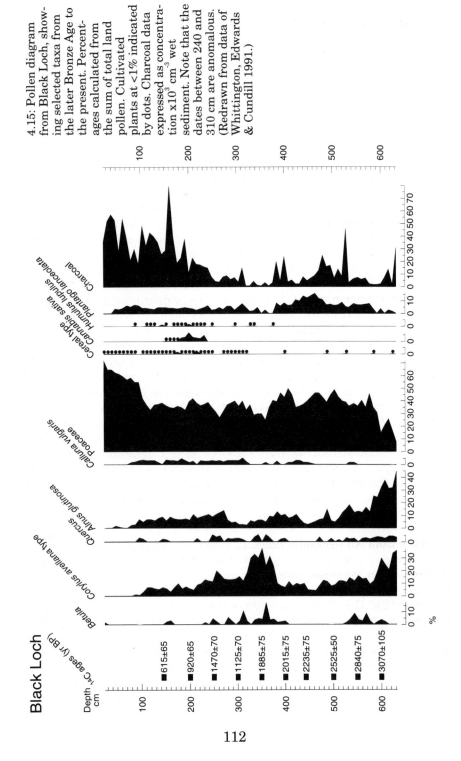

4.15: Pollen diagram from Black Loch, showing selected taxa from the later Bronze Age to the present. Percentages calculated from the sum of total land pollen. Cultivated plants at <1% indicated by dots. Charcoal data expressed as concentration x10³ cm⁻³ wet sediment. Note that the dates between 240 and 310 cm are anomalous. (Redrawn from data of Whittington, Edwards & Cundill 1991.)

pollen assemblages from this site is exaggerated by soil pollen from a previous phase of woodland.

Further south, on-site pollen data are also available from the Dod, a late Iron Age hill-fort in the Borders (Innes & Shennan 1991). A pollen sequence from the ditch had a basal date of 1905±50 BP (GU-1269, 30 cal BC-cal AD 230), and was dominated by grasses, suggesting an open environment locally in the late Iron Age or early Roman period.

Closer to Hadrian's Wall, the pollen sequence from Burnfoothill Moss shows major woodland clearance beginning in the late Iron Age or early Roman period, at a level where the 'humic' and 'humin' fractions of the peat were dated separately to 2015±45 BP (120 cal BC-cal AD 80) and 1965±45 BP (90 cal BC-cal AD 120) respectively (Tipping 1995a, b). Alder and birch seem to have been most severely affected by this clearance, and corresponding increases of grasses and ribwort plantain suggest the spread of grassland. Possible records of cereal pollen immediately above this level may be linked with local arable activity.

Beyond the Antonine Wall, in eastern Scotland, a pollen diagram from Black Loch, Fife, illustrates the vegetational history of an area which, despite its position north of the Roman border, was still affected by Roman incursions (Whittington, Edwards & Cundill 1991; Whittington & Edwards 1993). Interestingly, the Iron Age-Roman transition is marked by a major increase of hazel, a decline of grasses, and the temporary disappearance of plantain (Figure 4.15). There is also a marked decline in concentration of charcoal particles at this point. This suggests a period of land abandonment and woodland regeneration, quite in contrast to the record at most of the sites further south.

Further north, pollen sequences from Loch Davan and Braeroddach Loch are less securely dated, but also seem to show a phase of woodland regeneration similar to that at Blach Loch. Whittington and Edwards (1993) assign the regeneration phases in these three sequences to disruption of agricultural systems by the Roman army in Fife and Aberdeenshire, possibly due to destruction or confiscation of cattle and grain.

Turning to the environment of Scotland's islands, on Oronsay a pollen sequence from An t-Aoradh indicates an open landscape of heather moorland and grazed grassland (Beck & Gilbertson 1987), while on Arran a sequence from Machrie Moor indicates a mixture of woodland and open land in the Roman period, with an increase in the extent of woodland in the latter half (D.E. Robinson & Dickson 1988). There is a single record for pollen described as '*Cannabis / Humulus* type', which might reflect local hemp cultivation. At Machrie Moor the mire surface seems to have been burned in the Roman period, perhaps reflecting deliberate management as discussed earlier in relation to Fenton Cottage in Lancashire.

At Loch Meodal, on Skye, there was a mixture of woodland and open land in the Roman period, with a spread of heather just above a level dated

1930±50 BP (50 cal BC-cal AD 220) (Birks 1993b). In contrast, at Sheshader, Isle of Lewis, pollen analysis of blanket peat deposits indicated a virtually treeless environment of heather moorland (Newell 1988). Far to the north on Shetland, the pollen sequence from Dallican Water shows the presence of an open moorland landscape throughout the Roman period (K.D. Bennett *et al.* 1992).

Overall, it seems that much of the area crossed by the Antonine Wall was already fairly open before the arrival of the Roman army, although construction of the new frontier may have provided a temporary impetus to clearance. Parts of the region remained quite well wooded, however, and there seems to have been a trend towards woodland regeneration in the latter half of the Roman period. In eastern Scotland woodland regeneration also occurred, but may have begun earlier than at sites further south. There is no relevant information for mainland sites further north, but in the northern and western islands open moorland landscapes occurred throughout the Roman period, with variable amounts of woodland. Pollen evidence for cereal cultivation is limited to parts of southern Scotland close to the Hadrianic and Antonine Walls, suggesting the possibility that cereals were cultivated specifically to supply the military market.

Wales

Much of the pollen evidence for the Roman period in Wales comes from sites at relatively high altitudes, leaving the areas most favourable for agriculture under-represented. This is especially problematic for the southern half of Wales, where all the relevant sequences are from the hills and mountains.

In north Wales, Llyn Cororion lies on the plain between Snowdonia and the Menai Strait. The pollen sequence suggests that the area remained substantially wooded in the Roman period, but with a slight increase of clearance (Watkins 1990). At Bryn y Castell, in the uplands of Snowdonia, pollen sequences were obtained from wetland deposits close to a hill-fort that was the scene of iron-working activity in the late Iron Age and Roman period. Here the extent of woodland was limited in the early Roman period when iron-working was underway at the hill-fort (Mighall & Chambers 1995, 1997), later followed by some woodland recovery.

Evidence for iron-working also comes from the late prehistoric upland settlement of Crawcwellt West (Crew 1989, 1991). The adjacent pollen sequence shows major clearance from the late Bronze Age and throughout the Iron Age, resulting in a predominantly open environment (F.M. Chambers & Lageard 1993). In the Roman period birch and hazel woodland recovered, probably again connected with abandonment of the site, although much open land remained. To the west, at Moel y Gerddi, a pollen sequence was produced from close to the site of a late prehistoric enclosure (Kelly 1988; F.M. Chambers & Price 1988). Here major clearance began in the early Bronze Age, pre-dating the settlement, but substantial areas of woodland persisted throughout the Iron Age and Roman period.

Moving south to mid-Wales, at Cefn Gwernffrwd there was a phase of renewed clearance from a level dated 1900±45 BP (cal AD 0-230), continuing throughout the Roman period and resulting in an almost treeless landscape (F.M. Chambers 1983a). Increases of ribwort plantain, grasses and heather suggest that the woodland was largely replaced by moorland and grassland, although cereal cultivation also appears to have occurred locally.

From the uplands of south Wales, blanket peat deposits in the Brecon Beacons (F.M. Chambers 1982) and valley mire deposits from Cefn Glas (A.G. Smith & Green 1995) indicate an open landscape throughout the Roman period, while at Nant Helen, Mynydd y Drum, there were greater areas of woodland, increasing slightly in extent at approximately the end of the Roman period (F.M. Chambers, Lageard & Elliot 1990). In a lowland area of the Brecon Beacons, the sediments of Llangorse Lake change from organic muds to silty clays in the Roman period (R. Jones *et al.* 1985). This seems attributable to increased soil erosion resulting from woodland clearance and arable activity in the catchment.

Overall, the pollen evidence suggests that parts of north Wales remained wooded in the Roman period, and at some sites where major clearance had occurred in prehistory, woodland regeneration followed the Roman Conquest. Further south, the landscape seems to have been more open. To some extent this reflects the bias to upland sites, but all sequences suggest cereal cultivation in this area, and it seems that agricultural activity was more widespread in the southern half of Wales than in the north.

Pollen evidence for land-use change at the time of the Conquest

If we compare the overall extent of woodland in the late Iron Age with that for the Roman period it appears that at most sites (where a comparison is possible) there was a reduction in the extent of woodland in the Roman period, a pattern especially clear in the north of England (Figure 4.16). The stage at which the reduction in woodland occurred is, however, far from clear in most cases. The maps mask fluctuations in woodland in the course of the Roman period. A minor increase then major decline of woodland, for example, would appear only as an overall reduction. It is of interest to know what changes, if any, occurred specifically at the time of the Conquest. This question has already been approached in relation to the Hadrianic frontier, but here is addressed for Britain overall by examining the few sites with radiocarbon dates specifically for the conquest period, and where sampling is relatively detailed.

Table 4.2 lists sites where there is a radiocarbon date (with an error

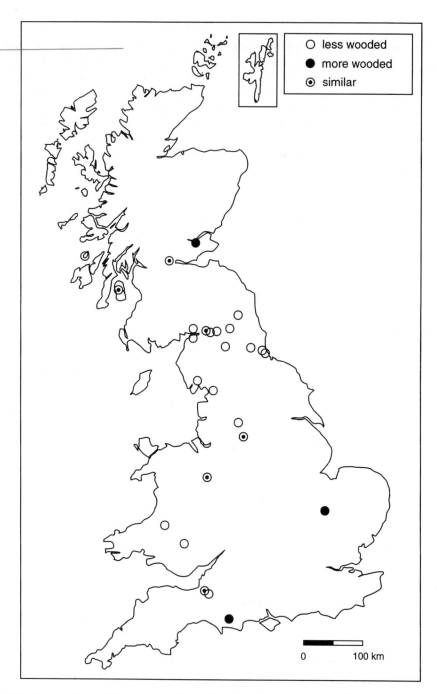

4.16: Comparison of the extent of woodland in the Roman period with that in the Iron Age, on the basis of average pollen percentages of trees and shrubs. ('Similar' is taken as values ±5%). For key to sites see Figure 4.6.

term not greater than ±80) relating to the period of the Conquest, and indicates whether or not any vegetational change occurred at this time (within the limits imposed by radiocarbon dating). Of course, the actual date at which different areas of Britain were incorporated into the Roman province varied: following invasion of the south-east in AD 43, Roman occupation spread west and north, leading to the conquest of Wales and northern England by AD 80, after which incursions into Scotland began (Millett 1995). However, for the purposes of comparison with the pollen record the difference is too small to be detectable on the basis of radiocarbon chronologies.

Table 4.2. Detailed pollen sequences with radiocarbon dates where the calibrated range of the date includes the Roman Conquest

For references and laboratory code numbers see Table 4.1.

Site	Radiocarbon date (BP)	Cal range (95.4% conf., highest probability)	Changes in vegetation
England			
Fairsnape Fell	2025±40	120 BC-AD 70	Decrease of alder and hazel, increase of heather
Fozy Moss	1820±45	AD 80-260	Decrease of trees, increase of heather, grasses and ribwort plantain
Glasson Moss	1860±40	AD 60-250	Decrease of oak, increase of grasses, cereals cease
Midgeholme Moss	1740±90 1970±60	AD 70-460 120 BC-AD 150	Decrease of trees and shrubs, increase of sedges
Redmere	1850±50	AD 50-260	Slight decrease of trees and increase of herbs
Rusland Moss	1963±50	100 BC-AD 130	Increase of hazel, decrease of grasses
Steng Moss	1970±60	120 BC-AD 150	Decrease of trees, increase of grasses and ribwort plantain
Walton Moss	1925±40	40 BC-AD 150	Increase of trees
Scotland			
Black Loch	2015±75	60 BC-AD 270	Increase of hazel, decrease of grasses and ribwort plantain
Burnfoothill Moss	1965±45	90 BC-AD 120	Decrease of birch, increase of grasses, sedges and plantain
Fannyside Muir	1925±45	40 BC-AD 210	Decrease of alder and hazel, increase of heather, grasses and sedges

Site	Radiocarbon date (BP)	Cal range (95.4% conf., highest probability)	Changes in vegetation
Wales			
Bryn y Castell (BYC 3VA)	2060±80	260 BC-AD 90	Little clear change
Cefn Gwernffrwd	1900±45 2030±45	AD 0-230 170 BC-AD 70	Decrease of hazel, alder and birch, increase of grasses

In considering Table 4.2 it should be noted that parts of a pollen sequence where change occurs are more likely to be chosen for radiocarbon-dating than periods where the nature of the pollen assemblages remains constant, so little can be read into the fact that most of the sites do show changes. Of interest here is the nature of this change.

The most striking point to emerge is that of the thirteen sequences under consideration, all but four show a reduction in the extent of woodland at the start of the Roman period. Only three show signs of increasing woodland cover.

At Walton Moss, north of Hadrian's Wall, local agricultural land seems to have been abandoned to woodland during the Roman occupation (Dumayne & Barber 1994), a pattern seen also at Black Loch in eastern Scotland (Whittington & Edwards 1993). Most sites near Hadrian's Wall show an increase of clearance at this time, however, as at Fozy Moss (Dumayne & Barber 1994) and Midgeholme Moss (Wiltshire 1997). At Glasson Moss, just 500m from Hadrian's Wall, cereal pollen ceases to occur at the same time as a decline of oak, suggesting an increase in the extent of open land but cessation of cereal cultivation (Dumayne & Barber 1994). This may reflect removal of areas of land from agricultural production to make way for military activities.

In Scotland, the two sites in the inter-wall zone – Burnfoothill Moss and Fannyside Muir – both seem to indicate woodland clearance at the start of the Roman period (Tipping 1995b; Dumayne-Peaty 1998). As already discussed, this clearance seems likely to reflect expansion of cereal cultivation and grazing to supply agricultural produce to the army.

Discussion of the significance of the pollen data in relation to the impact of the Roman Conquest is, of course, limited by the bias in its distribution to the north of England. It would be interesting to compare vegetational changes in this region with the picture beyond the Roman frontier in Scotland, and with areas of southern England that became strongly integrated into the villa economy, but too few sequences are available from these areas to enable any sort of conclusions to be reached at present. A wider coverage of well-dated pollen sequences with closely sampled Roman-period deposits is needed before pollen analysis can shed further light on the environmental consequences of the Roman Conquest.

While it might be assumed that most of the vegetational changes recorded at and after the Roman Conquest reflect fluctuations in agricultural activity, other facets of the Romano-British economy will have affected the landscape on a variety of scales. These include mining for minerals such as copper, lead and iron, quarrying for building stone, and production of pottery, tile, glass, salt and metalwork (B. Jones & Mattingly 1990; K. Dark & Dark 1997). Of these, iron-working and pottery production were particularly widespread, and form the subject of the next section.

Roman industry and the environment

The Roman period saw the establishment in Britain of industrial activity on an unprecedented scale (K. Dark 1996). Small-scale iron-working in the Iron Age and Roman periods, as at the north Welsh hillfort at Bryn y Castell, seems to have had only a minor impact on local woodland (Mighall & Chambers 1997), but the development of large-scale iron production in several parts of Britain in the Roman period might be expected to have had a more pronounced effect on woodland resources. A related issue is whether or not the presence of woodland influenced the location of these industries.

One of the most important areas of iron production in the Roman period was the Weald, the name of which means 'wood'. The area was described in the Anglo-Saxon Chronicle for 893 as 'the great wood which we call Andred' (Darby 1976), but this does not necessarily mean that it was heavily wooded in the Roman period. Unfortunately, there are no detailed pollen sequences from this area, or other major iron-production centres, such as the Forest of Dean. The environmental setting, and possible impact, of the iron industries is therefore uncertain. Henry Cleere (1976) has calculated that around 300km^2 of woodland would have been cleared in connection with Roman iron-making in the eastern part of the Weald, but this figure assumes total destruction of the trees. As Oliver Rackham (1980, p. 108) points out, it is more likely that some form of coppicing was used to ensure a continuous supply of fuel. Woodland would then have been conserved, rather than destroyed, as a result of the local iron industry.

Some idea of the range of trees and shrubs exploited is provided by the large quantity of charcoal generated by iron-working at Chesters villa, Woolaston, close to the Forest of Dean (Fulford & Allen 1992). Species represented included alder (*Alnus glutinosa*), field maple (*Acer campestre*), ash (*Fraxinus excelsior*), elm (*Ulmus*), willow (*Salix*), spindle (*Euonymus europaeus*), birch (*Betula*), hawthorn (*Crataegus monogyna*) and holly (*Ilex aquifolium*), although the assemblage was dominated by oak (*Quercus*) and hazel (*Corylus avellana*) (Figueiral 1992). In many of the oak and

119

hazel fragments the last annual rings were very close together, reflecting slow growth. This suggests that they may have grown in a coppice system, but the overall diversity of species suggests that at least some of the wood was collected fairly indiscriminately.

Pottery production would be expected to have had similar environmental impacts to iron working, as large quantities of fuel would have been required to fire the kilns. Experimental studies suggest that around 150kg of wood may have been required for a single kiln firing (Bryant 1973). Large pottery-production complexes developed in the late Roman period in areas such as the New Forest and Alice Holt Forest, Hampshire, and east of Oxford, in the area of the medieval Forest of Shotover and Stowood. In fact, the concentration of major pottery (and iron) production in areas that became medieval Forests is striking. Rackham (1990, pp. 164-6) has stressed that medieval Forests were not necessarily densely wooded – they were simply areas occupied by deer – although all of the examples mentioned above did have considerable expanses of woodland in the medieval period. The obvious interpretation of the apparent relationship between Roman potteries/iron works and later Forests is that these industries were sited to take advantage of woodland for fuel. This may not necessarily be true, however, as there is no reason to believe that these areas were densely wooded in the Roman period. Pollen evidence, of course, holds the key, but there is only one pollen sequence relating to a Roman pottery production centre, from Sidlings Copse in Oxfordshire (Day 1991, 1993).

The Oxfordshire pottery industry began in the second half of the first century AD and became one of the major pottery producers of Roman Britain by the early to mid-fourth century (Young 1977). Over thirty kiln sites are known from the area just to the east of Oxford, including a probable kiln less than 500m from Sidlings Copse. As discussed earlier, the Sidlings Copse pollen sequence indicates that local woodland was already sparse by the end of the Iron Age (Day 1991, 1993). During the course of the Roman period the remaining alder woodland was completely removed, leaving a limited amount of oak and hazel woodland on dry land, and willow on damper soils. It is unlikely that the final disappearance of alder was due to its removal for fuel, as this would have been a rather short-sighted policy in an area with so little woodland. In fact, it is possible that there was a deliberate attempt to increase fuel supplies by encouraging the growth of willow. Percentages of willow pollen increase in the Roman period, and the shrub could have been deliberately planted or encouraged as a renewable source of fuel (although natural encroachment of willow around the waterlogged deposits cannot be ruled out). Willow grows remarkably rapidly after cutting, and also flourishes on soils too damp for agriculture, so would have been the most obvious choice for this purpose. The small amount of oak/hazel woodland surviving on drier soils may also have been managed by coppicing. Oak actually increases slightly in the Roman period, possibly because it was preserved and encouraged as a source of timber.

For the area around Sidlings Copse, then, it could not be argued that fuel supplies were a factor in the positioning of the local kilns. Obviously, there may have been woodland in more distant parts of the pottery-production area (as on Shotover Hill), beyond the region reflected in the pollen diagram. Archaeological evidence suggests, however, that much of the medieval woodland on Shotover was of post-Roman origin (Day 1990). Sidlings Copse was within the Stowood portion of the Forest, and the pollen sequence indicates that here woodland regeneration occurred in the late Saxon or early medieval period (Day 1991, 1993).

Perhaps many of the centres of Roman industry later reverted to woodland because industrial activities made them unpopular places for settlement. Pottery manufacture required digging of local clay, and produced large mounds of waste material, creating a landscape of craters and tips that could have been farmed only with difficulty. Such a topography is visible today in Alice Holt Forest, site of part of the Alice Holt/Farnham industry (Lyne & Jefferies 1979). Similarly, slag tips from iron-working could be extensive: Cleere (1976) has estimated that iron production at Beauport Park in the Weald generated some 100,000 tonnes of slag, with a volume of 30,000 m³.

Managing the environment

Woodland management

The demand for fuel imposed by Roman industrial activity suggests that, at least in areas where woodland was sparse, it was likely to have been managed as a renewable resource. Domestic use (such as fuel for hearths, hypocausts and Roman baths) would also have exerted a drain on woodland resources, as would the use of wattle-work for construction purposes, such as wall panels and fencing.

Some woodland management practices are described in continental Roman textual sources, summarized by Meiggs (1982). Although they describe practices in Italy, the same methods might have been used in the more romanized areas of Britain. Cato, writing in the mid-second century BC, mentioned willow beds, coppice woods, orchards and 'mast-wood'. The latter could apply to oak or beech (*Fagus sylvatica*) woods, both of which provided nuts valued for feeding pigs. Cato also mentioned the planting of poplars (*Populus*) and elms as a source of leaf fodder for cattle and sheep.

References to coppice woods were also made by Columella, writing in the first century AD. He stated that the best woods for coppicing were oak and chestnut (*Castanea sativa*), chestnut being cut on a five-year cycle and the oak at seven years. He also described the planting of chestnut coppices. Chestnut is not a native British tree, but may have been introduced in the

Roman period (Godwin 1975, pp. 276-7). Some of the charcoal from iron-making at Chesters villa, mentioned above, has been tentatively identified as chestnut (Figueiral 1992). In relation to the possible existence of chestnut coppices in Roman Britain, it is notable that a coppice stool found in a Roman pit at Farmoor, Oxfordshire, has been identified as probably of oak but possibly chestnut (M. Robinson 1979, p. 81). Pollen evidence for the tree is lacking, but even if chestnut woods did occur, low pollen production and poor dispersal mean that they would be unlikely to be detected in the pollen record.

Evidence for the deliberate planting of willow groves is also sparse, and particularly difficult to detect in view of the native status of willows. As discussed above, at Sidlings Copse, Oxfordshire, willow increased significantly in the Roman period, possibly reflecting planting of willow or encouragement of existing stands.

Archaeological evidence for woodland management in Roman Britain is becoming increasingly abundant as more waterlogged sites with well-preserved wood remains are excavated. Wattle-work has been found used for fencing, as at Vindolanda by Hadrian's Wall (Manning *et al*. 1997), to line wells and pits, as at Barton Court Farm (M. Robinson 1986) and Farmoor in Oxfordshire (M. Robinson 1979, p. 81), and in buildings. Excavations at Castle Street, Carlisle, for example, have revealed the waterlogged remains of wooden buildings dating from the late first to early second century (McCarthy 1991). These contained predominantly oak and alder posts, stakes and wattle-work, with some wattles also of hazel and birch (Figure 4.17). Ring counts on some of the smaller wood remains suggested that most of the stems had been cut after less that ten years growth, and at least some of the alder and hazel could have come from coppice (J.P. Huntley 1991). Similarly, timber buildings from York, dated to the second to early third centuries, incorporated hazel rods with between four and ten annual rings (A.R. Hall & Kenward 1990, pp. 338-9), while some of the buildings in Roman London had wattle-and-daub walls, using rods that probably came from short-rotation coppice (Perring 1991a, pp. 74-7, 80-1).

Woodland management may, therefore, have been widespread in Roman Britain, providing a valuable source of building material and fuel. The practice would enable maximum use to be made of the little woodland remaining in many areas, and would have had the effect of conserving woodland against further clearance if the need for agricultural land increased.

Meadows

The pollen evidence indicates that grassland was widespread in Roman Britain, most of which owed its existence to human activity. In lowland areas with adequate drainage, grassland quickly reverts to woodland unless colonisation by trees is prevented by grazing or mowing. If grass-

4.17: Post and wattle building excavated at Castle Street, Carlisle. (Photograph provided by M.R. McCarthy, Carlisle Archaeological Unit.)

land is being managed to produce hay, animals must be excluded for most of the growing season to prevent loss of the hay crop. In Britain this practice seems to have begun in the Roman period, as mentioned previously.

The characteristic hay-meadow plants are rarely detected in the pollen record, because many lack distinctive pollen or their pollen is produced in small amounts or is poorly dispersed. Plant remains from archaeological sites have occasionally yielded direct evidence for meadows, however, such as the cut hay from a well at Farmoor (Lambrick & Robinson 1979, pp. 118-19) and the horse droppings containing hay-meadow plants from a well at Lancaster (Greig 1988). Other examples include remains of yellow rattle (*Rhinanthus* sp.), self heal (*Prunella vulgaris*) and bird's foot trefoil (*Lotus corniculatus*) from a fourth-century latrine pit at the temple site at Uley (Girling & Straker 1993). From Roman York remains of meadow-sweet (*Filipendula ulmaria*) and perhaps great burnet (*Sanguisorba officinalis*) inside a timber building were accompanied by grassland weevils, including *Apion* spp. and *Sitona lepidus*, suggesting the use of hay as stable litter (A.R. Hall & Kenward 1990, pp. 360, 400-4).

Moorland

Wide expanses of open moorland would have been a characteristic feature of the landscape of northern and western Britain by the Roman period, providing a variety of useful resources. Heather would have been an important source of browse for livestock, and could also be cut for thatch, bedding, or fuel. Remains of heather that may have been collected for these purposes have been found in Roman-period deposits from York (A.R. Hall *et al.* 1980, pp. 128, 135; A.R. Hall & Kenward 1990, pp. 341, 413-14) and Carlisle (Goodwin & Huntley 1991). On the south coast, Iron Age and Roman deposits from Hengistbury Head also contained heather, probably collected from heathland on the local sandy soils (Nye & Jones 1987, pp. 323-4).

Peat may also have been collected from moorland areas for fuel, perhaps explaining the discovery of charred fragments of mire plants, including *Sphagnum* moss and cotton grass (*Eriophorum vaginatum*), in excavations at York (A.R. Hall *et al.* 1980, pp. 128, 135; A.R. Hall & Kenward 1990, pp. 341, 413-14).

Heather moorland may be managed by periodic burning to increase its quality for grazing. Management in recent times has involved burning on a ten-year cycle, encouraging the nutritious new growth favoured by cattle and sheep (Gimingham 1972). Charcoal found in peat deposits may sometimes reflect this practice, as at the Antonine Wall enclosure at Wilderness Plantation (Newell 1983) and at Fenton Cottage, Lancashire (Middleton *et al.* 1995; Wells *et al.* 1997). It is, however, possible that the charcoal derives from natural or accidental fires, rather than representing a deliberate management strategy. High-resolution pollen and charcoal analysis might clarify the situation, if it was possible to detect cycles in charcoal and heather abundance, but there are currently no sufficiently detailed studies available.

If moorland areas were deliberately burned in the Roman period, it is unlikely that this period saw the introduction of the practice. Charcoal is common in prehistoric peat deposits, as at Fenton Cottage, where heather pollen and charcoal particles are abundant from the Bronze Age to the present (Figure 3.9).

The urban environment

The development of towns in Roman Britain created a new urban environment where a concentration of people, their animals and agricultural produce created conditions highly conducive to the spread of pests and diseases (Figure 4.18). The stores of cereal grain kept in towns, such as

4.18: Reconstruction of a Romano-British town. (Painting of Canterbury *c.* AD 300, by Ivan Lapper, © Canterbury Heritage Museum.)

Carlisle (Kenward *et al.* 1991) and York (Kenward 1979; A.R. Hall *et al.* 1980; Kenward, Hall & Jones 1986; A.R. Hall & Kenward 1990), were often hugely infested with insect pests, of which one of the commonest was the grain weevil, *Sitophilus granarius* (Figure 4.19). In some cases the insects were so abundant that they must have rendered the grain useless, or at least highly unpalatable!

4.19: Grain weevil, *Sitophilus granarius*. (Scanning electron micrograph by H.K. Kenward, reproduced by permission of the York Archaeological Trust.)

125

4. The Roman period

Remains of the black rat (*Rattus rattus*) have now been found in several Romano-British towns, including London and York, accompanied by bones of the house mouse (*Mus musculus*) (Armitage *et al.* 1984; J. Rackham 1979; A.R. Hall & Kenward 1990, p. 342) (Figure 4.20). Black rats are notorious for spreading bubonic plague via their fleas, and seem to have first arrived in Britain in the Roman period. The rat flea, *Nosopsyllus*, has also been recorded from York (A.R. Hall & Kenward 1990, p. 419), but it is not known whether outbreaks of plague occurred in Roman Britain (Figure 4.21b). Remains of black rat and house mouse are not confined to urban contexts, however. Both are recorded from the villas at Gorhambury, near St Albans (Locker 1990), and Dalton Parlours, West Yorkshire (Berg 1990), and from a granary at the fort of South Shields (Younger 1994).

Pests not only inhabited the streets and homes of Roman towns, but also lived on and in their human population. The human flea, *Pulex irritans*, has been recovered from Roman deposits in Carlisle (Kenward *et al.* 1991, p. 67) and York (A.R. Hall & Kenward 1990, p. 341) (Figure 4.21a), and human lice (*Pediculus humanus* or *capitis*) have come from Carlisle (Kenward *et al.* 1991, p. 67). Intestinal parasites also seem to have been prevalent, including the human whipworm (*Trichuris trichiura*) and

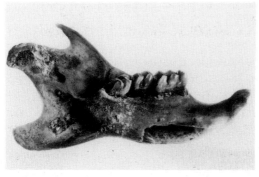

a

b

4.20: Remains of rodents from Roman York: (a) Left mandible of black rat, *Rattus rattus*, (b) Right mandible of house mouse, *Mus* sp. (Photographs by P.R. Tomlinson, reproduced by permission of the York Archaeological Trust.)

126

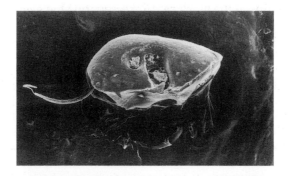

a

4.21: Heads of fleas from Roman York: (a) *Pulex irritans*, the human flea, (b) *Nosopsyllus ?fasciatus*, a rat and mouse flea. (Scanning electron micrographs by E.P. Allison, reproduced by permission of the York Archaeological Trust.)

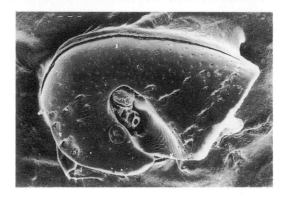

b

roundworm (*Ascaris*) (A.R. Hall & Kenward 1990, p. 343; A.K.G. Jones & Hutchinson 1991, pp. 70-1). These infestations are unlikely to have been life-threatening, but a more serious problem apparently connected with urban living comes from evidence for tuberculosis. The disease has been identified in human skeletal remains from Roman-period cemeteries at Ashton in Northamptonshire and Alington Avenue, near Dorchester in Dorset (Stirland & Waldron 1990), representing the earliest known cases of the disease from Britain.

Roman towns may have provided a home for a variety of livestock, doubtless increasing the prevalence of disease and parasitic infection. Mark Maltby has suggested that pigs were kept in some households in towns such as Winchester, Dorchester and Lincoln, probably accompanied by chickens (Maltby 1994, p. 98; Dobney, Jaques & Irving, nd, p. 44). Cats and dogs may have been kept as pets, although some Roman-period dog bones show signs of butchery, suggesting that they may have been eaten (Dobney, Jaques & Irving nd, pp. 46-7). Several of the wild animals familiar in urban areas today, including fox (*Vulpes vulpes*) and hedgehog (*Erinaceus europaeus*), have also been recorded from Roman urban sites (Maltby 1979). Foxes may have been attracted to towns by the opportunities for scavenging, although the remains may represent animals hunted for fur.

Another aspect of the Romano-British urban environment concerns an enigmatic deposit known as the 'dark earth'. This consists of a dark-coloured soil rich in charcoal and other materials, including slag, mortar and building materials. It usually dates from the late Roman or post-Roman period, and occurs in many towns, including London, York and Gloucester. Interpretation of the dark earth has important implications for the character of late Roman towns. Suggestions have included deliberate dumping of soil to create parks and gardens (Dixon 1992); farming activity (Reece 1980); natural accumulation of soil on abandoned sites, reflecting desertion of towns in the late Roman period (Esmonde Clearey 1989); or the remains of dense occupation in buildings of clay, and organic materials such as timber, wattle-work, turf and thatch (Yule 1990; K.R. Dark 1994, pp. 15-18; K. Dark & Dark 1997, pp. 120-2).

Micromorphological analysis of dark earth deposits tends to support the latter interpretation. Macphail (1994) suggests that the soil derives from decomposition and mixing of the remains of clay and timber buildings, combined with material from other activities such as horticulture, stabling of animals and rubbish tipping. These provided a broad range of ecological niches within a relatively restricted area, encouraging large populations of plants and animals that occurred only rarely in areas of more dispersed human settlement.

Conclusion

By the start of the Roman period much of the landscape, especially of southern England, had already been extensively cleared of woodland and converted to agriculture. In most of England there seems to have been a further impetus to clearance in the Roman period, presumably to increase the area available for pasture and cultivation of crops. This pattern is especially clear in the vicinity of Hadrian's Wall, where agricultural expansion seems to have been linked to the military market.

The increased clearance at many sites near the Hadrianic frontier, and to a lesser extent the Antonine Wall, contrasts with the situation further north, notably in eastern Scotland. Here there was a marked phase of woodland regeneration, apparently coinciding with the period of local Roman incursions. This suggests that – much as we might expect on other grounds – the nature of the relationship between Roman and native north of the Antonine Wall differed from that south of the border.

In relation to agriculture, cereal cultivation seems to have been more widespread than in the Iron Age, suggesting that some of the additional clearance may have been specifically to increase the area available for arable. Evidence for cereal cultivation in Scotland is limited, however, and appears predominantly in the frontier region. This might reflect cereal cultivation in response to military demand. The Roman period saw a diversification in the range of crops grown in some areas, and use of more intensive cultivation methods. Increased use of manuring, crop rotation and drainage, combined with more efficient types of plough, all helped to extend the types of land that could be cultivated, and increase the yields that could be obtained.

Further indications of the extension of arable activity are provided by signs of increased soil erosion, apparent from a period of country-wide alluviation coinciding with the Roman period (Macklin & Lewin 1993). Arguments that this may have resulted from increased rainfall rather than human activity find little support from the independent records of climate (Chapter 2). These suggest drier, rather than wetter, conditions in the Roman period compared to the Iron Age. In the latter half of the Roman period the climate may have become slightly warmer than that of today, potentially allowing expansion of cereal-growing into upland areas that would now be marginal for cultivation.

Agricultural produce may have been transported over considerable distances from its site of production, and evidence that grain was imported from abroad may hint at problems of obtaining sufficient supplies within Britain. Some of the largest stores of grain occurred in towns and forts, and this concentration of produce encouraged populations of pests of stored produce. The density of human population also seems to have increased the prevalence of parasitic infections and disease. Intriguingly, Paul Buckland has suggested that some of the increase in arable production in the Roman period was required to offset losses to pests of stored grain (Buckland 1978). Increasingly intensive farming methods may also have resulted in major losses to fungal diseases of crops in the field (P. Dark forthcoming).

The demand for woodland resources increased during the Roman period due to the need for fuel for large-scale manufacture of pottery, iron and so on, as well as for domestic heating and bathing requirements. This, combined with the evident reduction in the overall extent of woodland, probably resulted in an increase of woodland management practices such as coppicing.

The Roman period clearly brought significant changes to the environment of Britain, most notably an overall decline of woodland cover and extension of the area used for agriculture. For the new – more intensively farmed – landscape of the most romanised parts of Britain to persist, it would have to be actively maintained. In the next chapter we shall examine the environmental consequences of the social, political and economic changes that accompanied the end of Roman Britain.

5

The end of Roman Britain and the Anglo-Saxon period to AD 800

Introduction

Roman control over Britain was relinquished in AD 410, setting in motion a series of major social, political and economic changes (K. Dark 1994). Some of these changes may have had implications for the character of the environment, especially in terms of their effect on the supply of, and demand for, agricultural produce. During the course of the fifth and sixth centuries eastern England experienced a dramatic cultural transformation, associated with the migration of peoples from continental north-west Europe. This resulted in the emergence of early Anglo-Saxon England. In this zone urbanism, large-scale production and the villa economy probably ceased to operate in the fifth century, to be replaced by a landscape of small timber-built settlements and an entirely agricultural economy (Figure 5.1).

The conversion of the Anglo-Saxons to Christianity from the end of the sixth century onward gradually opened up their society and economy to new contacts with continental Europe. New settlement forms appeared, notably monasteries, associated with a major change in landscape organisation. By the end of the seventh century trade with continental Europe was centred on new urban centres (*wics*), as at London, York and Hamwic (near modern Southampton). These changes were contemporaneous with the growth of political centralization and the establishment of the Anglo-Saxon kingdoms.

The character of agricultural activity in the fifth to eighth centuries is currently less clearly understood even than for the Roman period, due to a sparsity of well-dated evidence. Little is known of field systems from this period, although open field cultivation, characteristic of much of the English Midlands in the Norman period and later, may be of late Anglo-Saxon origin (O. Rackham 1986, pp. 172-7; Hooke 1995, 1998).

Many of the plant and animal remains from archaeological sites of the fifth to eighth centuries are from middle Anglo-Saxon urban contexts, where they tell us more about the economy and human diet than about the environment. A particularly large assemblage of animal remains has, however, come from the early Anglo-Saxon settlement at West Stow, Suffolk (Crabtree 1985, 1989, 1994). Here the main domestic animals were

5.1: Reconstruction of an Anglo-Saxon village at West Stow, Suffolk.

sheep, goats, cattle and pigs, acompanied by domestic fowl and geese. Horse bones were also present, some bearing butchery marks suggesting that they had been used for food. Horse meat only formed a minor part of the diet, however, and the animals were probably more important for transport, traction and as symbols of status. Wild animal remains from the site included red deer (*Cervus elaphus*), roe deer (*Capreolus capreolus*), hare (*Lepus*), fox (*Vulpes vulpes*), beaver (*Castor fiber*), badger (*Meles meles*), and bear (*Ursus arctos*), all of which may have been hunted.

Interestingly, animal husbandry at West Stow shows continuity with that of the Iron Age and Roman periods, rather than resembling contemporary continental practices. From the Iron Age through to the Anglo-Saxon period there was an increase in the proportion of sheep and pig and decline of cattle and horses. Pig remains were particularly abundant in early fifth-century contexts, argued to reflect the need to establish herds in the initial stages of the Anglo-Saxon settlement.

Current knowledge of crops in Wales and Scotland in this period is minimal, but the principal crops in England seem to have been bread wheat (*Triticum aestivum*), rye (*Secale cereale*), barley (*Hordeum vulgare*) and oats (*Avena sativa*) (Greig 1991). Spelt (*Triticum spelta*) and emmer wheat (*Triticum dicoccum*) were also rare additions to the cereal assemblage at some sites. There are hints of regional variation in the range of crops grown. On sandy soils in eastern England, for example, rye seems to have been favoured, as in seventh-century contexts at West Stow (Murphy 1985). Rye is especially suited to cultivation on drier soils, because it is more drought-tolerant than most other cereals.

Other crops included peas (*Pisum sativum*), beans (*Vicia faba*), flax (*Linum usitatissimum*) and hemp (*Cannabis sativa*). While there are hints of hemp cultivation in the Roman period, and possibly even Iron Age, macroscopic remains of the plant only become frequent in the Anglo-Saxon period, at sites such as Staunch Meadow, Brandon (Murphy 1994). Fifth- to eighth-century pollen assemblages from some lakes, such as Crose Mere in Shropshire (Beales 1980), contain such high levels of hemp pollen that it seems probable that they were used for hemp retting. This involved soaking the plant in water for several weeks until the soft tissues rotted down, leaving the fibres free for rope-making (Bradshaw *et al.* 1981). Flax was also retted during fibre production, and its seeds provided linseed oil. Flax remains are common from sites of this period, again including Brandon, where remains of flax seeds in middle Saxon contexts were accompanied by stem fragments, suggesting processing of the plant (Murphy 1994).

Insofar as it is possible to tell from the minimal evidence available, it seems that the end of Roman Britain brought little change in the range of crops grown, although the cultivation of rye and oil- and fibre-producing plants apparently increased in the Anglo-Saxon period. A related question – for long debated in relation to the end of Roman Britain – is the extent to which agricultural systems were disrupted and land abandoned. Patterns of land-use and the scale of crop production and distribution must have been affected by Roman withdrawal, at least in parts of the country that had been most affected by romanisation. Such changes would be expected to leave their imprint in the pollen record, and particular attention has focused on the effect of land abandonment most easily reconstructed from such evidence – woodland regeneration.

Prior to the widespread use of radiocarbon dating, pollen sequences showing woodland regeneration after major clearance were often assumed to reflect the collapse of Romano-British agricultural systems (e.g. Moore 1968). The first application of radiocarbon dating to the issue, in the late 1970s, seemed to suggest a different pattern, however. On the basis of pollen sequences from north-eastern England, Judith Turner (1979) argued that much of the area was farmed throughout the Roman period until at least the sixth century. Woodland regeneration apparently occurred only after that date. The identification of initial post-Roman continuity rested on radiocarbon dates argued to be associated with woodland regeneration phases, but at some of the sites, such as Fellend Moss and Steng Moss in Northumberland, regeneration actually began *before* the radiocarbon-dated level. Most of the pollen sequences from this area probably do not, in fact, show a period of initial continuity, or are insufficiently detailed to enable any such period to be distinguished (K. Dark & Dark 1996).

In a later account of vegetation of the immediately post-Roman period, Turner incorporated further radiocarbon-dated pollen sequences, mainly from northern England and Scotland (J. Turner 1981). This led her to conclude that 'the majority of pollen diagrams indicate a regenerated forest and a lower proportion of arable and pasture land .... Some show no change and only a very small proportion indicate a higher level of activity than in the Iron Age' (J. Turner 1981, p. 71). This evidence was subsequently extrapolated to other areas, resulting in a general perception that abandonment of land and woodland regeneration were widespread after Roman withdrawal from Britain, a view first seriously challenged by Martin Bell (Bell 1989).

The question of post-Roman landscape continuity and change has most recently been addressed in an examination of all radiocarbon-dated pollen sequences from Britain spanning the period AD 400-800 (P. Dark 1996). This assessed whether there was environmental continuity from the Roman period, or whether vegetational change occurred at any stage in the four centuries after Roman withdrawal. The results showed that approximately half of the pollen sequences indicated reduced agricultural activity in the period AD 400-800, and of these, half were in northern England. These results will be discussed further later, but it is clear that the fifth to ninth centuries were not a general period of agricultural stagnation in Britain. In some areas there was an expansion of woodland clearance and agricultural activity.

An interesting additional perspective on the question of post-Roman woodland regeneration comes from examination of tree-ring sequences spanning the first millennium AD. No tree-ring samples from England have yet been dated to the fourth century AD, or rather, there are currently no samples with more than fifty rings (the number required to match a sample to existing chronologies) (Tyers, Hillam & Groves 1994). In other words, trees cut down in fourth-century England (and which have survived in archaeological contexts) seem to have been predominantly young. This contrasts with trees from first-century AD contexts, which were often two or three centuries old. The implication is that during the Roman period the supply of older and larger trees may have become exhausted.

After the gap in the fourth century, many of the tree-ring sequences for the Anglo-Saxon period began in the first half of the fifth century, including those from Brandon, Windsor and Tamworth (Tyers, Hillam & Groves 1994). This might reflect a period of woodland regeneration after Roman withdrawal, or perhaps cessation of management of coppiced woodland, resulting in the coppice stems growing on to timber. In Ireland there is no fourth-century gap, but there is a reduction in the number of trees represented in German tree-ring sequences for the same period (Tyers, Hillam & Groves 1994). This suggests that the pattern may be linked with the Roman occupation. The results need to be backed up by further tree-ring sequences from a wider geographical area, but they do offer hints of woodland regeneration in areas where pollen evidence is slight, such as south-east England and the Midlands.

We turn next to a detailed examination of pollen evidence for this period, both in terms of reconstructing the overall character of the landscape, and for signs of continuity and change in land use.

Pollen evidence for vegetation AD 400-800

Here pollen evidence is used to shed light on the nature of the environment in the fifth to eighth centuries on the basis of the relative extent of woodland and open land. As described in Chapter 3, tree/shrub pollen frequencies are mapped for sites where there is at least one radiocarbon date falling within the period, and where there are at least two relevant pollen samples. The sites, and their relevant radiocarbon dates, are listed in Table 5.1. Percentages of tree and shrub pollen have been calculated as an average figure for the period AD 400-800, and are plotted in Figure 5.2.

Crops represented in the pollen record for this period are cereals, hemp and/or hop ('*Cannabis* type' or Cannabaceae), and buckwheat (*Fagopyrum esculentum*). All are mapped by presence only, as they are severely underrepresented in the pollen record (Figures 5.3 and 5.4). The cereals are grouped together, although specific records for rye are indicated.

Results

As for the Roman period, the data are biassed to the north and west, away from the main Anglo-Saxon areas. This is unfortunate, as the south and east might be expected to have undergone the greatest changes in vegetation in the fifth to eighth centuries. Despite the limitations of the data, patterns do emerge. While some areas remained at least as open as in the Roman period, several pollen sequences show an increase in the extent of woodland. These are concentrated mainly in the north-west and north of England, and in parts of south-east Scotland. The possible significance of this pattern is discussed below.

5.2: Woodland AD 400-800. Percentages of tree and shrub pollen in radiocarbon-dated sequences spanning the period.

1. Dallican Water
2. Cross Lochs
3. Lochan an Druim
4. Little Loch Roag
5. Loch Lang
6. Lochan na Cartach
7. Carn Dubh
8. Letham Moss
9. Fannyside Muir
10. Blairbech Bog
11. Machrie Moor
12. Loch a'Bhogaidh
13. Burnfoothill Moss
14. Fellend Moss
15. Steng Moss
16. Quick Moss
17. Hallowell Moss
18. Rusland Moss
19. Fairsnape Fell
20. Willow Garth
21. Fenton Cottage
22. Knowsley Park
23. Lindow Moss
24. Featherbed Moss
25. Llyn Cororion
26. Bryn y Castell
27. Moel y Gerddi
28. Crose Mere
29. Swineshead
30. Hockham Mere
31. Coed Taf
32. Cefn Glas
33. Cefn Ffordd
34. Sidlings Copse
35. Snelsmore
36. Amberley
37. Meare Heath
38. The Chains

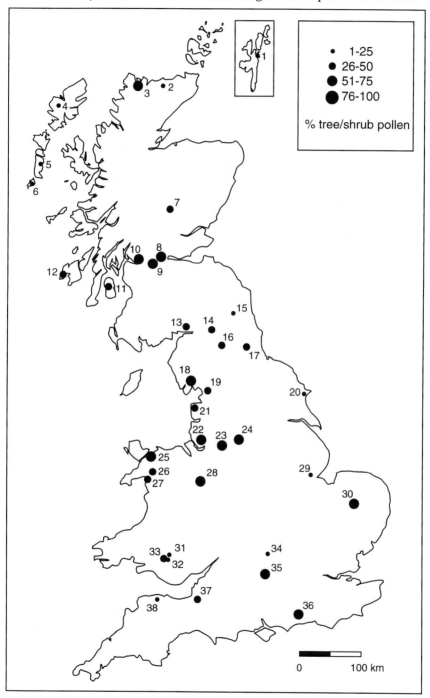

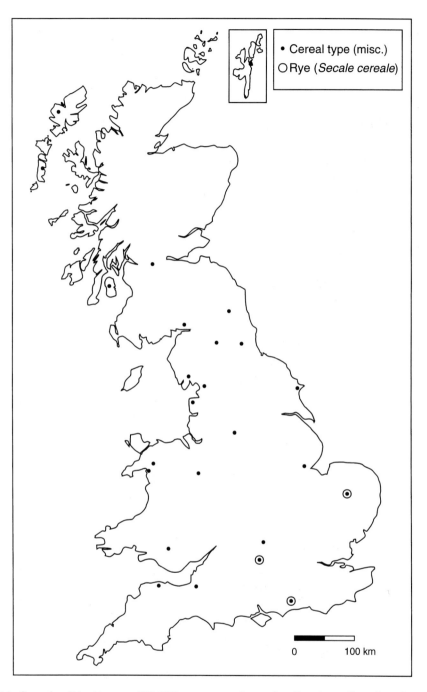

5.3: Cereal cultivation AD 400-800: presence of cereal pollen in radiocarbon-dated sequences spanning the period. For key to sites see Figure 5.2.

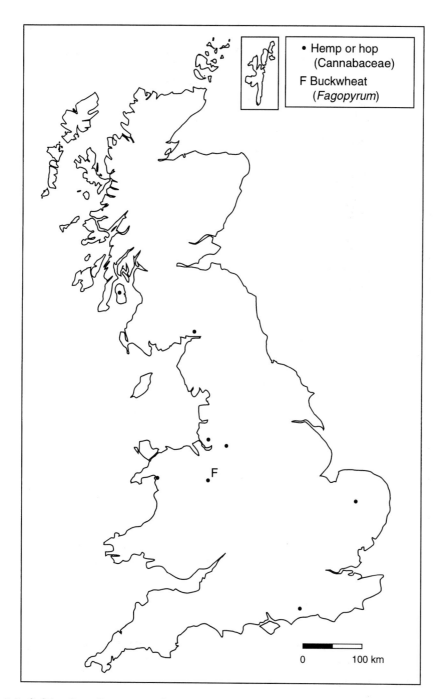

5.4: Cultivation of non-cereal crops AD 400-800: presence of pollen of hemp/hop and buckwheat in radiocarbon-dated sequences spanning the period. For key to sites see Figure 5.2.

5. The end of Roman Britain and the Anglo-Saxon period to AD 800

Table 5.1. Pollen sequences with radiocarbon dates and at least two pollen samples from the period AD 400-800

*detailed sequences – 7 or more relevant samples

Site	Radiocarbon date (BP)	Lab code	Cal range (AD) (95.4% conf.)	Reference
England				
*Amberley	1360±80	HAR-4234	540-880	Waton 1982, 1983
The Chains	1500±60	UB-816	420-650	Merryfield & Moore 1974; Moore et al. 1984
Crose Mere	1610±75	Q-1231	250-610	Beales 1980
Fairsnape Fell	1595±45	SRR-4504	340-570	Mackay & Tallis 1994
Featherbed Moss	1400±50	Q-852	540-720	Tallis & Switsur 1973
*Fellend Moss	1330±40	SRR-875	630-780	Dumayne & Barber 1994
*Fenton Cottage	1200±70	GU-5156	670-970	Middleton et al. 1995;
	1380±60	GU-5143	550-780	Wells et al. 1997
	1590±50	GU-5144	340-600	
Hallowell Moss	1522±65	SRR-412	410-650	Donaldson & Turner
	1355±50	SRR-413	600-780	1977
	1782±60	SRR-414	110-400	
Hockham Mere	1145±30	Q-1090	790-980	Sims 1978
Knowsley Park	1680±50	Birm-1177	220-460 (94.3%) 480-530 (1.1%)	Cowell & Innes 1994
Lindow Moss	1488±44	UB-3237	440-650	Branch & Scaife 1995
	1764±48	UB-3238	130-390	
Meare Heath	1414±45	SRR-910	550-680	Beckett & Hibbert 1979
	1746±45	SRR-911	180-400 (91.4%) 140-170 (4.0%)	
Quick Moss	1470±50		440-660	Rowell & Turner 1985
Rusland Moss	1361±55	SRR-125	590-780 (93.9%) 560-580 (1.5%)	Dickinson 1975
Sidlings Copse	1820±80	OxA-2047	20-400	Day 1991
Snelsmore	1290±80	HAR-4236	600-900	Waton 1982, 1983
*Steng Moss	1490±60	Q-1519	430-660	Davies & Turner 1979
Swineshead	1590±60	Q-2558	330-610	Waller & Alderton 1994
	1740±60	Q-2557	130-420	
Willow Garth	1170±50	SRR-2667	710-990	Bush & Flenley 1987
	1300±50	SRR-2668	640-860	

138

Site	Radiocarbon date (BP)	Lab code	Cal range (AD) (95.4% conf.)	Reference
Scotland				
Blairbech Bog	1750±45	SRR-4619	140-400	Dumayne-Peaty 1998
*Burnfoothill Moss	1365±45	SRR-3751	590-770	Tipping 1995 a,b
(paired dates)	1490±45		440-650	
Carn Dubh	1300±50	GU-3396	640-860	Tipping 1995c
Cross Lochs	1470±45	SRR-3707	450-660	Charman 1994
Dallican Water	1565±65	Q-2760	340-630	K.D. Bennett *et al.* 1992
Fannyside Muir	1550±40	SRR-4616	420-600	Dumayne-Peaty 1998
*Letham Moss	1465±40	SRR-4541	510-660 (92.5%) 450-490 (2.9%)	Dumayne-Peaty 1998
	1715±40	SRR-4542	230-420	
Little Loch Roag	1335±40	Q-1526	630-780	Birks & Madsen 1979
Loch a'Bhogaidh	1570±80	I-15258	330-640 (93.3%) 260-290 (2.1%)	Edwards & Berridge 1994
Lochan an Druim	1320±70	SRR-777	600-880	Birks 1993a
Lochan na Cartach	1540±45		420-610	Brayshay & Edwards 1996
Loch Lang	1415±45	Q-2702	550-680	K.D. Bennett *et al.* 1990
Machrie Moor	1120±60	GU-1348	780-1020	D.E. Robinson & Dickson
	1615±55	GU-1349	320-570 (91.0%) 250-300 (4.4%)	1988
Wales				
*Bryn y Castell	1655±50	GrN-17582	250-540	Mighall & Chambers 1995, 1997
Cefn Ffordd	1405±55	CAR-46	530-720 (94.0%) 740-770 (1.4%)	F.M. Chambers 1982
	1655±55	CAR-107	250-540	
Cefn Glas	1700±70	CAR-415	140-460 (91.9%) 480-530 (3.5%)	A.G. Smith & Green 1995
Coed Taf	1435±55	CAR-77	500-680 (92.4%) 450-490 (3.0%)	F.M. Chambers 1983b
Llyn Cororion	1585±65	SRR-3468	330-610 (93.9%) 260-290 (1.5%)	Watkins 1990
Moel y Gerddi	1665±60	CAR-660	240-540	F.M. Chambers & Price 1988

Cereal cultivation was widespread, but apparently less so than in the Roman period (cf Figure 4.7). Furthermore, records for rye pollen are confined to south-east England, whereas rye had been recorded at several sites near Hadrian's Wall in the Roman period. On some of Scotland's islands, however, cereals seem to have been grown for the first time. Pollen probably from hemp is recorded at several widely scattered sites, ranging from Amberley in Sussex (Waton 1983) to Machrie Moor on Arran (D.E. Robinson & Dickson 1988).

Regional patterns in the vegetation of Britain AD *400-800*

As in previous chapters, the pollen sequences are discussed here on a regional basis. Particular attention is given to the issue of environmental continuity and change after the end of the Roman period, and in this context some sites are included that lack direct dates for the period AD 400-800, but where the fifth-century deposits are sufficiently closely bracketed by earlier and later dates to enable any major changes to be detected. Note that laboratory codes for radiocarbon dates are given only for sites not listed in Table 5.1

South-east England

Just 5km east of the site of the Romano-British villa at Bignor, Sussex, lies Amberley Wild Brooks. Here the pollen sequence indicates that the environment had been predominantly open in the Roman period, but much of the landscape reverted to woodland in the late Roman or early post-Roman period (Waton 1982, 1983). In a region where agriculture would have been tightly geared to the villa economy, it is unsurprising that some land abandonment occurred in the wake of the Roman period. Agricultural activity did continue to a degree, however, as hemp and cereals, including rye, were grown locally. A similar pattern of late Roman or early post-Roman woodland regeneration occurred at Snelsmore in Berkshire, although again cereals continued to be grown locally (Waton 1982, 1983).

In Oxfordshire, however, a very different picture emerges from Sidlings Copse, close to the site of Headington Wick villa, and within the production area of Oxfordshire ware pottery. Here virtually all of the small area of woodland remaining on dry land had been removed at approximately the end of the Roman period (Day 1991, 1993). This created a local landscape almost devoid of trees, other than willow (*Salix*), and these open conditions persisted well into the post-Roman period (Figure 3.5). Here, then, it seems that the collapse of the pottery industry and villa economy produced no major effect on the environment. Intriguingly, woodland did regenerate later, at the end of the Anglo-Saxon period or in the early medieval period, giving rise to the medieval royal Forest of Stowood (Day 1991).

Archaeological evidence for an element of landscape continuity else-

140

where in the Oxford region comes from Barton Court Farm, near Abingdon. Here an Anglo-Saxon settlement was established from the fifth century adjacent to the site of a disused late Roman villa (Miles 1986). Assemblages of plant and animal remains from an Anglo-Saxon well suggest that there was little change in the overall character of the environment from that of the Roman period (M. Robinson 1986). There was a slight increase of tree and shrub pollen, but beetle assemblages contained no species requiring trees, suggesting that the landscape remained open. Continuity of arable farming is suggested by the occurrence of barley remains in the well, and flax probably also continued to be grown. The animal bones hint at a shift in the pastoral economy, however, with fewer cattle and more sheep (B. Wilson 1986).

Landscape continuity is also suggested by analysis of biological remains from Saxon wells near the Romano-British town of Dorchester in Oxfordshire. The beetle assemblages suggest open conditions on the gravel terraces in the fifth to sixth centuries, and there is evidence for cultivation of crops, again including flax and barley (M. Robinson 1981).

A further insight into the nature of agricultural activity in the Anglo-Saxon period may be provided by the rate of alluviation in the Upper Thames Valley. As discussed in previous chapters, alluviation had begun in the late Iron Age or Roman period. The rate of alluviation slowed, however, in the early and middle Saxon period, and then increased again from c. AD 800 (M. Robinson 1992). Given that alluviation probably reflects soil mobilisation due to agricultural activity, this might indicate a shift in agricultural emphasis from arable to grassland, a trend suggested elsewhere in southern England (see below).

One of the pollen sequences most frequently cited in relation to the Anglo-Saxon environment is from Epping Forest, Essex. This has been argued to reflect continuous woodland cover over the last four thousand years, but with a decline of lime (*Tilia*) in the Anglo-Saxon period (Baker, Moxey & Oxford 1978). There are several problems with the sequence, however, which mean that it must be interpreted with caution. The first concerns the poor temporal resolution of the sequence: the basal date of 4290±100 BP (Birm-525, 3350-2600 cal BC) is separated by only 35cm from a date of 1350±100 BP (Birm-690, cal AD 450-900), and there are only five pollen samples from the intervening period. Thus nearly three thousand years seem to be represented by just 35cm of deposit, with pollen samples some six hundred years apart. Part of the sequence could be missing, due to disturbance or a break in accumulation. Alternatively the basal date could be contaminated by the inwash of older material, a distinct possibility as the material dated was clay with low organic content. It is, therefore, possible that the sequence actually covers a much shorter period than initially appears to be the case.

Even if the basal date is not erroneous, the case for continuous woodland cover until the Anglo-Saxon period must be considered tenuous in

141

view of the large pollen sampling interval. The gap of around six hundred years between each sample could hide a considerable amount of vegetational change spanning, for example, virtually the entire Iron Age! This may explain the observation that the presence of a hill-fort of probable Iron Age date only 700m from the sampling site apparently produced 'no significant decline in tree species' (Baker *et al.* 1978, p. 647). The pollen diagram shows a decline of lime and increase of birch (*Betula*), hazel (*Corylus avellana*) and willow from the level dated 1350±100 BP, followed by an increase of beech (*Fagus sylvatica*) from 1110±160 BP (Birm-582, cal AD 600-1250). These changes were evidently accompanied by some clearance of woodland, as there is an increase of grasses and some other herbs. Tree and shrub pollen does remain dominant in the Anglo-Saxon period, however, suggesting that the site was substantially wooded, but a more detailed pollen sequence would be needed to establish the date of origin of this woodland.

An insight into the environment elsewhere in Essex is provided by a shorter sequence of organic deposits from an infilled channel in the Chelmer valley at Sandon Brook (Murphy 1994). The sequence apparently spanned the late Roman and Anglo-Saxon periods, and analysis of the macroscopic plant remains indicated that the local environment had remained predominantly open throughout this period, with no signs of woodland regeneration. Furthermore, remains of spelt wheat were present throughout the sequence, suggesting continuous local cultivation.

In conclusion, south-east England exhibits a variable pattern of vegetational change after the Roman period. At some sites agricultural land was abandoned and reverted to woodland, while at others the extent of farmland seems to have remained unchanged. Cereal cultivation continued, even where woodland regeneration occurred, but in some areas the extent of pasture may have been increased at the expense of arable.

East Anglia

Probably the most informative pollen evidence for the Anglo-Saxon period from East Anglia comes from Hockham Mere in Norfolk. As discussed in Chapter 3, the two radiocarbon-dated pollen sequences from the site (K.D. Bennett 1983; Sims 1978) have conflicting chronologies for the prehistoric parts of the sequence, although the date series are similar towards the end of the Roman period. Only the sequence produced by Sims contains post-Roman deposits. This sequence suggests the survival of quite substantial areas of woodland into the Anglo-Saxon period, but with some local agricultural activity, perhaps including cultivation of hemp. Pollen of cereals is less abundant than in the Roman period, and grasses and ribwort plantain (*Plantago lanceolata*) more so, suggesting a shift from cereal cultivation to pasture. This situation seems to have been reversed

142

immediately below 1145±30 BP (cal AD 790-980), with a major increase of cereals (including rye).

The only pollen sequence from the Fens with a radiocarbon date for the period AD 400-800 is from a narrow peat layer intercalated between clays at Swineshead (Waller & Alderton 1994). This shows very open conditions and possibly cereal cultivation, prior to marine inundation of the site after 1590±60 BP (cal AD 330-610).

In Suffolk, archaeological excavation of a Roman fort and settlement at Packenham was accompanied by sampling of the marginal deposits of an adjacent lake, Micklemere. Pollen analysis (by Pat Wiltshire, discussed in Murphy 1994) suggested that the environment remained open from the Roman period, with two phases of cereal cultivation – one Roman and one from approximately the middle Anglo-Saxon period – separated by an intervening lull. During this intervening period ribwort plantain continued to occur, suggested as a possible reflection of the maintenance of continued grazing after cereal cultivation ceased. This sequence thus suggests a similar pattern of land-use change to that implied elsewhere in East Anglia, and by alluviation in the Upper Thames Valley, i.e. a shift from arable to grassland.

South-west England

In the Somerset Levels the Meare Heath sequence shows increases of grasses and ribwort plantain at approximately the end of the Roman period, after which cereal pollen occurs more abundantly than at any earlier point in the sequence (Beckett & Hibbert 1979). This suggests an expansion of the area of open land and flourishing arable activity in the fifth to eighth centuries.

A contrasting pattern emerges, however, from analysis of blanket peat at The Chains on Exmoor (Merryfield & Moore 1974; Moore, Merryfield & Price 1984). Here a date of 1500±60 BP (cal AD 420-650) was obtained for an increase of birch and alder and decline of ribwort plantain, grasses, cereals and bracken (*Pteridium aquilinum*). This suggests that the area experienced a decline of agricultural activity and return of woodland, at least on poorer soils. Some cereal pollen occurred throughout the Dark Age deposits, however, suggesting that the area was not totally abandoned. At Hoar Moor, also on Exmoor, a decline of grasses and cereal-type pollen, and increase of heather (*Calluna vulgaris*) may also reflect abandonment of agricultural land at about this time (Francis & Slater 1990).

Once again, data from the south-west enable few general conclusions to be drawn. The abandonment of agricultural land on Exmoor, contrasting with the increased agricultural activity in the lowlands of the Somerset Levels, might suggest a response to climatic deterioration in the uplands, but more sequences are needed from both areas to investigate this suggestion further.

The Midlands

At Crose Mere, Shropshire, a decline of hazel at 1610±75 BP (cal AD 250-610) was immediately followed by a period of high levels of 'Cannabaceae' pollen, probably hemp, lasting until 1055±72 BP (Q-1230, cal AD 790-1160) (Beales 1980). The abundance of probable hemp pollen suggests that the mere may have been used for hemp retting, and need not necessarily indicate local cultivation of the crop. The fifth- to eighth-century deposits also produced the first local records for flax – another source of fibre – and for buckwheat – a crop that may have been grown for human or animal consumption. Cereal pollen is consistently present, and is accompanied by pollen of the cornflower (*Centaurea cyanus*), an arable weed rarely recorded in Britain before the Roman period (Figure 3.8).

Hemp also appears in the pollen sequence from the King's Pool, Stafford, at 1370±70 BP (WAT-275, cal AD 530-820) (Bartley & Morgan 1990), although less abundantly than at Crose Mere. There was a peak of cereals at the same point. The overall pattern of Roman and post-Roman vegetation change at this site is unfortunately uncertain, however, because deposits of the Iron Age, Roman and possibly early post-Roman period are mixed or missing.

Further north, at Featherbed Moss, Derbyshire, there was an increase of oak (*Quercus*) and decline of grasses, plantain, sorrel (*Rumex*) and bracken in this period, suggesting woodland regeneration (Tallis & Switsur 1973). Occasional records for cereals attest to at least some continuation of agriculture, however.

Overall, the Midlands present another mixed picture of regeneration at some sites and continuity at others. Hemp cultivation and processing again seem to have played an important role in the agricultural economy, as at sites further south.

North-west and north-east England

At Lindow Moss, Cheshire, the top of the pollen sequence has a date of 1488±44 BP (cal AD 440-650), so only the immediately post-Roman period is illustrated (Branch & Scaife 1995). This shows an increase of oak and hazel, and decline of heather, following a trend that began towards the end of the Roman period. There are no indications of local cereal cultivation, and the sequence suggests a reduction of grazing pressure and colonisation of some areas by woodland.

Further to the north, at Fenton Cottage a radiocarbon date of 1590±50 BP (cal AD 340-600) marks a decline of grasses and ribwort plantain, and increase of birch and oak (Middleton *et al.* 1995; Wells *et al.* 1997). The extent of woodland then exceeded that of the Roman period throughout the next four centuries (Figure 3.9). Charcoal also declines in abundance in the immediately post-Roman deposits, again suggesting a reduction in the levels of local human activity. Note, however, that plant macrofossil evidence from the site suggests a shift to wetter conditions, and this would reduce the likelihood of fires spreading, whatever their source of ignition.

At Fairsnape Fell in the central Pennines the end of the Roman period was accompanied by an increase of alder (*Alnus glutinosa*) and hazel and decline of grasses (Mackay & Tallis 1994). This again suggests local woodland regeneration, although much open moorland remained.

So, all sequences from the north-west of England show woodland regeneration in the centuries after Roman withdrawal. This contrasts with the picture presented from the only sequence with relevant dated deposits from the north-east, at Willow Garth (Bush 1993). Here the open landscape of the Roman period seems to have persisted into the post-Roman period virtually unchanged.

Northern England

Many pollen sequences from sites close to Hadrian's Wall indicate woodland regeneration after Roman withdrawal from the area, as mentioned earlier (K. Dark & Dark 1996). For example, at Fellend Moss, by the vallum, there was an increase of birch and decline of grasses and ribwort plantain at approximately the end of the Roman period (Davies & Turner 1979). There was then a further decline of grasses and disappearance of plantain at 1330±40 BP (cal AD 630-780). Cereals are absent from the Dark Age deposits, and it seems that some local areas of agricultural land were abandonded for several centuries. Despite this, much of the landscape remained open, probably due to grazing.

Other sites close to Hadrian's Wall also suggest woodland regeneration accompanying Roman withdrawal. At Fozy Moss hazel pollen increased in abundance, following its major decline in the Roman period (Dumayne & Barber 1994). Oak also increased slightly, but alder and birch seem not to have responded in the same way. These changes were accompanied by a decrease of grasses (Figure 4.11), followed by an increase of heather. Despite the evidence for land abandonment, some cultivation continued locally, suggested by the sporadic records of pollen of 'Avena-Triticum type'. After the initial period of regeneration, hazel declined again and grasses increased, and there seems to have been local cultivation of rye. Ribwort plantain increased to high frequencies, possibly reflecting local grazing. Here, then, a mixed agricultural economy seems to have emerged in the wake of a phase of land abandonment.

At Glasson Moss, near the western end of the wall, vegetational changes in the wake of Roman withdrawal are less marked than elsewhere along the frontier (Dumayne & Barber 1994). In this area some agricultural land may have been put out of use during the Roman occupation (Chapter 4,

Figure 4.11), so the effects of Roman withdrawal might be expected to have been less dramatic than elsewhere along the frontier.

At Walton Moss, north of the wall, there was an increase of hazel pollen and decline of grasses, again suggesting woodland regeneration (Figure 4.11), although the presence of rye, '*Avena-Triticum* type' and '*Cannabis* type' pollen suggests some local continuation of agriculture (Dumayne & Barber 1994). At nearby Bolton Fell Moss a sequence from the margin of the peat indicates an increase of birch, oak and alder, and decline of grasses at 1425±40 BP (SRR-4554, cal AD 550-670) (Dumayne-Peaty & Barber 1998). Again, agricultural activity obviously continued nearby, as suggested by the presence of pollen of rye, '*Avena-Triticum* type' and '*Cannabis* type'.

Woodland regeneration was not confined to sites closest to the wall, however. 20km to the north, at Steng Moss a similar pattern of post-Roman vegetational change occurred – an increase of birch and decline of grasses, cereals, ribwort plantain and sorrel (*Rumex acetosa*) (Davies & Turner 1979). To the south also, woodland regeneration at Quick Moss and Hallowell Moss seems to have occurred throughout the period AD 400-800, with declines of grasses, plantain, and bracken (Rowell & Turner 1985; Donaldson & Turner 1977). Further west, at Rusland Moss, Cumbria, there seems to have been an initial period of vegetational continuity before a decline of grasses and bracken and increase of birch (Dickinson 1975).

Almost all of the pollen sequences from the north of England show woodland regeneration after Roman withdrawal, although the evidence for cereal and possibly hemp cultivation indicates that agricultural activity continued to some extent. It seems most likely that the relaxation of land use at least partly reflects abandonment of areas that had been cleared specifically in response to the Roman occupation. The amount of woodland in the Dark Age phase is less than that of the Iron Age at most sites, however, so there was clearly not a simple return to pre-Roman levels of agricultural activity.

Scotland

After abandonment of the Antonine Wall in the late AD 160s Roman activity in Scotland was confined to the south. Roman incursions seem to have had little influence on native settlement, and the overall picture appears to be one of continuity in settlement throughout the first millennium AD (Ralston & Armit 1997).

In examining vegetational change in this period we begin with the pollen sequences from southern Scotland. At Letham Moss, north of the Antonine Wall, the extent of woodland had begun to increase in the late Roman period, from a level dated 1715±40 BP (cal AD 230-420), and peaked at 1465±40 BP (cal AD 510-660) (Dumayne-Peaty 1998) (Figure 4.14). Ribwort plantain was virtually absent during the period *c.* AD 400-800, in

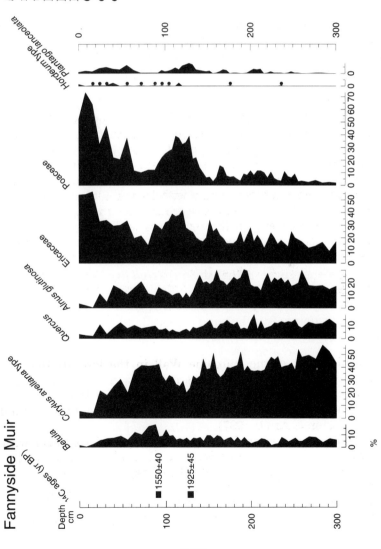

5.5: Pollen diagram from Fannyside Muir, showing selected taxa only. Percentages calculated from the sum of total land pollen excluding Ericaceae and Cyperaceae. Cereal pollen at <0.5% indicated by dots. (Redrawn from data of Dumayne-Peaty 1998.)

147

marked contrast to its previous abundance, and there is no evidence for local cereal cultivation. At Fannyside Muir, south of the wall, there was also an increase of woodland, peaking at 1550±40 BP (cal AD 420-600) (Dumayne-Peaty 1998) (Figure 5.5). This was accompanied by a decline of heather, grasses and ribwort plantain. The sporadic records of '*Hordeum* type' (probably barley) pollen suggest continued cereal cultivation in this area, however, despite the apparently limited extent of open land. At Blairbech Bog, near the western end of the wall, the landscape had already reverted largely to woodland in the Roman period, by 1750±45 BP (cal AD 140-400), and it remained so for several centuries after Roman withdrawal (Dumayne-Peaty 1998) (Figure 3.11). These sites, all lying within 10km of the Antonine Wall, therefore appear to mirror the pattern for the Hadrianic frontier in showing an increase in the extent of woodland after local Roman withdrawal.

Further south, at Bloak Moss, Strathclyde, there was a major peak of grasses and ribwort plantain between levels dated 1535±90 BP (Q722, cal AD 330-670) and 1370±105 BP (Q-721, cal AD 440-890), suggesting that in some parts of the inter-wall area there was renewed clearance in the post-Roman period (J. Turner 1965). Closer to Hadrian's Wall, however, at Burnfoothill Moss woodland regeneration is again suggested by a gradual increase of alder, birch and oak in approximately the fifth to ninth centuries, with a decline of grasses, ribwort plantain and cereal (Tipping 1995a, b).

North of the Antonine Wall, in south-east Scotland the Roman-period woodland regeneration seen at Black Loch seems to have been reversed, with a decline of trees and shrubs and increase of grasses, cereals, and ribwort plantain (Whittington, Edwards & Cundill 1991) (Figure 4.15). Unfortunately, the date of these changes is uncertain due to a reversal in the radiocarbon date series, but interpolation between the dates for the rest of the sequence suggests that they occurred in approximately the fifth century.

Closer to the coast, a layer of charcoal revealed in fossil sand dunes at Tentsmuir may derive from burning of heathland to improve its value for grazing (Whittington & McManus 1998). The burned layer extended over an area of more than a square kilometre, and was radiocarbon dated to 1530±80 BP (I-16,338, cal AD 340-660). Burning seems to have been sufficiently intense to destabilise the soil surface, and eventually encouraged replacement of the heather by grasses.

At Carn Dubh in Perthshire a date of 1300±50 BP (cal AD 640-860) corresponds with a major increase of grasses and decline of tree and shrub pollen (Tipping 1995c). These changes seem to mark near complete removal of local woodland and apparently its replacement by grassland.

On Scotland's islands and in the extreme north vegetational changes in this period are less marked, although at some sites there was an increase, or even the first occurrence, of cereal cultivation. For example, at Loch Lang, South Uist, the first record of cereal pollen occurs in deposits from approximately the sixth century (K.D. Bennett *et al.* 1990), while at Dallican Water, Shetland, cereal ('*Hordeum* type') pollen occurs fairly consistently from approximately the same date (K.D. Bennett *et al.* 1992). At Machrie Moor on Arran an increase of heather and decline of tree pollen from 1615±55 BP (cal AD 320-570) suggests an extension of open moorland, following an earlier trend towards woodland regeneration (D.E. Robinson & Dickson 1988). There is some pollen of cereal and hemp or hop, but the extent of agricultural activity was apparently limited by peat growth. On Islay a sequence from Loch a'Bhogaidh shows the maintenance of an open environment of heath and acid grassland throughout the fifth to ninth centuries (Edwards & Berridge 1994).

Further evidence for agricultural activity is provided by on-site deposits from the island of Iona, in the Hebrides, a site well-known in connection with the monastery founded by St Columba *c.* AD 563. Pollen analysis of the fill of a ditch, originally dug soon after the foundation of the monastery, revealed the presence of cereal pollen, suggesting arable activity nearby (Bohncke 1981). A notable feature of the deposits was the abundance of pollen and seeds of nettles (*Urtica dioica*) and elder (*Sambucus nigra*). Both plants are favoured by high nutrient levels, and may have been encouraged by use of the ditch for dumping rubbish.

In conclusion, parts of southern Scotland seem to have reverted to woodland after a period of increased clearance in the Roman period. At sites further north there is a variable pattern: some areas experienced a major increase of clearance in the fifth to ninth centuries, and several of the islands show the first signs of cereal cultivation. Much of the extreme north of Scotland had already become pemanently deforested in the Iron Age, and blanket peat was widespread.

Wales

As was the case for the Roman period, the post-Roman pollen sequences from Wales occur predominantly at higher altitudes, away from the areas likely to have been most productive agriculturally. There are, however, pronounced vegetational changes in most of the pollen sequences from Wales, coinciding approximately with the end of the Roman period. At Bryn y Castell in Snowdonia there was an increase of hazel and alder dated 1655±50 BP (cal AD 250-540) (Mighall & Chambers 1995, 1997). This may reflect recovery of local woodland after the cessation of iron-working at the local hill-fort, possibly as previously coppiced trees grew on to full size. There was then a gradual decline in the extent of woodland, probably reflecting an increase of grazing pressure in the area.

At Moel y Gerddi, also in north-west Wales, a date of 1665±60 BP (cal AD 240-540) was obtained for a decline of woodland and increase in the extent of open land (F.M. Chambers, Kelly & Price 1988). Cereal-type pollen occurs in the Dark Age deposits, suggesting local arable activity.

The *'Cannabis / Humulus'* pollen in these deposits is probably from hop, as there are records sporadically from the Mesolithic period onwards.

Further south, at Tregaron Bog a peak of ribwort plantain and grasses occurred just above a level dated 1477±90 BP (Q-391, cal AD 380-720) (J. Turner 1964). This followed clearance initiated towards the end of the Iron Age, suggesting continuity of agricultural activity. The date marks a change from weakly to highly humified peat, however, and the slow accumulation rate of the rest of the first-millennium deposits unfortunately obscures the detailed pattern of vegetational change.

From the uplands of south Wales, peat deposits at Cefn Glas show a decline of birch and hazel and increase of grasses at 1700±70 BP (cal AD 140-460) (A.G. Smith & Green 1995), while at Waun Fach South, in the Black Mountains, a sharp decline of ribwort plantain in perhaps the fifth or sixth century suggests a reduction in the extent of open land (Moore, Merryfield & Price 1984). At Coed Taf blanket peat accumulation began in the early post-Roman period in a virtually open landscape (F.M. Chambers 1983b).

So, pollen sequences from Wales show a variable pattern of vegetational change in the centuries after the end of the Roman period. More sequences are needed from lowland areas to highlight any changes of land use in the more agriculturally productive areas.

Pollen evidence for vegetational change and the end of Roman Britain: general conclusions

Turning to a more detailed consideration of the evidence for vegetational change at the end of the Roman period, Figure 5.6 presents a revised and updated version of the pollen data (cf P. Dark 1996). Pollen sequences spanning the end of the Roman period have been examined to assess

5.6: Pollen evidence for environmental continuity and change at the end of the Roman period: changes in the proportion of tree/shrub pollen in radiocarbon-dated sequences spanning the fourth to fifth centuries AD.

1. Dallican Water	15. Fellend Moss	29. Crose Mere
2. Loch Lang	16. Fozy Moss	30. Swineshead
3. Lochan na Cartach	17. Steng Moss	31. Hockham Mere
4. Carn Dubh	18. Quick Moss	32. Cefn Gwernffrwd
5. Loch Cholla	19. Hallowell Moss	33. Waun Fach South
6. Blairbech Bog	20. Rusland Moss	34. Brecon Beacons
7. Fannyside Muir	21. Fairsnape Fell	35. Cefn Glas
8. Letham Moss	22. Fenton Cottage	36. Sidlings Copse
9. Black Loch	23. Willow Garth	37. Snelsmore
10. Machrie Moor	24. Featherbed Moss	38. Amberley
11. Burnfoothill Moss	25. Lindow Moss	39. Meare Heath
12. Glasson Moss	26. Llyn Cororion	40. Aller Farm
13. Bolton Fell Moss	27. Bryn y Castell	41. Hoar Moor
14. Walton Moss	28. Moel y Gerddi	42. The Chains

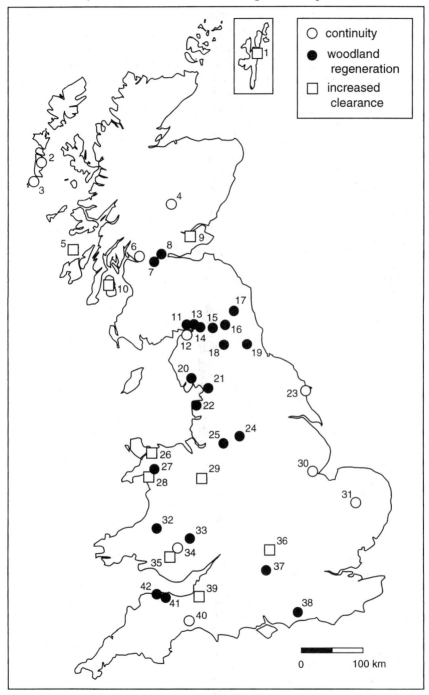

whether they show continuity, woodland regeneration, or increased clearance. Sites are included where relevant deposits are either directly radiocarbon dated, or can be dated by interpolation, based on radiocarbon date series where the relevant dates have error terms not greater than ±80.

A pattern of regional variability in land-use change after the Roman period appears. In the south there seems to have been land abandonment and woodland regeneration in some areas, as at Snelsmore in Berkshire and Amberley in Sussex, but at other sites continuity is indicated, as at Sidlings Copse in Oxfordshire. Where woodland regeneration is not apparent, there are hints of a shift from arable production to a more pastoral economy, as perhaps at Hockham Mere, but this did not totally replace cereal cultivation.

In the north of England and in southern Scotland there is a fairly consistent picture of woodland regeneration at most sites at some stage in the period AD 400-800. This is seen close to both the Hadrianic and Antonine frontiers. The most obvious explanation for this relaxation of land-use is that it reflects a previous reliance on markets provided by the Roman army, which could not be replaced by local demand once the troops were withdrawn (K. Dark & Dark 1996).

How closely these changes coincided with the end of the Roman period is, of course, uncertain, because of the age ranges for the radiocarbon dates. It is, therefore, impossible to establish a precise relationship between the date of official Roman withdrawal and vegetation change. The distribution of pollen sequences is biassed towards those areas that were least romanised in the fourth century, where least change might be expected. Furthermore, little pollen evidence is available from the areas of early Anglo-Saxon influence. The bias of the pollen data to the north and west of Britain unfortunately means that the pollen evidence has an almost inverse distribution to the area of *primary* Anglo-Saxon occupation. This obviously limits the extent to which pollen analysis can be used to shed light on the environmental impacts of the Anglo-Saxon occupation. It is, for example, impossible to tell whether any changes in the extent of agricultural land were triggered by the adoption of Anglo-Saxon agricultural practices, although there are hints of a shift from arable to pasture in some areas (mentioned earlier).

With reference to the effects of climatic deterioration in this period (Chapter 2), the rather mixed pattern of land-use change suggests that this deterioration was not severe enough to have had a detrimental effect on agriculture across the whole of Britain. If the pattern of vegetational change is compared with site altitude (Table 5.2) it becomes apparent, however, that most sites with evidence for reduced human activity are at altitudes greater than 150m, while sites showing continuity or increased activity are mainly at lower altitudes. This is illustrated in the south-west, where an expansion of agricultural activity at Meare Heath in the Somerset Levels contrasts with a reduced intensity of land use on the uplands of

152

Exmoor. It is, therefore, possible that climatic deterioration may have caused land abandonment in some areas that were already marginal for agriculture. This pattern of land abandonment could also lend support to the suggestion of upland soil deterioration due to acidification by volcanic emissions (Chapter 2), but the available evidence does not allow separation of the effects of soil acidification by volcanic gases from the effects of increased rainfall.

Table 5.2. Altitudes of sites shown in Figure 5.6, in relation to evidence for environmental continuity and change (continued overleaf)

	Altitude				
	0-150m	151-300m	301-450m	451-600m	601m+
Continuity					
Aller Farm	+				
Blairbech Bog	+				
Brecon Beacons					+
Carn Dubh			+		
Glasson Moss	+				
Hockham Mere	+				
Loch Lang	+				
Lochan na Cartach	+				
Swineshead	+				
Willow Garth	+				
Increased clearance					
Black Loch	+				
Cefn Glas				+	
Crose Mere	+				
Dallican Water	+				
Llyn Cororion	+				
Loch Cholla	+				
Machrie Moor	+				
Meare Heath	+				
Moel y Gerddi	+				
Sidlings Copse	+				
Woodland regeneration					
Amberley	+				
Bolton Fell Moss	+				
Bryn y Castell			+		
Burnfoothill Moss	+				

153

	0-150m	151-300m	301-450m	451-600m	601m+
Cefn Gwernffrwd			+		
Fairsnape Fell				+	
Fannyside Muir		+			
Featherbed Moss				+	
Fellend Moss		+			
Fenton Cottage	+				
Fozy Moss		+			
Hallowell Moss	+				
Hoar Moor			+		
Letham Moss	+				
Lindow Moss	+			+	
Quick Moss					
Rusland Moss	+				
Snelsmore	+				
Steng Moss			+		
The Chains				+	
Walton Moss	+				
Waun Fach					+

There are problems in disentangling 'cultural' and environmental factors in relation to land-use change. Abandonment of upland sites might be expected, irrespective of external environmental factors, if contraction of agricultural activity occurred, as one would expect a concentration on the more productive lowland areas. Alternatively, environmental change may have tipped the balance to land-abandonment in areas where, for example, reduced demand for agricultural produce itself encouraged relaxation of land-use. The role of climatic and/or soil deterioration in leading to abandonment of upland sites in this period, therefore, remains unclear.

In addition to changes in agricultural activity in this period, the question also arises of whether or not Roman-period levels of exploitation of natural resources continued to be employed, notably of woodland.

Woodland management

We have seen that the Roman industries such as pottery and iron production probably relied heavily on managed woodland as a source of fuel, so woodland management practices might be expected to decline when production was halted before or during the fifth century. While the need for mass consumption of wood after the Roman period was probably reduced, requirements for fuel and building purposes would have remained, how-

154

ever. Coppice management was not a Roman introduction to Britain, so it seems unlikely that such practices would have been abandoned.

Construction in the post-Roman period relied heavily on wood and timber (e.g. Rahtz 1976), and wattle-work was widely used. Archaeological evidence for the use of wattle-work comes from many sites, including the middle Saxon settlement at Hamwic (Southampton), where wattle-impressed burnt daub was a common find (Andrews 1997). At Barton Court Farm, Oxfordshire, a well of probable fifth-century date was lined with oak, hazel and willow rods woven around oak and hazel uprights (Miles 1986, p. 36). Other examples include wattle-lined wells from a fifth/sixth-century site near Dorchester, Oxfordshire (M. Robinson 1981, p. 269), and an eighth-century well from Aldwincle, Northamptonshire (M. Robinson & Wilson 1987, p. 60). In Scotland, excavations of the hill-fort at Dundurn, Perthshire, revealed a wattle floor of hazel (Alcock, Alcock & Driscoll 1989), two samples of which were radiocarbon dated to 1510 ± 60 BP (GU 1042, cal AD 420-650) and 1390 ± 60 BP (HAR 2519, cal AD 540-780), indicating that they were cut at some time in the fifth to eighth centuries.

While woodland management probably continued to be widespread after the Roman period, there are hints that some coppices may have ceased to be managed. In particular, the tree-ring studies mentioned earlier might be interpreted as reflecting cessation of coppicing in some areas, allowing young shoots to grow on to timber. Similarly, it could be argued that the increase of tree pollen seen in some pollen diagrams in the centuries after Roman withdrawal might also reflect cessation of coppicing, enabling shoots previously cut before they could flower to produce pollen. The effect on the pollen record would depend on the tree species concerned. Hazel is likely to have been favoured by coppicing, as the new shoots can flower in their second year (O. Rackham 1990, p. 71). Other trees take longer to flower, however, so may have been unable to produce pollen if coppiced. If coppicing stopped it might, therefore, produce a decline of hazel but increase of other trees. This effect would occur rapidly – within perhaps a decade – in contrast to colonisation of an area by trees, which would take several decades. These differences would not be detectable in most pollen sequences, however, due to the relatively coarse sampling interval.

While some apparent instances of post-Roman woodland recovery may actually reflect cessation of coppicing, it would be unrealistic to suggest that this is the case in most pollen sequences. Other changes in the pollen record – notably falls in abundance of cereal and ribwort plantain pollen – suggest that the extent of pasture and arable land declined at the same time.

155

Conclusion

In conclusion, then, we see a pattern of regional variation in land-use change in the period AD 400-800. In northern Scotland the picture is predominantly of continuity, or even increased clearance, as one might expect away from the main centres of romanisation. In England there is something of a north-south divide in vegetational change. Some sites in the southern half of England show continuity or an increased level of agricultural activity after Roman withdrawal, while at others there is woodland regeneration. In the south-east there seem to have been a trend towards greater pastoral as opposed to arable farming. Moving north towards the former Roman border region there are increasing signs of woodland regeneration, to the extent that almost all sites within 20km of Hadrian's Wall show a reduced intensity of land use at some point in the period AD 400-800. Most sites near the Antonine Wall show regeneration also, but beginning at an earlier date. The north of England and southern Scotland had experienced a particularly dramatic increase in the level of agricultural acitivity in the Roman period, so to some extent this woodland regeneration can be argued to reflect a direct response to loss of the military market. At most sites, however, woodland did not return to its pre-Roman abundance.

In some areas the trend towards woodland regeneration was accompanied by a cessation of cereal cultivation, but elsewhere cereals continued to be grown, despite the spread of woodland. Rye and hemp seem first to have been widely cultivated from the middle Anglo-Saxon period, as evidenced from both pollen and macroscopic remains.

Overall, then, many of the regions that had undergone the greatest change in vegetation and agriculture in the Roman period seem to have experienced a relaxation in the intensity of land use in the post-Roman period. Probably the most productive soils were maintained for arable, as around Sidlings Copse in Oxfordshire, while less fertile soils were converted to pasture or even allowed to revert to woodland. In a few cases it is possible that the apparent woodland regeneration reflects a cessation of coppicing, but woodland management certainly continued in many areas into the Anglo-Saxon period.

6

Late Anglo-Saxon England and the Viking Age

Introduction

From the end of the eighth century AD Britain was subjected to sporadic attacks by Scandinavian raiders – the Vikings. Initially the Vikings were apparently concerned solely with looting, but from the mid-ninth century their interests turned towards permanent settlement. The extent of Viking influence is documented in written sources, and by the distribution of Scandinavian place-names (Hill 1981; Richards 1991; Ritchie 1993). These indicate that the main areas of settlement were in eastern and north-western England, and in the west and north of Scotland, although the scale of colonisation in terms of numbers of people is uncertain. Little is known of the character of Viking Age rural settlement in Britain, but the increasing interest in town life in this period is evidenced at several sites, including York and London (Clarke & Ambrosiani 1991; Richards 1991).

The Viking period coincided with major landscape change in late Anglo-Saxon England, notably settlement nucleation and the formation of villages (Lewis, Mitchell-Fox & Dyer 1997). This change seems to have been accompanied by a reorganisation of agricultural land and the origin of the open field system in parts of central southern England and the Midlands (Hooke 1995, 1998; Lewis *et al.* 1997).

Evidence for the nature of agriculture in this period is slight, as there are few excavated rural settlements with large assemblages of plant and animal remains. The main crops apparently continued to be bread wheat (*Triticum aestivum*), barley (*Hordeum vulgare*), rye (*Secale cereale*) and oats (*Avena*), with some 'Celtic bean' (*Vicia faba*) and peas (*Pisum sativum*). Hemp (*Cannabis sativa*) and flax (*Linum usitatissimum*) also seem to have been widely grown, probably as a source of fibre and oil. Evidence for the use of hemp comes both from macroscopic remains, as at York (A.R. Hall *et al.* 1983; Kenward & Hall 1995, p. 478) and Norwich (Ayers & Murphy 1983), and from pollen records (see later). As discussed previously, there are problems in separating pollen of hemp and hop (*Humulus lupulus*), but the macrofossil records from York and Norfolk suggest that both were used in this period (A.R. Hall *et al.* 1983; Kenward & Hall 1995, p. 478; Ayers & Murphy 1983). Hops may be used in dying and in medicine, as well as for brewing. They are native to Britain, growing naturally in fen environments and hedgerows, but where large quantities of hops were required they may have been deliberately culti-vated. An example is provided by the substantial assemblage of hops recovered from a tenth-century boat found at Graveney in Kent (D.G. Wilson 1975; D.G. Wilson & Connolly 1978).

Macroscopic remains of flax have been found at rural sites ranging from Birsay Bay (Donaldson & Nye 1989; Nye 1996) and Freswick Links (J.P. Huntley with Turner 1995) in northern Scotland, to Springfield Lyons (Murphy 1994) and West Cotton (Campbell 1994) in eastern England. At West Cotton a silted river channel contained waterlogged capsules and seeds of flax, probably reflecting retting of the plant for fibre production. The channel also contained the remains of hay-meadow plants, such as clover (*Trifolium* sp.), yellow rattle (*Rhinanthus minor*), and ox-eye daisy (*Leucanthemum vulgare*), suggesting the presence of managed grassland.

Assemblages of plant remains from towns also frequently contain flax, as at Stafford (Moffett 1994), Norwich (Ayers & Murphy 1983), London (G. Jones, Straker & Davis 1991) and York (A.R. Hall *et al.* 1983; Kenward & Hall 1995). These finds cannot necessarily be linked with local cultivation of the plant – its importance as a source of fibre and linseed oil means that it may have been transported over considerable distances. From York, tenth-century deposits yielded not only plant remains suggesting fibre production for textiles, but also plants used for dying, including woad (*Isatis tinctoria*), dyer's greenwood (*Genista tinctoria*) and madder (*Rubia tinctorum*) (Kenward & Hall 1995).

In terms of the possible environmental impacts of human activity in this period, there are several aspects that might be expected to leave traces in the palaeoecological record. The initial phases of Viking raiding probably caused some land to be abandoned, but this would presumably have been mainly in coastal areas most prone to sudden attack. The later Viking settlement phase would presumably have led to changes in land tenure, and these might be reflected in the pollen record if they were accompanied by changes in land use. The growth of urbanism in this period (Clarke & Ambosiani 1991) may also have had implications for the scale of farming activity, as the movement of some of the population to towns would have exerted pressure on the rural populace to increase productivity. Perhaps most significant in central southern England and the Midlands is the change in landscape organisation arising from settlement nucleation and open field agriculture.

An increase in agricultural productivity may have been facilitated by climatic amelioration at this time. The Viking Age coincided with the beginning of warm period that lasted for several centuries (Chapter 2), and this may have provided an impetus to agriculture by enabling cereals to be grown in areas where the climate had previously been unfavourable. With these points in mind we now turn to the pollen evidence for the character of vegetation in the Viking Age.

Pollen evidence for vegetation in the Viking Age

Site selection

Following the criteria adopted in previous chapters, pollen sequences with radiocarbon dates (with error terms not greater than ±80) for the Viking Age and with at least two pollen samples from the relevant deposits have been mapped in Figure 6.1. This shows the percentages of tree and shrub pollen (calculated on the basis of a sum including all pollen and spores of vascular plants, excluding obligate aquatics) as an indication of the extent of woodland surviving in this period. The occurrence of pollen of crops in these deposits is indicated in Figure 6.2 by presence only. Details of the sites and the relevant radiocarbon dates are given in Table 6.1.

Table 6.1. Pollen sequences with radiocarbon dates and at least two pollen samples for the period AD 800-1000

Site	Radiocarbon date (BP)	Lab code	Cal range (AD) (95.4% conf.)	Reference
England				
Crose Mere	1055±72	Q-1230	790-1160	Beales 1980
Featherbed Moss	1023±50	Q-851	890-1060 (83.9%) 1070-1160 (11.5%)	Tallis & Switsur 1973
Fellend Moss	945±40	SRR-874	1000-1180	Davies & Turner 1979
Fenton Cottage	1200±70	GU-5156	670-970	Middleton *et al.* 1995; Wells *et al.* 1997
Glasson Moss	960±40	SRR-4532	1000-1170	Dumayne & Barber 1994
Hockham Mere	1145±30	Q-1090	790-980	Sims 1978
Snelsmore	1290±80	HAR-4236	600-900	Waton 1982, 1983
Steng Moss	1085±35	SRR-1041	880-1010	Davies & Turner 1979
Willow Garth	1170±50	SRR-2667	710-990	Bush & Flenley 1987
Scotland				
Black Loch	920±65	UB-2291	1000-1250	Whittington *et al.* 1991
Burnfoothill Moss	1045±45	SRR-3750	880-1040	Tipping 1995a, b
(paired dates)	1100±45		850-1020 (92.7%) 810-840 (2.7%)	
Machrie Moor	1120±60	GU-1348	780-1020	D.E. Robinson & Dickson 1988
Wales				
Coed Taf (A)	1195±50	CAR-78	680-960	F.M. Chambers 1983b

6. Late Anglo-Saxon England and the Viking Age

6.1: Woodland in the late Anglo-Saxon period and Viking Age. Percentages of tree and shrub pollen in radiocarbon-dated sequences spanning the period AD 800-1000.

1. Black Loch
2. Machrie Moor
3. Burnfoothill Moss
4. Glasson Moss
5. Fellend Moss

6. Steng Moss
7. Fenton Cottage
8. Willow Garth
9. Featherbed Moss
10. Crose Mere

11. Hockham Mere
12. Coed Taf
13. Snelsmore

Results

Analysis of vegetational change in this period is affected to an even greater extent than for earlier periods by a lack of well-dated pollen sequences. Northern Scotland and south-west England lack any relevant closely dated sequences, and sites elsewhere are thinly scattered. Of these, most show a similar extent of woodland to that in the preceding period. Records for cereal and hemp/hop pollen are too sparse and widely scattered to enable any regional patterns in cultivation to be identified.

Discussion here focuses on the sites listed in Table 6.1 where the Viking Age deposits are directly dated, but is augmented by other pollen sequences where the deposits can be reasonably dated by interpolation. Regions separated in previous chapters are here lumped together due to the sparsity of the evidence. Note that laboratory codes for radiocarbon dates are given in the text only for sites not listed in Table 6.1.

Regional patterns in the vegetation of Britain in the Viking Age

South-east England and East Anglia

Contrasting patterns of vegetational change in this region are highlighted by comparison of the pollen sequences from Snelsmore, in Berkshire, and Sidlings Copse, in Oxfordshire. At Snelsmore woodland had regenerated in the late Roman or early Anglo-Saxon period, and much of the landscape seems to have remained wooded throughout the late Anglo-Saxon period (Waton 1982, 1983). At Sidlings Copse, however, the post-Roman landscape remained almost completely open until the late Anglo-Saxon or early Norman period, when some woodland regeneration began (Day 1991, 1993) (Figure 3.5). As discussed in Chapter 5, this regeneration could have resulted from changes in land-use when Forest Law was imposed on the area in the early Norman period, as the site was part of the Royal Forest of Shotover and Stowood recorded in Domesday Book (Day 1990).

In East Anglia, the pollen record from Hockham Mere indicates an increase of cereals, especially rye, and decline of ribwort plantain (*Plantago lanceolata*) and grasses immediately below a level dated 1145±30 BP

161

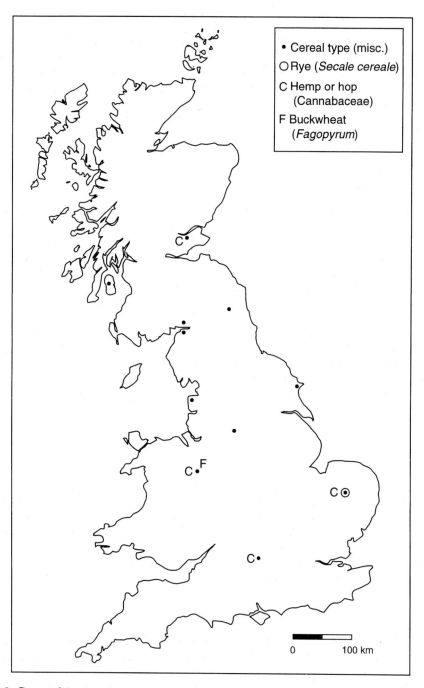

6.2: Crop cultivation in the late Anglo-Saxon period and Viking Age. Presence of pollen of cereals, hemp/hop and buckwheat in radiocarbon-dated sequences spanning the period AD 800-1000. For key to sites see Figure 6.1.

(cal AD 790-980) (Sims 1973). This suggests the possibility of a shift from pasture to arable agriculture in the area. Percentages of Cannabaceae (probably hemp) pollen increased immediately above this, reflecting either local cultivation of the crop, or hemp retting in the lake. Cannabaceae pollen is abundant in lake sediments elsewhere in Norfolk, as at Old Buckenham Mere (Godwin 1967), Quidenham Mere (Peglar 1993a) and Diss Mere (Peglar 1993b), in deposits thought to belong to the Anglo-Saxon period, but unfortunately these sites lack radiocarbon dates.

The Midlands

At Crose Mere in Shropshire a date of 1055±72 BP (cal AD 790-1160) marks an increase of grasses and ribwort plantain, following a major decline of Cannabaceae pollen – again presumed to be hemp (Beales 1980). Cereals also decline slightly, and buckwheat (*Fagopyrum esculentum*) ceases to occur (Figure 3.8). This pattern suggests a change in land use, with an increase in the extent of grassland at the expense of crops.

At Featherbed Moss, Derbyshire, there were increases of grasses, plantain, bracken (*Pteridium aquilinum*), and sorrel (*Rumex*), and a continuous curve for '*Urtica* type' (probably nettle – *Urtica dioica*) pollen from 1023±50 BP (cal AD 890-1060) (Tallis & Switsur 1973). This followed a period of woodland regeneration from approximately the eighth-ninth century. At the same time alder (*Alnus glutinosa*) and hazel decline. These changes may reflect an increase in the use of the area for grazing, but cereal pollen also increases, suggesting some expansion of local arable activity.

North-west and north-east England

In the north-west, at Fenton Cottage, the extent of woodland continued to increase in the Viking Age, following a trend initiated at approximately the end of the Roman period (Middleton, Wells & Huckerby 1995; Wells, Huckerby & Hall 1997). Cereals do seem to have been grown locally, however (Figure 3.9). In the north-east, at Willow Garth there is an increase of cereal pollen and herbs of disturbed ground (Bush 1993), suggesting a new impetus to agricultural activity in the Viking Age.

Northern England

At Fellend Moss, Northumberland, the extent of open land declined in the Viking Age, followed at 945±40 BP (cal AD 1000-1180) by a major peak of heather (*Calluna vulgaris*), grasses, cereals, ribwort plantain and other herbs, and a record for hemp pollen, suggesting renewed clearance and agricultural activity (Davies & Turner 1979). A similar pattern occurs at Bolton Fell Moss, where the Viking Age coincided with an increase of woodland, especially of birch (*Betula*) and oak (*Quercus*), and decline of ribwort plantain (Barber 1981; Dumayne-Peaty & Barber 1998). This was followed at 920±70 BP (Hv-3082, cal AD 990-1250) by a decline of tree and shrub pollen and increase of grasses, '*Avena-Triticum* type' (oat or wheat), rye and ribwort plantain.

At Fozy Moss the extent of woodland had begun to decline in approximately the seventh to ninth centuries, following its post-Roman increase, and this trend continued (Dumayne & Barber 1994). At the same time there was an increase of grasses and presence of '*Avena-Triticum* type' pollen (Figure 4.11). Similarly, at Glasson Moss there was also an increase in the extent of open land and cereal cultivation in the Viking Age (Dumayne & Barber 1994) (Figure 4.11). At Steng Moss there was a steep decline of tree and shrub pollen and peak of grasses, cereals, ribwort plantain and heather at 1085±35 BP (cal AD 880-1010) (Davies & Turner 1979).

Clearly then, some sites in the north of England show an increased impetus to clearance and agricultural activity in the Viking Age, while others experienced abandonment of land and woodland regeneration.

Scotland

In south-west Scotland, at Burnfoothill Moss an increase of grasses, ribwort plantain and probable cereal pollen from approximately the beginning of the Viking Age suggest an expansion of agriculture (Tipping 1995a, b). In the east, at Black Loch, conditions were already predominantly open, and the Viking Age deposits show an increase of several herb types associated with disturbed ground (Whittington, Edwards & Cundill 1991). A slight increase of cereal pollen suggests some extension of arable, and pollen specifically identified as hemp becomes quite abundant, reflecting either local cultivation of the plant or retting of hemp fibres in the lake (Figure 4.15).

At Machrie Moor on Arran a date of 1120±60 BP (cal AD 780-1020) marks a peak of grasses and decline in abundance of tree and shrub pollen to very low levels (D.E. Robinson & Dickson 1988). Cereal-type pollen is present, and ribwort plantain peaks immediately above this level. These changes suggest a major increase in human activity at the site, perhaps including expansion of cereal cultivation in response to climatic warming (D.E. Robinson & Dickson 1988).

In Caithness, a pollen sequence has been analysed from an area of blanket peat at Hill of Harley, 1.5km west of the Norse settlement at Freswick Links (J.P. Huntley 1995). At the time of occupation the landscape appears to have resembled that of today, with areas of moorland, grassland and some mixed farming. The excavation at Freswick Links revealed the charred remains of several crops, including barley, oats, bread wheat, Celtic bean and flax (J.P. Huntley with Turner 1995). The occurrence of a few cereal pollen grains in the pollen sequence suggests that at least some of the cereals were grown locally. The site also produced charred seaweed fragments, perhaps reflecting attempts to increase soil fertility (J.P. Huntley with Turner 1995). Such a practice is still followed today in the Western Isles, although seaweed can also be used in making soap.

All of these Scottish sites show an increase of clearance in the Viking Age, usually with evidence for cereal cultivation. The effects of climatic improvement in this period may have been especially marked in Scotland, where much of the land was probably marginal for growing cereals. A warmer climate would have provided the opportunity for arable production in some areas that had previously been suitable only for pasture.

Wales

Little can be said of vegetational change in Wales in this period, as the only published sequences with relevant dates come from high-altitude blanket peat at Cefn Glas and Coed Taf in south Wales. At Coed Taf blanket peat formation had begun between approximately the sixth and seventh centuries AD, in a predominantly open landscape (F.M. Chambers 1983b). There was some increase in the local abundance of trees from a level dated 1195±50 BP (cal AD 680-960), but the extent of woodland remained small. At Cefn Glas there was some reduction of woodland at 1120±60 BP (CAR-354, cal AD 780-1020), in an already predominantly open landscape (A.G. Smith & Green 1995). There are problems with the radiocarbon dates from this sequence, however, and the pollen sampling interval is wide, so the detailed chronology of vegetational change is uncertain.

Woodland management

Overall, the ninth and tenth centuries seem to have seen only minor changes in the extent of woodland in most areas. As in earlier periods, much of this woodland is likely to have been managed as a valued resource. Anglo-Saxon charters refer to various aspects of woodland management and exploitation, including coppicing, pollarding and pannage (O. Rackham 1980, 1986, 1990). Pollarding resembles coppicing, but the trees are cut several feet above ground level so that the new shoots are beyond the reach of animals. This practice meant that livestock could be grazed in the woods without the need to fence off newly cut areas. Pannage involved releasing pigs into woodland in autumn to feed on acorns or beech mast. Some coppice woods were probably embanked in this period to assist in controlling access of livestock and wild animals (especially deer) to areas of woodland at different stages in the coppice cycle (O. Rackham 1980, 1990).

6.3: Wattle-lined pit from Coppergate, York. (Photographed by M.S. Duffy, reproduced by permission of the York Archaeological Trust.)

Archaeological evidence indicates that in many areas Viking Age buildings were predominantly of wood, and included a large component of wattle-work. For example, tenth-century buildings in York had wattle walls and were on plots of land defined by wattle fences (Kenward & Hall 1995). Wattle-work was also employed to line pits with a variety of functions, including use for storage or as cesspits (Figure 6.3). The main tree species used at York were hazel and willow, and the sheer abundance of stems would seem to suggest that woodland was managed to ensure a continuous supply. Analysis of a large sample of the roundwood from 16-22 Coppergate, however, indicated that it was of variable age, and had been selected on the basis of size for particular functions (Kenward & Hall 1995, pp. 528, 722). This suggests that the wood was not entirely the product of coppicing, as such a practice would produce even-aged poles. Wood at this and other sites was probably gathered from a variety of sources, in addition to managed woodland, including hedges and areas being cleared of trees and scrub for agricultural purposes.

The urban environment

Our greatest insight into the character of towns in the Viking Age is provided by excavations at York, especially Coppergate. Here, analysis of a range of biological remains has enabled a detailed reconstruction of the home environment, suggesting that it was far from hygienic (A.R. Hall *et al.* 1983; Kenward & Hall 1995). Large quantities of organic material accumulated in the town during the tenth century, supporting a host of insects. Many of these were associated with rotting material of various kinds, ranging from faeces to structural timbers (A.R. Hall *et al.* 1983). Various domestic animals were kept in the town, including pigs and chickens as well as cats and dogs, all adding to the accumulation of foul materials (Hall *et al.* 1983, pp. 217-18).

Excavations at 16-22 Coppergate located many pits containing faecal material, and these evidently attracted swarms of flies, including the house fly (*Musca domestica*) (Kenward & Hall 1995). The combination of exposed human waste and flies would obviously have encouraged the spread of various diseases, such as poliomyelitis and cholera. Direct evidence relating to human health comes from the eggs of the intestinal parasites, maw worm (*Ascaris lumbricoides*) and whipworm (*Trichuris trichiura*), in the faecal material (Figure 6.4), suggesting that at least part of the population suffered from heavy parasitic infections (Kenward & Hall 1995). These parasites have also been found in samples from late Saxon pits in London (De Rouffignac 1991). From York there is also evidence for external parasites, including fleas (*Pulex irritans*) and lice (*Pediculus humanus*) (A.R. Hall *et al.* 1983, p. 218; Kenward & Hall 1995).

Pests, parasites and disease had already been a feature of town life in the Roman period, so the question arises as to whether Viking Age towns were any more squalid. At York the thick layers of organic material from the Viking town contrast with the low organic content of the Roman deposits, suggesting that much more rubbish was left lying around in the former (A.R. Hall *et al.* 1983, pp. 222-3).

A further contrast between the Viking and Roman towns is the scarcity of evidence for pests of stored produce in the Viking Age contexts, in contrast with their abundance in the Roman period. This could reflect differences in methods of grain storage, but may be linked with a cessation of mass transport and storage of grain (A.R. Hall *et al.* 1983, p. 224; Kenward & Hall 1995, pp. 760-1).

The insect remains from York also shed additional light on the climate in this period. For example, the bug *Heterogaster urticae* was found in several samples from the site, yet its current distribution does not extend as far north as York, suggesting that temperatures there may have been higher in the tenth century (Addyman *et al.* 1976; A.R. Hall *et al.* 1983, pp. 219-20; Kenward & Hall 1995, p. 781). This, of course, accords with

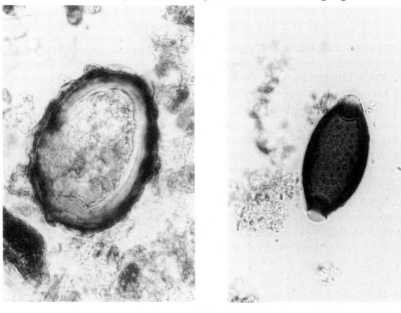

a   b

6.4: Parasite eggs from Viking York: (a) Maw worm, *Ascaris*, (b) Whipworm, *Trichuris*. (Photographs by A.K.G. Jones, reproduced by permission of the York Archaeological Trust.)

evidence from a range of other sources for warmer temperatures at this time (Chapter 2), and may have been important for the cultivation of exotic crop plants such as madder and woad (Kenward & Hall 1995, p. 781).

Conclusion

The scarcity of pollen sequences covering the late Anglo-Saxon period/ Viking Age imposes severe constraints on discussion of the effects of human activity on environmental change in relation to the questions outlined earlier in this chapter. There is, for example, too little evidence from the main areas of settlement nucleation and open field agriculture to illustrate vegetational changes associated with the major landscape reorganisation that these movements involved. Yet some clear trends do emerge in other areas. In Scotland, there seems to be a consistent pattern of increased clearance and agricultural activity, perhaps attributable to climatic amelioration enabling expansion of agriculture to previously marginal areas. In northern England several sites show a similar trend. A general increase of woodland clearance and agriculture may provide an explanation for the observation by Macklin and Lewin (1993) that the period 1200-800 BP (*c.* cal AD 800-1250) was one of widespread valley floor sedimentation in the uplands of northern and western Britain.

Woodland continued to be managed by coppicing or pollarding in many areas, and provided an important resource not only for wood and timber, but also for hunting wild game and feeding livestock. Venison would presumably have been a welcome addition to the human diet, and in areas of oak and beech woodland pigs were left to feed on acorns and beech mast during the autumn. Wooded areas also provided a home for several large mammals that would be eradicated from Britain in later centuries, including wild boar (*Sus scrofa*), wolf (*Canis lupus*) and bear (*Ursus arctos*).

Much more research is required into the nature of the environment of the Late Anglo-Saxon period and the Viking Age, especially as this period was pivotal in the formation of the modern landscape. It would be particularly interesting to compare the amount of woodland in the ninth and tenth centuries, reconstructed by pollen analysis, with the records for woodland compiled for Domesday Book in 1086 (see Rackham 1980, 1986, 1990). Current evidence enables such a multidisciplinary approach to be applied only on a relatively small scale (e.g. Day 1990), but as palaeo-ecological data accumulate in the future the potential for such studies will increase. There are major opportunities for comparison of archaeological, textual and 'environmental' information for the final centuries of the first millennium AD (Bell & Dark 1998). It is to be hoped that the relative neglect of this period will be remedied in the early years of the third millennium.

7

Discussion

The preceding chapters have examined the character of the environment of Britain in the first millennium AD, within the framework of the archaeological record. While recognising the problems of such an approach, it has been adopted to enhance the opportunities for integrating the 'environmental' and archaeological data.

Pollen analysis has provided the principal method for environmental reconstruction. This is because it provides a long-term perspective on the general character of the environment in terms of vegetation cover. An attempt has been made, for each period, to examine all well-dated pollen sequences on a regional basis. A severe constraint on the use of pollen analysis in examining regional variations in the environment is the skewed distribution of the data. Most pollen sequences come from the north and west of Britain, yet many key archaeological questions relate to other areas. For example, the distributions of Roman villas, and pollen sequences spanning the Roman period, are almost mutually exclusive. This obviously limits the use of pollen analysis in examining the environmental consequences of the collapse of the villa economy.

Despite the problems, one possible benefit of the environmental 'marginality' of many of the sites that have produced pollen sequences for the first millennium is that they may be especially sensitive indicators of climatic and economic change. Areas where agriculture was strongly constrained by poor soils and unfavourable climate might be expected to be the first to be abandoned at times of environmental or cultural stress.

Macroscopic plant remains from archaeological sites have been used largely to provide information on environmental exploitation such as woodland and grassland management and agriculture. Animal remains have played a lesser role in this account because they have been less widely used in illustrating the general character of the environment of the first millennium AD. The many assemblages of animal bones from archaeological sites are principally a source for diet and animal exploitation, but smaller animal remains, notably insects, provide important information about domestic living conditions.

7. Discussion

General trends

Climate

Climate during the first millennium AD began rather wetter and cooler than that of today, becoming warmer and drier in the Roman period. The end of the Roman period coincided approximately with a phase of climatic deterioration that is widely recorded from a variety of sources, suggesting both cooler and wetter conditions. During the middle-late Anglo-Saxon period there seems to have been a trend towards an increasingly warm and dry climate, which lasted well into the medieval period. There are hints that at least one major volcanic eruption may have affected the climate of Britain temporarily in the first millennium, but its environmental consequences are unlikely to have lasted for more than a few years.

Sea level

At the start of the first millennium AD parts of the coastline differed considerably from that of today, especially in areas of gentler coastal topography. The combination of sea-level rise, uplift, silting and erosion have combined to produce a regionally variable pattern of coastal change, confounding attempts to map the coastline of the whole of Britain at any stage in the first millennium. Detailed work on the East Anglian Fens and Severn Estuary Levels illustrates local changes in areas where relative sea level has risen by c. 4m and 1m respectively since the Roman period. More such studies are required on post-prehistoric deposits to complement the extensive work on coastal change in prehistory, but problems of disturbance of later sequences by drainage, ploughing and construction for coastal defences hamper such attempts.

Soils

By the beginning of the first millennium AD the soils of many upland areas of northern and western Britain had already become nutrient depleted and begun to accumulate peat deposits. Human activity seems to have triggered peat formation at some sites, due to hydrological changes brought about by woodland clearance. Sandy soils in lowland areas were also showing signs of nutrient depletion, and these trends continued into the first millennium. Attempts to overcome soil nutrient loss are indicated by the practices of manuring and crop rotation. Soil erosion had been a problem since the Bronze Age in some areas, but there were further episodes of major erosion, detectable on a regional scale by increased river alluviation, in the Roman period and late Saxon period.

By the Iron Age cultivation was already exploiting a range of soils, including heavy clays and areas prone to waterlogging. The Roman period

171

apparently saw the beginning of extensive organised land drainage schemes, ranging from individual fields to large areas of countryside such as the Fens and Severn Estuary Levels. This might hint at increased pressure on the land, to the point where it was economically worth the expense of major drainage initiatives.

Vegetation

After climate and sea level, a key determinant of the overall character of the landscape for human occupation is the relative extent of woodland and open land. The natural vegetation of most of Britain was woodland, and many areas first experienced sustained woodland clearance and extensive agricultural activity in the Bronze Age, especially in the south and east. Clearance continued in many areas in the Iron Age, becoming widespread in the north. In southern England and Wales there appears to have been some relaxation in the intensity of land-use in the middle Iron Age, leading to a period of woodland regeneration. The late Iron Age saw a major impetus to clearance, particularly in areas of northern England that had hitherto remained substantially wooded.

In most areas clearance of new land seems to have continued into the Roman period, and in northern England agricultural expansion may have been linked with the need to supply the Roman army. In eastern Scotland, however, woodland regeneration indicates that the effect of a Roman military presence was not always to encourage local agricultural production.

At the end of the Roman period there are signs of woodland regeneration in some areas, especially the north of England. Here the loss of the military market may have led to a relaxation of land use, as local demand for agricultural produce dwindled. Elsewhere, especially in the west of Britain, there are signs of continuity of agricultural activity, or even increased levels of clearance, in the immediately post-Roman period. Unfortunately, as mentioned earlier, the pollen evidence is biassed away from areas of southern and eastern England where the villa economy had been well developed, so the environmental consequences of its end are unclear.

The Viking Age saw an extension of clearance in many areas, apparently involving an increase in cereal cultivation. In the Midlands, north-east and south of England, this may have been connected with reorganisation of the agricultural landscape in this period. Clearance is especially noticeable in Scotland, however, where it may be attributable to climatic amelioration facilitating expansion of agriculture into previously marginal areas.

Environmental management

During the first millennium AD there is abundant evidence for manipulation of 'natural' vegetational communities to maximise their output of useful materials. The most obvious of these is woodland management, which probably involved some form of coppicing. Woodland management seems to have been practised in Britain from as early as the Neolithic period, and apparently continued throughout the first millennium AD. The need for coppicing must have been especially great in the Roman period, due to the fact that many areas had little remaining woodland – in some regions probably no more than exists today – and the 'industrial' scale of production of pottery, tile, metal-work etc. Buildings also made use of wattle-work throughout most of the first millennium, and of course fuel – mostly wood – for domestic fires was a universal requirement. Where moorland was extensive there are hints of the use of peat and heather for fuel, suggesting that woodland resources may have been too scarce to be allowed to go up in smoke! It is possible that some areas of managed woodland ceased to be maintained after the Roman period, but the evidence is currently slight.

The Roman period provides the first clear indications of grassland management to produce hay. Little can be said about grassland management practices between the end of the Roman period and the late Saxon period, however, due to a scarcity of evidence.

Agriculture

Pollen and macroscopic plant remains provide complementary information relating to cereal cultivation, as the pollen record is biassed to the north and west of Britain, while macroscopic cereal remains come predominantly from the south and east. Caution must be exercised in inferring local cereal cultivation from macroscopic cereal remains on archaeological sites, however, as they may represent long-distance transport. From the Roman period considerable movement of agricultural produce seems to have occurred to fill the granaries of the towns and forts, perhaps even including imports from the Continent. The pollen record is more likely to reflect local cultivation, although it probably severely underestimates the extent of cereal cultivation due to the low production and poor transport of most cereal pollen.

From the pollen record it is clear that cereals were grown in both upland and lowland areas throughout the first millennium AD. Cereal pollen is recorded less frequently in Scotland than in England and Wales, although an absence of cereal pollen need not necessarily imply an absence of cereal cultivation. Many of the available pollen sequences are from areas unlikely to have been used to grow crops due to their waterlogged nature.

The detail of what was cultivated, especially for the non-cereal crops, is provided by macroscopic plant remains from archaeological sites. These indicate considerable changes in crop exploitation in the first millennium AD. In the Iron Age the main cereals were barley (*Hordeum vulgare*) and spelt wheat (*Triticum spelta*). Evidence for non-cereals is less extensive, but 'Celtic bean' (*Vicia faba*) and peas (*Pisum sativum*) were used at some sites. Flax (*Linum usitatissimum*) is also evidenced from the macrofossil record, while off-site pollen sequences suggest the possibility of hemp (*Cannabis sativa*) cultivation. Both flax and hemp may have provided a source of fibre or oil. The problems of distinguishing hemp pollen from that of hop (*Humulus lupulus*), and uncertainties over the chronology of the possible Iron Age hemp pollen records, urge caution in interpreting the pollen record as indicating hemp cultivation in this period.

The Roman period saw increasing use in some areas of bread wheat (*Triticum aestivum*), rye (*Secale cereale*) and oats (*Avena sativa*), but spelt wheat and barley remained an important element of the cereal assemblage. Beans, peas and flax continued to be recorded at some sites, and there is firmer evidence that hemp was grown. More specialised cultivation included grapes (*Vitis vinifera*) and a range of horticultural products, while the existence of ornamental gardens at villas attests an increasing interest in aesthetic aspects of plant cultivation.

After the Roman period, bread wheat came to dominate the crop assemblage at many sites, accompanied by rye, barley and oats. Flax and hemp became particularly prominant in the Anglo-Saxon period and Viking Age, probably as a source of fibre. Textile production seems to have been an important aspect of the economy of some Viking Age towns, and plants used for dying, including woad (*Isatis tinctoria*) and madder (*Rubia tinctorum*), may have been grown for this purpose.

Throughout the first millennium AD arable fields provided a haven for a variety of weeds that were apparently rare or absent prior to the late Iron Age. These included the cornflower (*Centaurea cyanus*), corncockle (*Agrostemma githago*) and stinking mayweed (*Anthemis cotula*), plants that are now rare due to the use of herbicides. The change in weed floras towards the end of the Iron Age is presumably linked with changes in cultivation regime, including increasingly deep ploughing (M. Jones 1988).

Animal husbandry was principally based on cattle, sheep and pigs throughout the first millennium AD, although the relative proportions of the different species varied regionally, by site type, and over time. Cattle seem to have been particularly important in the late Iron Age and Roman period, perhaps reflecting their vital role in pulling ploughs at a time of rapid agricultural expansion.

Overall, the first millennium AD was a period of major change in sea level, climate, soils and vegetation, interacting with variations in the character and intensity of human activity to produce a highly variable pattern of landscapes. The next section examines some of the different perspectives on land-use change offered by environmental evidence from this period.

7. Discussion

Off-site palaeoecological sequences and the archaeological record

Analysis of pollen and other components of the off-site palaeoecological record can achieve much more than the simple provision of an environmental backdrop against which human events are played out. It can help to answer questions relating directly to the character and duration of human settlement on a variety of spatial and temporal scales.

The landscape scale

Archaeological projects are increasingly moving from examination of isolated sites to consideration of whole landscapes, including settlements, field systems, trackways and so on. Palaeoecological information is obviously an important adjunct to 'landscape archaeology', and can approach questions that have proved difficult to answer purely from an archaeological perspective. For example, pollen analysis has been used to address the problem of the date and period of use of a later prehistoric field system in the Peak District (D.J. Long, Chambers & Barnatt 1998).

Pollen sequences from large lake basins or peat deposits may provide a picture of vegetational change integrated over an area of perhaps several square kilometres. If many sequences are available from an area, especially if their pollen source areas overlap, they can be used to provide detailed information on landscape change, again complementing the archaeological record.

There are few areas of Britain with a sufficient density of pollen sequences to look at detailed spatial variability for a single region, but where events might be expected to affect land-use over wide areas the examination of all available pollen sequences has proved useful. For example, the nature of the end of Roman Britain can be viewed from a variety of perspectives on the basis of the archaeological record, ranging from events at a single site (did use of a particular villa continue into the fifth century?) to the fate of whole towns, production systems and so on. The palaeoecologial record enables us to examine the broader question of whether there was any detectable change in landscape use. If farming systems were disrupted over a prolonged period, we might expect to see widespread woodland regeneration in the pollen record. As we have seen in Chapter 5, the vegetation of many parts of Britain seems to have been unaffected by Roman withdrawal, but regeneration did happen in some areas, especially in the Hadrianic frontier zone. This area had experienced a particularly marked expansion of agricultural activity in response to Roman occupation, and once the military market was lost there was presumably insufficient demand for agricultural produce to sustain the same levels of production (K. Dark & Dark 1996).

Pollen analysis can also help us to examine the effects of the establishment and end of some of the major industries of Roman Britain. Unfortunately only one well-dated pollen sequence is currently available from such an area – associated with the Oxfordshire ware pottery industry. This indicates landscape continuity after the end of the Roman period, suggesting that the local economy was not so strongly linked to the industry that major change in land-use followed its demise (Day 1991, 1993). More research is required from other Roman industrial areas to establish whether or not this was a general pattern.

Site-specific questions

If an off-site pollen sequence is closely associated with an excavated archaeological site, then it can help to shed light on the character of the occupation and to answer questions relating specifically to activity at that site, such as the period over which it was used. Such off-site sequences may be of considerably greater value than an on-site record because they are less likely to have suffered disturbance by human activity, and may span the period before, during, and after occupation of the site.

Of course, our ability to examine all of these issues is hampered by the difficulty of chronological correlation between the palaeoecological and archaeological records. The usual reliance on radiocarbon chronologies for pollen sequences imposes the problem of the impossibility of precise correlation due to the fact that radiocarbon 'dates' are actually age ranges. This problem is made even worse when the archaeological site cannot be dated on the basis of characteristic artefacts, such as coins or pottery, and has to be dated by radiocarbon as well! To some extent the problem can be reduced if a large number of dates is available from a sequence, so that Bayesian analysis of the series can be used to reduce the age-ranges of the dates, but the frequently limited allocation of radiocarbon dates means that this approach has rarely been used.

Another approach is to establish a direct link between specific archaeological sites and an adjacent pollen sequence by identification of 'markers' generated by human activity at the site in the pollen-bearing deposits. This method has been adopted for sequences of lake deposits next to Hadrian's Wall and the Stanegate, in an attempt to ascertain whether clearance of local woodland was undertaken in connection with the establishment of the frontier, or at an earlier date (P. Dark forthcoming).

Future directions for research

The most obvious need to arise from the present study is for more pollen sequences from many areas of Britain for the first millennium AD, especially the whole of southern and eastern England, the Midlands, and lowland areas of Wales. These areas lack the obvious expanses of peat and lakes of the uplands of the north and west, and even where peat does occur it has often been disturbed by drainage or peat cutting. The location of suitable deposits relies on time-consuming fieldwork to locate the smaller areas of organic accumulation.

Even where pollen sequences are available, their temporal resolution is often poor. Greater use of high resolution pollen analysis is required, of the type more usually applied to deposits of the Mesolithic and early Neolithic periods. Pollen analysis at Fairsnape Fell (Mackay & Tallis 1994), Fozy Moss and Glasson Moss (Dumayne & Barber 1994), has employed this approach, but it is needed at a far greater variey of sites. Multiple pollen analyses from a single site, as at Bryn y Castell (Mighall & Chambers 1997), are also of value in cautioning against over-interpretation of a single sequence, illustrating the degree to which local vegetational change may mask wider changes.

While our principal source for the general character of the terrestrial environment in the first millennium is pollen analysis, there are frequently problems in using the pollen record alone to identify the effects of human activity on the environment. Pollen-bearing lake sediments and peat deposits contain a variety of other types of biological and inorganic materials that can shed light on many aspects of the environment. There is a need for more integrated studies involving analysis of the fullest possible range of these other aspects of the palaeoecological record.

The most obvious of these is microscopic charcoal particles. Most types of vegetation in Britain rarely burn naturally, so the occurrence of charcoal in pollen-bearing deposits can provide a valuable independent indicator of human activity. More problematic is the nature of this activity: the charcoal could derive from domestic hearths, 'industrial' sources such as pottery kilns, or from burning of vegetation, whether by accident or design. The analysis of charcoal from deposits of the first millennium AD is now being undertaken more widely, for example in relation to the Iron Age and Roman iron smelting at Bryn y Castell in north Wales (Mighall & Chambers 1997) and pottery production in Oxfordshire (Day 1991), but is still far from universal.

Another component of sediments that is of value in interpreting environmental history is the mineral content (determined by loss-on-ignition analysis). A high mineral/low organic content may be linked to soil erosion, such as might occur following forest clearance or ploughing. Magnetic analysis of this mineral component may indicate its source, providing the potential to link human activity to exploitation of specific soil types (Thompson & Oldfield 1986).

Much could be gained by analysis of other biological components of lake sediments and peat deposits. Fungal spores offer considerable scope for enhanced interpretation of the biological record, although there are problems both in their identification – most can currently only be assigned type numbers – and ecological implications (van Geel 1986). In relation to the Peak District field systems, spores of fungi connected with deposition of animal dung were analysed, providing a possible indicator of pastoral land-use (D.J. Long *et al.* 1998).

Another aspect largely neglected is the role of fungi as pathogens. The large-scale storage of crops in the Roman period was associated with grain storage pests, which evidently led to considerable crop losses, but what of losses in the field due to other insect pests and fungal disease? We currently know remarkably little about the problems involved in crop production in the pre-modern period, but the increasingly intensive nature of arable activity in the Roman and later Anglo-Saxon periods means that loss of crops to pests and diseases must have been a principal factor in reducing yields. In this context it is interesting to note the tentative identification of spores resembling those of the fungus causing covered smut (*Ustilago hordei*), a disease most commonly affecting barley, among the stomach contents of Lindow Man (Scaife 1986). From continental north-west Europe there are several records of fungal crop pathogens from late Iron Age and Roman-period contexts. Best known of these are the spores of *Ustilago hordei* and sclerotia of the ergot fungus (*Claviceps purpurea*) in the stomach of the Danish Iron Age bog bodies, Tollund Man and Grauballe Man (Helbaek 1958). Such records represent merely the 'tip of the iceberg' in terms of the overall extent of crop disease in the later prehistoric and early historic periods (P. Dark forthcoming).

In the first millennium AD we must also consider the possibility of environmental pollution at levels detectable in the palaeoecological record. Atmospheric pollution is usually assumed only to have become a problem since the Industrial Revolution, but analysis of the lead content of Swedish lake sediments suggests that air quality was falling long before this (Renberg, Persson & Emteryd 1994). Lead levels in the sediments first began to rise above background at around 2600 BP (*c.* 800 cal BC), and reached a small peak about five times above background levels at 2000 BP (*c.* 0 cal AD). After this peak, lead concentrations fell until approximately 1000 BP (*c.* cal AD 1000), when a major and sustained increase began. This pattern mirrors the history of lead production in Europe, suggesting that the data reflect long-range transport of air-borne pollutants. Even more remarkable is the fact that increased lead levels have also been found to follow a similar pattern in the Greenland ice sheet (Hong *et al.* 1994), suggesting that lead mining and smelting were polluting the atmospheric on at least an hemispheric scale for more than two millennia before the Industrial Revolution!

Another potential source of atmospheric pollution in the first millennium AD is coal burning. Use of coal for fuel first became widespread in Britain in the Roman period (Webster 1955; Dearne & Branigan 1995; A.H.V. Smith 1996, 1997), and would have added a further source of particulates to an atmosphere already laden with fine ash from burning of wood and peat. Characteristic 'spherical carbonaceous particles' produced by coal burning are abundant in sediments dating to the mid-nineteenth and twentieth centuries, but appear not to occur in significant quantities in deposits from the first millennium AD (Wik & Natkanski 1990). Microscopic charcoal particles are, however, often abundant in such deposits – especially from the Iron Age and Roman periods – at sites such as Fenton Cottage, Lancashire (Wells, Huckerby & Hall 1997), and Crawcwellt in Gwynedd (F.M. Chambers & Lageard 1993). If, as mentioned above, charcoal particle analysis was undertaken more widely than at present, it could also shed light on contemporary air quality.

The problem of chronology

Crucial to all future areas of research lies the problem of chronology. Greater chronological control in the first millennium AD is of vital importance, especially in view of the rapidity of cultural change in this period.

The thin tephra layers found in some peat sequences present the exciting possibility of dating to individual years where a link can be made to a specific historically dated eruption. Even where this is not possible, tephra layers provide chronological markers to compare sites, as elegantly demonstrated for pollen sequences from Northern Ireland (V.A. Hall, Pilcher & McCormac 1993). Unfortunately, however, few tephra layers have been identified from deposits of the first millennium AD. Furthermore, the approach seems likely to be available only for deposits in northern Britain and Ireland due to patterns of tephra dispersal from the Icelandic eruptions that seem to be the principal tephra source.

Radiocarbon dating will probably remain the main means of providing chronological control for 'environmental' sequences in the forseeable future, but refinements in methodology and approaches to data analysis are making marked improvements in the level of precision available. As already discussed, the application of Bayesian analysis will require more radiocarbon dates for sequences covering this period than have usually been obtained. Similarly, 'wiggle-matching' of date series to the calibration curve provides another potential way forward. Again, however, this relies on the availability of a large number of closely-spaced radiocarbon dates. This method has been employed successfully for the early Mesolithic site at Star Carr, where twelve radiocarbon accelerator dates were available for a sequence spanning just 70cm in depth, and could be matched to a radiocarbon 'plateau' at 9600 BP (Day & Mellars 1994; P. Dark 1998c).

Conclusion

One of the goals of this book has been to highlight the increasing body of data available for reconstruction of first-millennium AD environments, and to attempt to offset the general bias in discussion of environmental change towards prehistory. Despite the problems of chronological imprecision and patchy distribution of the data, it has been possible to illustrate a number of trends in environmental change directly resulting from, or with implications for, human activity. These include the timing of the first major extensive woodland clearance, subsequent patterns of woodland regeneration and clearance in relation to land-use fluctuations, and issues of continuity and change in the landscape in relation to social, economic and cultural forces.

Many of the consequences of human activity in the first millennium AD remain with us today, despite the sweeping changes in agricultural land-use and industrialisation in the second millennium AD. At a time of increasing concern over the global effects of environmental degradation, the long-term perspective provides a vital context for understanding these effects, and taking action to minimise them.

References

Addyman, P.V., Hood, J.S.R., Kenward, H.K., MacGregor, A. & Williams, D. 1976. Palaeoclimate in urban environmental archaeology at York, England: problems and potential. *World Archaeology* 8, 220-33

Aitken, M.J. 1990. *Science-based Dating in Archaeology.* Longman, London/New York

Alcock, L., Alcock, E.A. & Driscoll, S.T. 1989. Reconnaissance excavations on Early Historic fortifications and other royal sites in Scotland, 1974-84: 3, Excavations at Dundurn, Strathearn, Perthshire, 1976-77. *Proceedings of the Society of Antiquaries of Scotland* 119, 189-226

Alderton, A. & Waller, M. 1994a. Railway Crossing. In M. Waller, *The Fenland Project, Number 9: Flandrian Environmental Change in Fenland*, 230-4. East Anglian Archaeology Report 70, Cambridgeshire County Council, Cambridge

Alderton, A. & Waller, M. 1994b. New Bridge Road. In M. Waller, *The Fenland Project, Number 9: Flandrian Environmental Change in Fenland*, 234-8. East Anglian Archaeology Report 70, Cambridgeshire County Council, Cambridge

Allen, J.R.L. 1991. Salt-marsh accretion and sea-level movement in the inner Severn Estuary, southwest Britain: the archaeological and historical contribution. *Journal of the Geological Society, London*, 148, 485-94

Allen, J.R.L. & Fulford, M.G. 1986. The Wentlooge Level: a Romano-British saltmarsh reclamation in southeast Wales. *Britannia* 17, 91-117

Allen, J.R.L. & Fulford, M.G. 1987. Romano-British settlement and industry on the wetlands of the Severn Estuary. *Antiquaries Journal* 67, 237-74

Allen, J.R.L. & Fulford, M.G. 1992. Romano-British and later geoarchaeology at Oldbury Flats: reclamation and settlement on the changeable coast of the Severn Estuary. *Archaeological Journal* 149, 82-123

Allen, J.R.L., Bradley, R.J., Fulford, M.G., Mithen, S.J., Rippon, S.J. & Tyson, H.J. 1997. The archaeological resource: chronological overview. In M. Fulford, T. Champion & A. Long (eds) *England's Coastal Heritage*, 103-53. English Heritage, London

Allen, T.G., Darvill, T.C., Green, L.S. & Jones, M.U. 1993. *Excavations at Roughground Farm, Lechlade, Gloucestershire: a Prehistoric and Roman Landscape.* Oxford University Committee for Archaeology, Oxford

Andersen, S.T. 1979. Identification of wild grass and cereal pollen. *Danmarks Geologiske Undersogelse*, Yearbook 1978, 69-92

Andrews, P. 1997. *Excavations at Hamwic Volume 2: Excavations at Six Dials.* CBA Research Report 109, York

Armitage, P.L., Locker, A. & Straker, V. 1987. Environmental archaeology in London: a review. In H.C.M. Keeley (ed.) *Environmental Archaeology: a Regional Review*, 252-331. HBMCE, London

Armitage, P.L., Rudling, D. & Parfitt, S. 1995. Larger vertebrates. In F. Aldsworth

& D. Rudling, Excavations at Bignor Roman villa, West Sussex 1985-90, 172-3. *Sussex Archaeological Collections* 133, 103-88

Armitage, P.L., West, B. & Steedman, K. 1984. New evidence of black rat in Roman London. *London Archaeologist* 4, 375-83

Armour-Chelu, M. 1991. The faunal remains. In N.M. Sharples, *Maiden Castle. Excavations and Field Survey 1985-6*, 139-51. English Heritage, London

Atherden, M.A., 1976. Late Quaternary vegetational history of the North York Moors. III. Fen Bogs. *Journal of Biogeography* 3, 115-24

Ayers, B. & Murphy, P. 1983. A waterfront excavation at Whitefriars Street Car Park, Norwich, 1979. *East Anglian Archaeology Report* No. 17, 1-60

Baillie, M.G.L. 1994. Dendrochronology raises questions about the nature of the AD 536 dust-veil event. *The Holocene* 4, 212-7

Baillie, M.G.L. 1995. *A Slice Through Time*. Batsford, London

Baillie, M.G.L. & Munro, M.A.R. 1988. Irish tree rings, Santorini and volcanic dust veils. *Nature* 332, 344-6

Baker, C.A., Moxey, P.A. & Oxford, P.M. 1978. Woodland continuity and change in Epping Forest. *Field Studies* 4, 645-69

Balaam, N.D., Smith, K. & Wainwright. G.J. 1982. The Shaugh Moor Project, fourth report: environment, context and conclusions. *Proceedings of the Prehistoric Society* 48, 203-78

Barber, K.E. 1981. *Peat Stratigraphy and Climatic Change*. A.A. Balkema, Rotterdam

Barber, K.E. 1982. Peat-bog stratigraphy as a proxy climate record. In A.F. Harding (ed.) *Climatic Change in Later Prehistory*, 103-33. Edinburgh University Press, Edinburgh

Barber, K.E., Chambers, F.M., Maddy, D., Stoneman, R. & Brew, J.S. 1994. A sensitive high-resolution record of late Holocene climatic change from a raised bog in northern England. *The Holocene* 4, 198-205

Barber, K.E. & Twigger, S.N. 1987. Late Quaternary palaeoecology of the Severn basin. In K.J. Gregory & J.B. Thornes (eds) *Palaeohydrology in Practice*, 217-50. John Wiley & Sons Ltd, Chichester

Bartley, D.D. 1975. Pollen analytical evidence for prehistoric forest clearance in the upland area west of Rishworth, W. Yorkshire. *New Phytologist* 74, 375-81

Bartley, D.D. & Chambers, C. 1992. A pollen diagram, radiocarbon ages and evidence of agriculture on Extwistle Moor, Lancashire. *New Phytologist* 121, 311-20

Bartley, D.D., Chambers, C. & Hart-Jones, B. 1976. The vegetational history of parts of south and east Durham. *New Phytologist* 77, 437-68

Bartley, D.D. & Morgan, A.V. 1990. The palynological record of the King's Pool, Stafford, England. *New Phytologist* 116, 177-94

Beales, P.W. 1980. The late Devensian and Flandrian vegetational history of Crose Mere, Shropshire. *New Phytologist* 85, 133-61

Beck, R.B. & Gilbertson, D.D. 1987. An t-Aoradh, Oronsay. In P. Mellars, *Excavations on Oronsay*, 57-62. Edinburgh University Press, Edinburgh

Beckett, S.C. & Hibbert, F.A. 1979. Vegetational change and the influence of prehistoric man in the Somerset Levels. *New Phytologist* 83, 577-600

Behre, K.-E. 1981. The interpretation of anthropogenic indicators in pollen diagrams. *Pollen et Spores* 23, 225-45

Bell, M. 1981. Valley sediments and environmental change. In M. Jones & G. Dimbleby (eds) *The Environment of Man: the Iron Age to the Anglo-Saxon Period*, 75-91. BAR British Series, Oxford

182

References

Bell, M. 1989. Environmental archaeology as an index of continuity and change in the medieval landscape. In M. Aston, D. Austin & C. Dyer (eds), *The Rural Settlement of Medieval England*, 269-86. Blackwell, Oxford

Bell, M. 1992a. *Field Survey and Excavation at Goldcliff 1992.* Severn Estuary Levels Research Committee Annual Report 1992, 15-29

Bell, M. 1992b. *Goldcliff Excavation 1991.* Severn Estuary Levels Research Committee Annual Report 1991, 13-19

Bell, M.G. 1992c. The prehistory of soil erosion. In M.G. Bell & J. Boardman (eds) *Past and Present Soil Erosion: Archaeological and Geographical Perspectives*, 21-35. Oxbow, Oxford

Bell, M. 1995. People and nature in the Celtic world. In M.J. Green (ed.) *The Celtic World*, 145-58. Routledge, London

Bell, M. 1996. Environment in the first millennium BC. In T.C. Champion & J.R. Collis (eds) *The Iron Age in Britain and Ireland; Recent Trends*, 5-16. J.R. Collis Publications, Sheffield

Bell, M. & Dark, P. 1998. Continuity and change: environmental archaeology in historic periods. In J. Bayley (ed.) *Science in Archaeology: an Agenda for the Future*, 179-93. English Heritage, London

Bell, M. & Neumann, H. 1997. Prehistoric intertidal archaeology and environments in the Severn Estuary, Wales. *World Archaeology* 29, 95-113

Bell, M. & Walker, M.J.C. 1992. *Late Quaternary Environmental Change. Physical and Human Perspectives.* Longman, London

Bennett, J. 1983. The examination of Turret 10A and the Wall and Vallum at Throckley, Tyne and Wear, 1980. *Archaeologia Aeliana*, 5th series, 11, 27-60

Bennett, K.D. 1983. Devensian late-glacial and Flandrian vegetational history at Hockham Mere, Norfolk, England. *New Phytologist* 95, 457-87

Bennett, K.D. 1984. The post-glacial history of *Pinus sylvestris* in the British Isles. *Quaternary Science Reviews* 3, 133-55

Bennett, K.D. 1994a. *Annotated catalogue of pollen and pteridophyte spore types of the British Isles.* Unpub. manuscript, University of Cambridge

Bennett, K.D. 1994b. 'psimpoll' version 2.23: a C program for analysing pollen data and plotting pollen diagrams. *INQUA Commission for the Study of the Holocene: Working Group on Data-Handling Methods Newsletter* 11, 4-6

Bennett, K.D., Boreham, S., Sharp, M.J. & Switsur, V.R. 1992. Holocene history of environment, vegetation and human settlement on Catta Ness, Lunnasting, Shetland. *Journal of Ecology* 80, 241-73

Bennett, K.D., Fossitt, J.A., Sharp, M.J. & Switsur, V.R. 1990. Holocene vegetational and environmental history at Loch Lang, South Uist, Western Isles, Scotland. *New Phytologist* 114, 281-98

Bennett, K.D., Simonson, W.D. & Peglar, S.M. 1990. Fire and man in post-glacial woodlands of Eastern England. *Journal of Archaeological Science* 17, 635-42

Berg, D. 1990. Mammal bones from Well 1. In S. Wrathmell & A. Nicholson (eds) *Dalton Parlours Iron Age Settlement and Roman Villa*, 245-59. West Yorkshire Archaeology Service, Wakefield

Biddick, K. 1984. Pig husbandry on the Peterborough Abbey Estate from the twelfth to the fourteenth century AD. In C. Grigson & J. Clutton-Brock (eds) *Animals and Archaeology, 4: Husbandry in Europe*, 161-77. BAR International Series 227, Oxford

Bidwell, P.T. & Watson, M. 1996. Excavations on Hadrian's Wall at Denton, Newcastle upon Tyne, 1986-89. *Archaeologia Aeliana*, 5th series, 24, 1-56

Birks, H.J.B. 1980. *Quaternary Vegetational History of West Scotland.* Excursion Guide, 5th International Palynological Congress, Cambridge

183

References

Birks, H.J.B. 1993a. Lochan an Druim. In J.E. Gordon & D.G. Sutherland (eds) *Quaternary of Scotland*, 141-3. Chapman & Hall, London

Birks, H.J.B. 1993b. Loch Ashik, Loch Cleat and Loch Meodal. In J.E. Gordon & D.G. Sutherland (eds) *Quaternary of Scotland*, 399-401. Chapman & Hall, London

Birks, H.J.B. 1993c. Loch Cill an Aonghais. In J.E. Gordon & D.G. Sutherland (eds) *Quaternary of Scotland*, 350-2. Chapman & Hall, London

Birks, H.J.B. & Birks, H.H. 1980. *Quaternary Palaeoecology*. Edward Arnold, London

Birks, H.J.B. & Madsen, B.J. 1979. Flandrian vegetational history of Little Loch Roag, Isle of Lewis, Scotland. *Journal of Ecology* 67, 825-42

Blackford, J.J. & Chambers, F.M. 1991. Proxy records of climate from blanket mires: evidence for a Dark Age (1400 BP) climatic deterioration in the British Isles. *The Holocene* 1, 63-7

Blagg, T.F.C. 1989. Richborough. In V.A. Maxfield, *The Saxon Shore: a Handbook*, 140-5. University of Exeter, Exeter

Bohncke, S. 1981. The pollen diagram from Ditch 1. In J.W. Barber, Excavations on Iona, 1979, 346-8. *Proceedings of the Society of Antiquaries of Scotland* 111, 282-380

Boon, G.C. 1980. Caerleon and the Gwent Levels in early historic times. In F.H. Thompson (ed.) *Archaeology and Coastal Change*, 24-36. Society of Antiquaries of London, London

Bowden, M., Ford, S. & Mees, G. 1993. The date of the ancient fields on the Berkshire Downs. *Berkshire Archaeological Journal* 71 (1991-3), 109-33

Bowman, S. 1990. *Radiocarbon Dating*. British Museum, London

Boyd, W.E. 1984. Environmental change and Iron Age land management in the area of the Antonine Wall, central Scotland: a summary. *Glasgow Archaeological Journal* 11, 75-81

Boyd, W.E. 1985a. Palaeobotanical evidence from Mollins. *Britannia* 16, 37-48

Boyd, W.E. 1985b. The problem of the time span represented by pollen spectra in podzol turves, with examples from the Roman sites at Bar Hill and Mollins, central Scotland. In Fieller *et al.* (eds) *Palaeobiological Investigations*, 189-201. BAR S266, Oxford

Boyd, W.E. 1988. Cereals in Scottish antiquity. *Circaea* 5, 101-10

Bradley, R.S. 1988. The explosive volcanic eruption signal in northern hemisphere continental temperature records. *Climatic Change* 12, 221-43

Bradshaw, R.H.W., Coxon, P., Greig, J.R.A. & Hall, A.R. 1981. New fossil evidence for the past cultivation and processing of hemp (*Cannabis sativa* L.) in eastern England. *New Phytologist* 89, 503-10

Bramwell, D. 1978. The bird bones. In M. Parrington, *The Excavation of an Iron Age Settlement, Bronze Age Ring-ditches and Roman Features at Ashville Trading Estate, Abingdon (Oxfordshire) 1974-76*, 133. Oxfordshire Archaeological Unit/CBA Archaeology, Oxford/London

Branch, N.P. & Scaife, R.G. 1995. The stratigraphy and pollen analysis of peat sequences associated with the Lindow III bog body. In R.C. Turner & R.G. Scaife (eds), *Bog Bodies. New Discoveries and New Perspectives*, 19-30. British Museum Press, London

Brayshay, B. & Edwards, K. 1996. Late-glacial and Holocene vegetational history of South Uist and Barra. In D. Gilbertson, M. Kent & J. Grattan (eds) *The Outer Hebrides – The Last 14,000 Years*, 13-26. Sheffield Academic Press, Sheffield

Breeze, D.J. & Dobson, B. 1987. *Hadrian's Wall*, 3rd edn. Penguin, Harmondsworth

References

Briffa, K.R., Bartholin, T.S., Eckstein, D., Jones, P.D., Karlen, W., Schweingruber, F.H. & Zetterberg, P. 1990. A 1,400-year tree-ring record of summer temperatures in Fennoscandia. *Nature* 346, 434-9

Bronk Ramsey, C. 1995. Radiocarbon calibration and analysis of stratigraphy: the OxCal program. In G.T. Cook, D.D. Harkness, B.F. Miller & E.M. Scott (eds) *Proceedings of the 15th International ¹⁴C Conference. Radiocarbon* 37, 425-30

Brown, A.G. 1997. *Alluvial Geoarchaeology*. Cambridge University Press, Cambridge

Brown, A.G. 1988. The palaeoecology of *Alnus* (alder) and the postglacial history of floodplain vegetation. Pollen percentage and influx data from the West Midlands, United Kingdom. *New Phytologist* 110, 425-36

Brown, A.G. & Barber, K.E. 1985. Late Holocene paleoecology and sedimentary history of a small lowland catchment in central England. *Quaternary Research* 24, 87-102

Brown, T.A., Nelson, D.E., Mathewes, R.W., Vogel, J.S. & Southon, J.R. 1989. Radiocarbon dating of pollen by accelerator mass spectrometry. *Quaternary Research* 32, 205-12

Bryant, G.F. 1973. Experimental Romano-British kiln firings. In A. Detsicas (ed.) *Current Research in Romano-British Coarse Pottery*, 149-60. CBA Research Report 10, London

Buck, C.E., Kenworthy, J.B., Litton, C.D. & Smith, A.F.M. 1991. Combining archaeological and radiocarbon information: a Bayesian approach to calibration. *Antiquity* 65, 808-21

Buck, C.E., Litton, C.D. & Smith, A.F.M. 1992. Calibration of radiocarbon results pertaining to related archaeological events. *Journal of Archaeological Science* 19, 497-512

Buckland, P.C. 1978. Cereal production, storage, and population: a caveat. In S. Limbrey & J.G. Evans (eds) *The Effect of Man on the Landscape: the Lowland Zone*, 43-5. CBA Research Report 21, London

Buckland, P.C., Dugmore, A.J. & Edwards, K.J. 1997. Bronze Age myths? Volcanic activity and human response in the Mediterranean and North Atlantic regions. *Antiquity* 71, 581-93

Bulleid, A. & Gray, H. St G. 1911. *The Glastonbury Lake Village, Vol. I*. Glastonbury Antiquarian Society, Glastonbury

Bulleid, A. & Gray, H. St G. 1917. *The Glastonbury Lake Village, Vol. II*. Glastonbury Antiquarian Society, Glastonbury

Bulleid, A. & Gray, H. St G. 1948. *The Meare Lake Village, Vol. I*. Privately published, Taunton Castle

Bulleid, A. & Gray, H. St G. 1953. *The Meare Lake Village, Vol. II*. Privately published, Taunton Castle

Burnham, C.P. 1989. The coast of south-east England in Roman times. In V.A. Maxfield (ed.) *The Saxon Shore: a Handbook*, 12-17. University of Exeter, Exeter

Bush, M.B. 1993. An 11400 year paleoecological history of a British chalk grassland. *Journal of Vegetation Science* 4, 47-66

Bush, M.B. & Flenley, J.R. 1987. The age of the British chalk grassland. *Nature* 329, 434-36

Campbell, G. 1994. The preliminary archaeobotanical results from Anglo-Saxon West Cotton and Raunds. In J. Rackham (ed.) *Environment and Economy in Anglo-Saxon England*, 65-82. CBA Research Report 89, York

Caseldine, A.E. 1986. The environmental context of the Meare lake villages. *Somerset Levels Papers* 12, 73-96

185

References

Caseldine, A.E. 1988. A reinterpretation of the pollen sequence from Meare. *Somerset Levels Papers* 14, 53-6

Caseldine, A.E. 1990. *Environmental Archaeology in Wales*. Department of Archaeology, St David's University College, Lampeter

Caseldine, C.J. & Hatton, J.M. 1996. Into the mists? Thoughts on the prehistoric and historic environmental history of Dartmoor. *Devon Archaeological Society Proceedings* 52 (1994), 35-47

Caseldine, C.J. & Maguire, D.J. 1981. A review of the prehistoric and historic environment on Dartmoor. *Devon Archaeological Society Proceedings* 39, 1-16

Chambers, C. 1978. A radiocarbon-dated pollen diagram from Valley Bog, on the Moor House National Nature Reserve. *New Phytologist* 80, 273-80

Chambers, F.M. 1982. Two radiocarbon-dated pollen diagrams from high-altitude blanket peats in south Wales. *Journal of Ecology* 70, 445-59

Chambers, F.M. 1983a. The palaeoecological setting of Cefn Gwernffrwd – a prehistoric complex in mid-Wales. *Proceedings of the Prehistoric Society* 49, 303-16

Chambers, F.M. 1983b. Three radiocarbon-dated pollen diagrams from upland peats north-west of Merthyr Tydfil, South Wales. *Journal of Ecology* 71, 475-87

Chambers, F.M. 1989. The evidence for early rye cultivation in north west Europe. In A. Milles, D. Williams & N. Gardner (eds) *The Beginnings of Agriculture*, 165-75. BAR International Series 496, Oxford

Chambers, F.M., Barber, K.E., Maddy, D. & Brew, J. 1997. A 5500-year proxy-climate and vegetation record from blanket mire at Talla Moss, Borders, Scotland. *The Holocene* 7, 391-9

Chambers, F.M. & Jones, M.K. 1984. Antiquity of rye in Britain. *Antiquity* 58, 219-24

Chambers, F.M., Kelly, R.S. & Price, S.-M. 1988. Development of the late-prehistoric cultural landscape in upland Ardudwy, north-west Wales. In H.H. Birks, H.J.B. Birks, P.E. Kaland & D. Moe (eds) *The Cultural Landscape – Past, Present and Future*, 333-48. Cambridge University Press, Cambridge

Chambers, F.M. & Lageard, J.G.A. 1993. Vegetational history and environmental setting of Crawcwellt, Gwynedd. *Archaeology in Wales* 33, 23-5

Chambers, F.M., Lageard, J.G.A. & Elliot, L. 1990. Field survey, excavation and pollen analysis at Mynydd y Drum, Ystradgynlais, Powys, 1983 and 1987. *Bulletin of the Board of Celtic Studies* 37, 215-46

Chambers, F.M. & Price, S.-M. 1988. The environmental setting of Erw-wen and Moel y Gerddi: prehistoric enclosures in upland Ardudwy, North Wales. *Proceedings of the Prehistoric Society* 54, 93-100

Charles, M., Jones, G. & Hodgson, J.G. 1997. FIBS in archaeobotany: functional interpretation of weed floras in relation to husbandry practices. *Journal of Archaeological Science* 24, 1151-61

Charman, D.J. 1994. Late-glacial and Holocene vegetation history of the Flow Country, northern Scotland. *New Phytologist* 127, 155-68

Clark, J.S. 1988. Particle motion and the theory of charcoal analysis: source area, transport, deposition, and sampling. *Quaternary Research* 30, 67-80

Clarke, H. & Ambrosiani, B. 1991. *Towns in the Viking Age*. Leicester University Press, Leicester

Clausen, H.B., Hammer, C.U., Hvidberg, C.S., Dahl-Jensen, D., Steffensen, J.P., Kipfstuhl, J. & Legrand, M. 1997. A comparison of the volcanic records over the past 4000 years from the Greenland Ice Core Project and Dye 3 Greenland ice cores. *Journal of Geophysical Research* 102, 26,707-23

Cleere, H. 1976. Some operating parameters for Roman ironworks. *Bulletin of the Institute of Archaeology* 13, 233-46

Cloutman, E. 1994. Haddenham, the Lower Delphs and Foulmire Fen. In M. Waller, *The Fenland Project, Number 9: Flandrian Environmental Change in Fenland*, 164-70. East Anglian Archaeology Report 70, Cambridgeshire County Council, Cambridge

Coles, B. & Coles, J. 1986. *Sweet Track to Glastonbury: the Somerset Levels in Prehistory*. Thames & Hudson, London.

Coles, J.M. 1987. Meare Village East: the excavations of A. Bulleid and H. St George Gray 1932-1956. *Somerset Levels Papers* 13

Coles, J. & Minnitt, S. 1995. *'Industrious and Fairly Civilized': the Glastonbury Lake Village*. Somerset Levels Project/Somerset County Council Museums Service

Coles, J.M. & Orme, B.J. 1977. Neolithic hurdles from Walton Heath, Somerset. *Somerset Levels Papers* 3, 6-29

Courty, M.A., Goldberg, P. & Macphail, R. 1989. *Soils and Micromorphology in Archaeology*. Cambridge University Press, Cambridge

Cowell, R.W. & Innes, J.B. 1994. *The Wetlands of Merseyside*. Lancaster University Archaeological Unit, Lancaster

Coy, J. 1984. The bird bones. In B.W. Cunliffe, *Danebury: an Iron Age Hillfort in Hampshire Vol. 2: the Excavations, 1969-1978: the Finds*, 527-30. CBA Research Report 52, London

Crabtree, P. 1985. The faunal remains. In S. West, *West Stow, The Anglo-Saxon Village Volume 1: Text*, 85-96. Suffolk County Planning Department, Ipswich

Crabtree, P. 1989. *West Stow, Suffolk: Early Anglo-Saxon Animal Husbandry*. Suffolk County Planning Department, Ipswich

Crabtree, P. 1994. Animal exploitation in East Anglian villages. In J. Rackham (ed.) *Environment and Economy in Anglo-Saxon England*, 40-54. CBA Research Report 89, York

Crew, P. 1989. Excavations at Crawcwellt West, Merioneth, 1986-89: a late prehistoric upland iron-working settlement. *Archaeology in Wales* 29, 11-16

Crew, P. 1991. Crawcwellt West, Trawsfynydd. *Archaeology in Wales* 31, 7

Cunliffe, B.W. 1971. *Excavations at Fishbourne 1961-1969, Vol. I: the Site*. Report of the Research Committee of the Society of Antiquaries of London 26, Leeds

Cunliffe, B.W. 1977. The Romano-British village at Chalton, Hants. *Proceedings of the Hampshire Field Club and Archaeological Society* 33, 45-67

Cunliffe, B.W. 1984. *Danebury: an Iron Age Hillfort in Hampshire Vol. 1: the Excavations, 1969-1978: the Site*. CBA Research Report 52, London

Cushing, E.J. 1967. Evidence for differential pollen preservation in Late Quaternary sediments in Minnesota. *Review of Palaeobotany and Palynology* 4, 87-101

Darby, H.C. 1976. The Anglo-Scandinavian foundations. In H.C. Darby (ed.) *A New Historical Geography of England Before 1600*, 1-38. Cambridge University Press, Cambridge

Dark, K.R. 1994. *Civitas to Kingdom*. Leicester University Press, Leicester

Dark, K.R. 1996. Proto-industrialisation and the end of the Roman economy. In K.R. Dark (ed.) *External Contacts and the Economy of Late Roman and Post-Roman Britain*, 1-21. Boydell Press, Woodbridge

Dark, K.R. & Dark, S.P. 1996. New archaeological and palynological evidence for a sub-Roman reoccupation of Hadrian's Wall. *Archaeologia Aeliana*, 5th series, 24, 57-72

Dark, K. & Dark, P. 1997. *The Landscape of Roman Britain*. Sutton Publishing, Stroud

187

References

Dark, (S.) P. 1996. Palaeoecological evidence for landscape continuity and change in Britain *ca.* AD 400-800. In K.R. Dark (ed.) *External Contacts and the Economy of Late Roman and Post-Roman Britain*, 23-51. Boydell Press, Woodbridge

Dark, P. 1998a. Comparison and correlation of lake-edge sequences. In P. Mellars & P. Dark *Star Carr in Context*, 147-52. McDonald Institute, Cambridge

Dark, P. 1998b. Lake-edge sequences: results. In P. Mellars and P. Dark, *Star Carr in Context*, 125-46. McDonald Institute, Cambridge

Dark, P. 1998c. Radiocarbon dating of the lake-edge deposits. In P. Mellars & P. Dark, *Star Carr in Context*, 119-24. McDonald Institute, Cambridge

David, C., Dearing, J. & Roberts, N. 1998. Land-use history and sediment flux in a lowland lake catchment: Groby Pool, Leicestershire, UK. *The Holocene* 8, 383-94

Davies, G. & Turner, J. 1979. Pollen diagrams from Northumberland. *New Phytologist* 82, 783-804

Day, S.P. 1990. *History and Palaeoecology of Woodlands in the Oxford Region.* Unpub. D.Phil. thesis, University of Oxford

Day, S.P. 1991. Post-glacial vegetational history of the Oxford region. *New Phytologist* 119, 445-70

Day, S.P. 1993. Woodland origin and 'ancient woodland indicators': a case-study from Sidlings Copse, Oxfordshire, UK. *The Holocene* 3, 45-53

Day, S.P. 1996. Devensian late-glacial and early Flandrian environmental history of the Vale of Pickering, Yorkshire, England. *Journal of Quaternary Science* 11, 9-24

Day, S.P. & Mellars, P.A. 1994. 'Absolute' dating of Mesolithic human activity at Star Carr, Yorkshire: new palaeoecological studies and identification of the 9600 BP radiocarbon 'plateau'. *Proceedings of the Prehistoric Society* 60, 417-22

Dearne, M.J. & Branigan, K. 1995. The use of coal in Roman Britain. *Antiquaries Journal* 75, 71-105

De Rouffignac, C. 1991. Parasite remains. In A. Vince (ed.) *Aspects of Saxo-Norman London: II Finds and Environmental Evidence*, 386-8. London and Middlesex Archaeological Society, London

Dickinson, W. 1975. Recurrence surfaces in Rusland Moss, Cumbria (formerly North Lancashire). *Journal of Ecology* 63, 913-35

Dimbleby, G.W. 1985. *The Palynology of Archaeological Sites.* Academic Press, London

Dixon, P. 1992. 'The cities are not populated as once they were'. In J. Rich (ed.) *The City in Late Antiquity*, 145-60. Routledge, London/New York

Dobney, K.M., Jaques, S.D. & Irving, B.G. nd. *Of Butchers and Breeds. Report on Vertebrate Remains from Various Sites in the City of Lincoln.* Lincoln Archaeology Unit

Donaldson, A.M. & Nye, S. 1989. The botanical remains. In C.D. Morris, *The Birsay Bay Project Volume 1, Coastal Sites beside the Brough Road, Birsay, Orkney Excavations 1976-1982*, 262-7. University of Durham, Durham

Donaldson, A.M. & Turner, J. 1977. A pollen diagram from Hallowell Moss, near Durham City, U.K. *Journal of Biogeography* 4, 25-33

Dugmore, A. 1989. Icelandic volcanic ash in Scotland. *Scottish Geographical Magazine* 105, 168-72

Dugmore, A.J., Larsen, G. & Newton, A.J. 1995. Seven tephra isochrones in Scotland. *The Holocene* 5, 257-66

Dumayne, L. 1993. Invader or native? – vegetation clearance in northern Britain during Romano-British time. *Vegetation History and Archaeobotany* 2, 29-36

Dumayne, L. 1994. The effect of the Roman occupation on the environment of

Hadrian's Wall: a pollen diagram, from Fozy Moss, Northumberland. *Britannia* 25, 217-24

Dumayne, L. & Barber, K.E. 1994. The impact of the Romans on the environment of northern England: pollen data from three sites close to Hadrian's Wall. *The Holocene* 4, 257-66

Dumayne, L., Stoneman, R., Barber, K. & Harkness, D. 1995. Problems associated with correlating calibrated radiocarbon-dated pollen diagrams with historical events. *The Holocene* 4, 118-23

Dumayne-Peaty, L. 1998. Human impact on the environment during the Iron Age and Romano-British times: palynological evidence from three sites near the Antonine Wall, Great Britain. *Journal of Archaeological Science* 25, 203-14

Dumayne-Peaty, L. & Barber, K. 1998. Late Holocene vegetational history, human impact and pollen representivity variations in northern Cumbria, England. *Journal of Quaternary Science* 13, 147-64

Edwards, K.J. & Berridge, J.M.A. 1994. The Late-Quaternary vegetational history of Loch a'Bhogaidh, Rinns of Islay S.S.S.I., Scotland. *New Phytologist* 128, 749-69

Edwards, K.J., Hirons, K.R. & Newell, P.J. 1991. The palaeoecological and prehistoric context of minerogenic layers in blanket peat: a study from Loch Dee, southwest Scotland. *The Holocene* 1, 29-39

Edwards, K.J. & Rowntree, K.M. 1980. Radiocarbon and palaeoenvironmental evidence for changing rates of erosion at a Flandrian stage site in Scotland. In R.A. Cullingford, D.A. Davidson & J. Lewin, *Timescales in Geomorphology*, 207-23. John Wiley & Sons, Chichester

Edwards, K.J. & Whittington, G. 1997. Vegetation change. In K.J. Edwards & I.B.M. Ralston, *Scotland: Environment and Archaeology, 8000 BC – AD 1000*, 63-82. John Wiley & Sons, Chichester

Faegri, K. & Iversen, J. 1989. *Textbook of Pollen Analysis*, 4th edn (revised by K. Faegri, P.E. Kaland & K. Krzywinski). John Wiley & Sons, Chichester

Figueiral, I. 1992. The charcoals. In M.G. Fulford & J.R.L. Allen, Iron-making at the Chesters Villa, Woolaston, Gloucestershire: survey and excavation 1987-91, 188-91. *Britannia* 23, 159-215

Fleming, A. 1987. Coaxial field systems: some questions of time and space. *Antiquity* 61, 188-202

Fleming, A. 1988. *The Dartmoor Reaves*. Batsford, London

Fowler, P.J. 1983. *The Farming of Prehistoric Britain*. Cambridge University Press, Cambridge

Francis, P.D. & Slater, D.S. 1990. A record of vegetational and land use change from upland peat deposits on Exmoor. Part 2: Hoar Moor. *Proceedings of the Somerset Archaeology and Natural History Society* 134, 1-25

Francis, P.D. & Slater, D.S. 1992. A record of vegetational and land use change from upland peat deposits on Exmoor. Part 3: Codsend Moors. *Proceedings of the Somerset Archaeology and Natural History Society* 136, 9-28

French, C.N. & Moore, P.D. 1986. Deforestation, *Cannabis* cultivation and schwingmoor formation at Cors Llyn (Llyn Mire), Central Wales. *New Phytologist* 102, 469-82

Frere, S.S., Rivet, A.L.F. & Sitwell, N.H.H. 1987. *Tabula Imperii Romani. Britannia Septentrionalis*. Oxford University Press, New York

Fulford, M.G. & Allen, J.R.L. 1992. Iron-making at the Chesters Villa, Woolaston, Gloucestershire: survey and excavation 1987-91. *Britannia* 23, 159-215

Fulford, M.G., Allen, J.R.L. & Rippon, S.J. 1994. The settlement and drainage of the Wentlooge Level, Gwent: excavation and survey at Rumney Great Wharf 1992. *Britannia* 25, 175-211

Gaffney, V. & Tingle, M. 1989. *The Maddle Farm Project: an Integrated Survey of Prehistoric and Roman Landscapes on the Berkshire Downs*. BAR British Series 200, Oxford

Gearey, B. & Charman, D. 1996. Rough Tor, Bodmin Moor: testing some archaeological hypotheses with landscape palaeoecology. In D.J. Charman, R.M. Newnham & D.G. Croot (eds) *Devon and East Cornwall Field Guide*, 101-19. Quaternary Research Association, London

Gelling. M. 1974. Some notes on Warwickshire place-names. *Birmingham and Warwickshire Archaeological Society Transactions* 86, 59-79

Gelling. M. 1984. *Place-names in the Landscape*. Dent & Sons Ltd, London

Gimingham, C.H. 1972. *Ecology of Heathlands*. Chapman & Hall, London

Girling, M. & Straker, V. 1993. Plant macrofossils, arthropods and charcoal. In A. Woodward & P. Leach, *The Uley Shrines*, 250-3. English Heritage, London

Godwin, H. 1943. Coastal peat-beds of the British Isles and North Sea. *Journal of Ecology* 31, 199-247

Godwin, H. 1967. Pollen-analytical evidence for the cultivation of *Cannabis* in England. *Review of Palaeobotany and Palynology* 4, 71-80

Godwin, H. 1975. *History of the British Flora*, 2nd edn. Cambridge University Press, Cambridge

Godwin, H. 1978. *Fenland: its Ancient Past and Uncertain Future*. Cambridge University Press, Cambridge

Goodwin, K. and Huntley, J.P. 1991. The waterlogged plant remains and woodland management studies. In M.R. McCarthy, *The Structural Sequence and Environmental Remains from Castle Street, Carlisle: Excavations 1981-2*, 54-64. Cumberland and Westmorland Antiquarian and Archaeological Society, Kendal

Grant, A. 1971. Animal bones. In B. Cunliffe, *Excavations at Fishbourne 1961-1969, Vol. II: the Finds*, 377-88. Report of the Research Committee of the Society of Antiquaries of London 27, Leeds

Grant, A. 1984. Animal husbandry in Wessex and the Thames Valley. In B. Cunliffe & D. Miles (eds) *Aspects of the Iron Age in Central Southern Britain*, 102-19. Oxford University Committee for Archaeology, Oxford

Grant, A. 1989. Animals in Roman Britain. In M. Todd (ed.) *Research on Roman Britain: 1960-89*, 135-46. Britannia Monograph no. 11, London

Grant, A. 1991. Animal husbandry. In B. Cunliffe & C. Poole, *Danebury: an Iron Age Hillfort in Hampshire Volume 5. The Excavations, 1979-88: the Finds*, 447-78. CBA, London

Grattan, J. & Charman, D.J. 1994. Non-climatic factors and the environmental impact of volcanic volatiles: the implications of the Laki fissure eruption of AD 1783. *The Holocene* 4, 101-6

Grattan, J.P. & Gilbertson, D.D. 1994. Acid-loading from Icelandic tephra falling on acidified ecosystems as a key to understanding archaeological and environmental stress in northern and western Britain. *Journal of Archaeological Science* 21, 851-9

Greig, J.R.A. 1976. The plant remains. In P.C. Buckland, *The Environmental Evidence from the Church Street Roman Sewer System*, 23-8. CBA, London

Greig, J.R.A. 1988. Some evidence of the development of grassland plant communities. In M. Jones (ed.) *Archaeology and the Flora of the British Isles*, 39-54. Oxford University Committee for Archaeology, Oxford

References

Greig, J.R.A. 1991. The British Isles. In W. van Zeist, K. Waslikowa & K.-E. Behre, *Progress in Old World Palaeoethnobotany*, 299-334. Balkema, Rotterdam

Hall, A.R. & Kenward, H.K. 1990. *Environmental Evidence from the Colonia: General Accident and Rougier Street*. CBA, London

Hall, A.R., Kenward, H.K. & Williams, D. 1980. *Environmental Evidence from Roman Deposits in Skeldergate*. CBA, London

Hall, A.R., Kenward, H.K., Williams, D. & Greig, J.R.A. 1983. *Environment and Living Conditions at Two Anglo-Scandinavian Sites*. CBA, London

Hall, D. & Coles, J. 1994. *Fenland Survey: an Essay in Landscape and Persistence*. English Heritage, London

Hall, V.A., Pilcher, J.R. & McCormac, F.G. 1993. Tephra-dated lowland landscape history of the north of Ireland, AD 750-1150. *New Phytologist* 125, 193-202

Hammer, C.U., Clausen, H.B. & Dansgaard, W. 1980. Greenland ice sheet evidence of post-glacial vulcanism and its climatic impact. *Nature* 288, 230-5

Hanson, W.S. 1996. Forest clearance and the Roman army. *Britannia* 27, 354-8

Hanson, W.S. & Maxwell, G.S. 1986. *Rome's North-West Frontier: the Antonine Wall*, 2nd edn. Edinburgh University Press, Edinburgh

Harcourt, R. 1979. The animal bones. In G.J. Wainwright, *Gussage All Saints. An Iron Age Settlement in Dorset*, 150-60. HMSO, London

Hatton, J.M. & Caseldine, C.J. 1992. Vegetation change and land-use history during the first millennium AD at Aller Farm, east Devon as indicated by pollen analysis. *Devon Archaeological Society Proceedings* 49, 107-14

Hayes, A.J. 1996. On-site pollen. In J. May, *Dragonby: Report on Excavations at an Iron Age and Romano-British Settlement in North Lincolnshire, Volume 1*, 179-97. Oxbow Monograph 61, Oxford

Helbaek, H. 1958. Graubailemandens Sidste Maltid. *Kuml. 1958*, 83-116. Arhus

Hibbert, F.A. 1980. Possible evidence for sea-level change in the Somerset Levels. In F.H. Thompson (ed.) *Archaeology and Coastal Change*, 103-5. Society of Antiquaries of London, London

Hicks, S.P. 1971. Pollen-analytical evidence for the effect of prehistoric agriculture on the vegetation of north Derbyshire. *New Phytologist* 70, 647-67

Higham, N.J. 1991. Soldiers and settlement in northern England. In R.F.J. Jones (ed.) *Britain in the Roman Period: Recent Trends*, 93-101. J.R. Collis Publications, Department of Archaeology and Prehistory, University of Sheffield, Sheffield

Hill, D. 1981. *An Atlas of Anglo-Saxon England*. Blackwell, Oxford

Hillam, J., Groves, C.M., Brown, D.M., Baillie, M.G.L., Coles, J.M. & Coles, B.J. 1990. Dendrochronology of the English Neolithic. *Antiquity* 64, 210-20

Hillman, G. 1981. Reconstructing crop husbandry practices from charred remains of crops. In R. Mercer (ed.) *Farming Practice in British Prehistory*, 123-62. Edinburgh University Press, Edinburgh

Hong, S., Candelone, J.-P., Patterson, C.C. & Boutron, C.F. 1994. Greenland ice evidence of hemispheric lead pollution two millennia ago by Greek and Roman civilizations. *Science* 265, 1841-3

Hooke, D. 1981. *Anglo-Saxon Landscapes of the West Midlands: the Charter Evidence*. BAR British Series 95, Oxford

Hooke, D. 1985. *The Anglo-Saxon Landscape: The Kingdom of the Hwicce*. Manchester University Press, Manchester

Hooke, D. 1995. The mid-late Saxon period: settlement and land use. In D. Hooke & S. Burnell (eds) *Landscape and Settlement in Britain AD 400-1066*, 95-114. Exeter University Press, Exeter

References

Hooke, D. 1998. *The Landscape of Anglo-Saxon England.* Leicester University Press, London & Washington

Housley, R.A. 1988a. The environment. In J. Coles & S. Minnitt, *'Industrious and Fairly Civilized': the Glastonbury Lake Village*, 121-36. Somerset Levels Project and Somerset County Council Museums Service

Housley, R.A. 1988b. The environmental context of Glastonbury lake village. *Somerset Levels Papers* 14, 63-82

Huntley, B. 1981. The past and present vegetation of the Caenlochan National Nature Reserve, Scotland II. Palaeoecological investigations. *New Phytologist* 87, 189-222

Huntley, B. & Birks, H.J.B. 1983. *An Atlas of Past and Present Pollen Maps for Europe: 0-13,000 Years Ago.* Cambridge University Press, Cambridge

Huntley, J.P. 1991. Woodland management studies. In M.R. McCarthy, *The Structural Sequence and Environmental Remains from Castle Street, Carlisle: Excavations 1981-2,* 60-4. Cumberland and Westmorland Antiquarian and Archaeological Society, Kendal

Huntley, J.P. 1995. Pollen analytical investigations. In C.D. Morris, C.E. Batey & D.J. Rackham *Freswick Links, Caithness. Excavation and Survey of a Norse Settlement,* 8-16. Historic Scotland, Inverness

Huntley, J.P. & Stallibrass, S. 1995. *Plant and Vertebrate Remains from Archaeological Sites in Northern England.* Architectural and Archaeological Society of Durham and Northumberland, Durham

Huntley, J.P. & Turner, J. 1995. Carbonised plant remains. In C.D. Morris, C.E. Batey & D.J. Rackham *Freswick Links, Caithness. Excavation and Survey of a Norse Settlement,* 220-4. Historic Scotland, Inverness

Innes, J.B. & Shennan, I. 1991. Palynology of archaeological and mire sediments from Dod, Borders Region, Scotland. *Archaeological Journal* 148, 1-45

Jacobson, G.L. & Bradshaw, R.H.W. 1981. The selection of sites for palaeovegetational studies. *Quaternary Research* 16, 80-96

Jenkins, D., Lacelles, B. & Williams, J. 1995. Hiraethog's changing vegetation. *Clwyd Archaeology News.*

Jewitt, L. 1851. On Roman remains recently discovered at Headington, near Oxford. *Journal of the British Archaeological Association* 6, 52-67

Johnsen, S.J., Clausen, H.B., Dansgaard, W., Fuhrer, K., Gundestrup, N., Hammer, C.U., Iversen, P., Jouzel, J., Stauffer, B., & Steffensen, J.P. 1992. Irregular glacial interstadials recorded in a new Greenland ice core. *Nature* 359, 311-13

Johnson, N. & Rose, P. 1994. *Bodmin Moor. An Archaeological Survey, Volume 1: the Human Landscape to c 1800,* English Heritage/RCHME, London

Johnson, S. 1989. *Hadrian's Wall.* Batsford, London

Jones, A.K.G. & Hutchinson, A.R. 1991. The parasitological evidence. In M.R. McCarthy, *The Structural Sequence and Environmental Remains from Castle Street, Carlisle: Excavations 1931-2,* 68-72. Cumberland and Westmorland Antiquarian and Archaeological Society, Kendal

Jones, B. & Mattingly, D. 1990. *An Atlas of Roman Britain.* Blackwell, Oxford

Jones, G., Straker, V. & Davis, A. 1991. Early medieval plant use and ecology. In A. Vince (ed.) *Aspects of Saxo-Norman London: II Finds and Environmental Evidence,* 347-85. London and Middlesex Archaeological Society, London

Jones, M. 1978. The plant remains. In M. Parrington, *The Excavation of an Iron Age Settlement, Bronze Age Ring-ditches and Roman Features at Ashville Trading Estate, Abingdon (Oxfordshire) 1974-76,* 93-110. Oxfordshire Archaeological Unit/CBA, Oxford/London

Jones, M. 1981. The development of crop husbandry. In M. Jones & G. Dimbleby

References

(eds), *The Environment of Man: the Iron Age to the Anglo-Saxon Period*, 95-128. BAR British Series 87, Oxford

Jones, M. 1984. The plant remains. In B.W. Cunliffe, *Danebury: an Iron Age Hillfort in Hampshire Vol. 2: the Excavations, 1969-1978: the Finds*, 483-95. CBA Research Report 52, London

Jones, M. 1996. Plant exploitation. In T.C. Champion & J.R. Collis (eds) *The Iron Age in Britain and Ireland: Recent Trends*, 29-40. J.R. Collis Publications, Sheffield

Jones, M. 1988. The arable field: a botanical battleground. In M. Jones (ed.) *Archaeology and the Flora of the British Isles*, 86-92. Oxford University Committee for Archaeology, Oxford

Jones, M. 1989. Agriculture in Roman Britain: the dynamics of change. In M. Todd (ed.) *Research on Roman Britain: 1960-89*, 127-34. Britannia Monograph no. 11, London

Jones, M. 1991. Food consumption and production – plants. In R.F.J. Jones (ed.) *Britain in the Roman Period: Recent Trends*, 21-7. J.R. Collis Publications, Department of Archaeology and Prehistory, University of Sheffield, Sheffield

Jones, M. & Dimbleby, G. 1981 (eds) *The Environment of Man: the Iron Age to the Anglo-Saxon Period*. BAR British Series 87, Oxford

Jones, M. & Nye, S. 1991. The plant remains: a quantitative analysis of crop debris. In B. Cunliffe & C. Poole, *Danebury: an Iron Age Hillfort in Hampshire Vol. 5: the Excavations, 1979-88: the Finds*, 439-47. CBA, London

Jones, M. & Robinson, M. 1986. The crop plants. In D. Miles (ed.) *Archaeology at Barton Court Farm, Abingdon, Oxon*, microfiche chapter 9. Oxford Archaeological Unit/CBA, Oxford/London

Jones, M.E. 1996. *The End of Roman Britain*. Cornell University Press, Ithaca/London

Jones, R., Benson-Evans, K. & Chambers, F.M. 1985. Human influence upon sedimentation in Llangorse Lake, Wales. *Earth Surface Processes and Landforms* 10, 227-35

Karlen, W. 1991. Glacier fluctuations in Scandinavia during the last 9000 years. In L. Starkel, K.J. Gregory & J.B. Thornes (eds) *Temperate Palaeohydrology*, 395-412. John Wiley & Sons, Chichester

Keeley, H.C.M. (ed.) 1984. *Environmental Archaeology: a Regional Review*. Department of the Environment, London

Keeley, H.C.M. (ed.) 1987. *Environmental Archaeology: a Regional Review Vol II*. HBMCE, London

Kelly, R.S. 1988. Two late prehistoric circular enclosures near Harlech, Gwynedd. *Proceedings of the Prehistoric Society* 54, 101-51

Kenward, H.K. 1979. The insect remains. In H.K. Kenward & D. Williams, *Biological Evidence from the Roman Warehouses in Coney Street*, 62-78. CBA, London

Kenward, H.K. 1982. Insect communities and death assemblages past and present. In A.R. Hall & H.K. Kenward (eds) *Environmental Archaeology in the Urban Context*, 71-8. CBA Research Report 43, London

Kenward, H.K., Hall, A.R. & Jones, A.K.G. 1986. *Environmental Evidence from a Roman Well and Anglian Pits in the Legionary Fortress*. CBA, London

Kenward, H.K., Allison, E.P. & Morgan, L.M. 1991. The insect remains. In M.R. McCarthy, *The Structural Sequence and Environmental Remains from Castle Street, Carlisle: Excavations 1981-2*, 65-8. Cumberland and Westmorland Antiquarian and Archaeological Society, Kendal

References

Kenward, H.K. & Hall, A.R. 1995. *Biological Evidence from 16-22 Coppergate.* CBA, York

Kerney, M.P. 1966. Snails and man in Britain. *Journal of Conchology* 26, 3-14

King, A.C. 1978. A comparative survey of bone assemblages from Roman sites in Britain. *Institute of Archaeology Bulletin* 15, 207-32

King, A.C. 1984. Animal bones and the dietary identity of military and civilian groups in Roman Britain, Germany and Gaul. In T.F.C. Blagg & A. King (eds) *Military and Civilian in Roman Britain,* 187-218. BAR British Series 136, Oxford

King, A.C. 1991. Food production and consumption – meat. In R.F.J. Jones (ed.) *Britain in the Roman Period: Recent Trends,* 15-20. J.R. Collis Publications, Department of Archaeology and Prehistory, University of Sheffield, Sheffield

Knights, B.A., Dickson, C.A., Dickson, J.H. & Breeze, D.J. 1983. Evidence concerning the Roman military diet at Bearsden, Scotland, in the 2nd century AD. *Journal of Archaeological Science* 10, 139-52

Lamb, H.H. 1981. Climate from 1000 BC to 1000 AD. In M. Jones & G. Dimbleby (eds) *The Environment of Man: the Iron Age to the Anglo-Saxon Period,* 53-65. BAR British Series 87, Oxford

Lamb, H.H. 1995. *Climate, History and the Modern World,* 2nd edn. Routledge, London/New York

Lambrick, G. 1992. The development of late prehistoric and Roman farming on the Thames gravels. In M.G. Fulford & E. Nichols (eds), *The Archaeology of the British Gravels: a Review,* 78-105. Society of Antiquaries, London

Lambrick, G. & Robinson, M. (eds) 1979. *Iron Age and Roman Riverside Settlements at Farmoor, Oxfordshire.* Oxford Archaeological Unit/CBA, Oxford/London

Lambrick, G. & Robinson, M. 1988. The development of floodplain grassland in the Upper Thames Valley. In M. Jones (ed.) *Archaeology and the Flora of the British Isles,* 55-75. Oxford University Committee for Archaeology, Oxford

Leemann, A. & Niessen, F. 1994. Holocene glacial activity and climatic variations in the Swiss Alps: reconstructing a continuous record from proglacial lake sediments. *The Holocene* 4, 259-68

Lewis, C., Mitchell-Fox, P. & Dyer, C. 1997. *Village, Hamlet and Field. Changing Medieval Settlements in Central England.* Manchester University Press, Manchester

Locker, A. 1990. The mammal, bird and fish bones. In D.S. Neal, A. Wardle & J. Hunn, *Excavation of the Iron Age, Roman and Medieval Settlement at Gorhambury, St Albans,* 205-12. HBMCE, London

Long, A., Davis, O.K. & De Lanois, J. 1992. Separation and ^{14}C dating of pure pollen from lake sediments: nanofossil AMS dating. *Radiocarbon* 34, 557-60

Long, A.J. & Roberts, D.H. 1997. Sea-level change. In M. Fulford, T. Champion & A. Long (eds) *England's Coastal Heritage,* 25-49. English Heritage, London

Long, D.J., Chambers, F.M. & Barnatt, J. 1998. The palaeoenvironment and the vegetation history of a later prehistoric field system at Stoke Flat on the gritstone uplands of the Peak District. *Journal of Archaeological Science* 25, 505-19

Lowe, J.J. & Walker, M.J.C. 1997. *Reconstructing Quaternary Environments,* 2nd edn. Longman, London

Luff, R.-M. 1982. *A Zooarchaeological Study of the Roman North-western Provinces.* BAR International Series 137, Oxford

Lyne, M.A.B. & Jefferies, R.S. 1979. *The Alice Holt / Farnham Roman Pottery Industry.* CBA Research Report 30, London

194

References

Mackay, A.W. & Tallis, J.H. 1994. The recent vegetational development of the Forest of Bowland, Lancashire, UK. *New Phytologist* 128, 571-84

Macklin, M.G. & Lewin, J. 1993. Holocene river alluviation in Britain. In I. Douglas & J. Hagendorm (eds) *Geomorphology and Geoecology: Fluvial Geomorphology*. Gebruder Borntraeger, Berlin/Stuttgart

Macphail, R.I. 1994. The reworking of urban stratigraphy by human and natural processes. In A.R. Hall & H.K. Kenward, *Urban-Rural Connexions: Perspectives from Environmental Archaeology*, 13-43. Oxbow Monograph 47, Oxford

McCarthy, M.R. 1991. *The Structural Sequence and Environmental Remains from Castle Street, Carlisle: Excavations 1981-2.* Cumberland and Westmorland Antiquarian and Archaeological Society, Kendal

Maltby, M. 1979. *Faunal Studies on Urban Sites: the Animal Bones from Exeter 1971-1975.* Department of Prehistory and Archaeology, University of Sheffield, Sheffield

Maltby, M. 1981. Iron Age, Romano-British and Anglo-Saxon animal husbandry: a review of the faunal evidence. In M. Jones & G. Dimbleby (eds), *The Environment of Man: the Iron Age to the Anglo-Saxon Period*, 155-203. BAR British Series 87, Oxford

Maltby, M. 1994. The meat supply in Roman Dorchester and Winchester. In A.R. Hall & H. Kenward (eds) *Urban-rural Connexions: Perspectives from Environmental Archaeology*, 85-102. Oxbow Monograph no. 47, Oxford

Maltby, M. 1996. The exploitation of animals in the Iron Age: the archaeo-zoological evidence. In T.C. Champion & J.R. Collis (eds) *The Iron Age in Britain and Ireland: Recent Trends*, 17-27. J.R. Collis Publications, Sheffield

Manning, A., Birley, R. & Tipping, R. 1997. Roman impact on the environment at Hadrian's Wall: precisely dated pollen analysis from Vindolanda, northern England. *The Holocene* 7, 175-86

Matthews, J.A. & Karlen, W. 1992. Asynchronous neoglaciation and Holocene climatic change reconstructed from Norwegian glaciolacustrine sedimentary sequences. *Geology* 20, 991-4

May, J. 1996. *Dragonby.* 2 volumes. Oxbow Monograph 61, Oxford

Meadows, I. 1996. Wollaston: the Nene Valley, a British Moselle? *Current Archaeology* 150, 212-15

Meiggs, R. 1982. *Trees and Timber in the Ancient Mediterranean World.* Clarendon Press, Oxford

Merryfield, D.L. & Moore, P.D. 1974. Prehistoric human activity and blanket peat initiation on Exmoor. *Nature* 250, 439-41

Middleton, R., Wells, C.E. & Huckerby, E. 1995. *The Wetlands of North Lancashire.* Lancaster Imprints 4

Mighall, T.M. & Chambers, F. 1995. Holocene vegetation history and human impact at Bryn y Castell, Snowdonia, North Wales. *New Phytologist* 130, 299-321

Mighall, T.M. & Chambers, F.M. 1997. Early ironworking and its impact on the environment: palaeoecological evidence from Bryn y Castell hillfort, Snowdonia, North Wales. *New Phytologist* 63, 199-219

Miles, D. (ed.) 1986. *Archaeology at Barton Court Farm, Abingdon, Oxon.* Oxford Archaeological Unit/CBA, Oxford/London

Millett, M. 1995. *Roman Britain.* English Heritage/Batsford, London

Moffett, L. 1994. Charred cereals from some ovens/kilns in late Saxon Stafford and the botanical evidence for the pre-*burh* economy. In J. Rackham (ed.) *Environment and Economy in Anglo-Saxon England*, 55-64. CBA Research Report 89, York

References

Moore, P.D. 1968. Human influence upon vegetational history in north Cardigan-shire. *Nature* 217, 1006-7

Moore, P.D. 1985. Forests, man and water. *International Journal of Environmental Studies* 25, 159-66

Moore, P.D. 1988. The development of moorlands and upland mires. In M. Jones (ed.) *Archaeology and the Flora of the British Isles*, 116-22. Oxford Committee for Archaeology, Oxford

Moore, P.D. 1993. The origin of blanket mire, revisited. In F.M. Chambers (ed.) *Climate Change and Human Impact on the Landscape*, 217-24. Chapman & Hall, London

Moore, P.D., Webb, J.A. & Collinson, M.E. 1991. *Pollen Analysis*, 2nd edn, Oxford

Moore, P.D., Merryfield, D.L. & Price, M.D.R. 1984. The vegetation and development of blanket mires. In P.D. Moore (ed.) *European Mires*, 203-35. Academic Press, London

Morgan, R.A. 1983. Tree-ring studies in the Somerset Levels: the examination of modern hazel growth in Bradfield Woods, Suffolk, and its implications for prehistoric data. *Somerset Levels Papers* 9, 44-8

Murphy, P. 1985. The cereals and crop weeds. In S. West, *West Stow: the Anglo-Saxon Village, Volume 1: Text*, 100-8. East Anglian Archaeology Report 24, Suffolk County Planning Department

Murphy, P. 1994. The Anglo-Saxon landscape and rural economy: some results from sites in East Anglia and Essex. In J. Rackham (ed.) *Environment and Economy in Anglo-Saxon England*, 23-39. CBA Research Report 89, York

Musson, C.R. with Britnell, W.J. & Smith, A.G. 1991. *The Breiddin Hillfort*. CBA Research Report 76, London

Newell, P.J. 1983. Pollen analysis report. In W.S. Hanson & G.S. Maxwell, Minor enclosures on the Antonine Wall at Wilderness Plantation. *Britannia* 14, 227-43

Newell, P.J. 1988. A buried wall in peatland by Sheshader, Isle of Lewis. *Proceedings of the Society of Antiquaries of Scotland* 118, 79-93

Noddle, B.A. 1984. A comparison of the bones of cattle, sheep, and pigs from ten Iron Age and Romano-British sites. In C. Grigson & J. Clutton-Brock (eds) *Animals and Archaeology, 4: Husbandry in Europe*, 105-23. BAR International series 227, Oxford

Nye, S. 1996. Botanical remains. In C.D. Morris *The Birsay Bay Project Volume 2 Sites in Birsay Village and on the Brough of Birsay, Orkney*, 184-6. University of Durham, Durham

Nye, S. & Jones, M. 1987. The carbonised plant remains. In B.W. Cunliffe, *Hengistbury Head, Dorset, Vol. 1: The Prehistoric and Roman Settlement, 3500 BC-AD 500*, 323-8. Oxford University Committee for Archaeology, Oxford

Oldfield, F. 1991. Environmental magnetism – a personal perspective. *Quaternary Science Reviews* 10, 73-85

Orme, B.J., Coles, J.M. & Sturdy, C.R. 1979. Meare Lake Village West: a report on recent work. *Somerset Levels Papers* 5, 6-17

Parker Pearson, M. & Sydes, R.E. 1997. The Iron Age enclosures and prehistoric landscape of Sutton Common, South Yorkshire. *Proceedings of the Prehistoric Society* 63, 221-59

Patterson III, W.A., Edwards, K.J. & Maguire, D.J. 1987. Microscopic charcoal as a fossil indicator of fire. *Quaternary Science Reviews* 6, 2-23

Pearson, E. & Giorgi, J. 1992. The plant remains. In C. Cowan, A possible mansio in Roman Southwark: Excavations at 15-23 Southwark Street, 1980-86, 165-70. *Transactions of the London and Middlesex Archaeological Society* 43, 3-191

References

Peglar, S.M. 1979. A radiocarbon-dated pollen diagram from Loch of Winless, Caithness, north-east Scotland. *New Phytologist* 82, 245-63

Peglar, S.M. 1993a. Mid- and late-Holocene vegetation history of Quidenham Mere, Norfolk, UK interpreted using recurrent groups of taxa. *Vegetation History and Archaeobotany* 2, 15-28

Peglar, S.M. 1993b. The development of the cultural landscape around Diss Mere, Norfolk, UK, during the past 7000 years. *Review of Palaeobotany and Palynology* 76, 1-47

Pennington, W. 1964. Pollen analyses from the deposits of six upland tarns in the Lake District. *Philosophical Transactions of the Royal Society of London* Series B, 248, 205-44

Pennington, W. 1970. Vegetation history in the north-west of England: a regional synthesis. In D. Walker & R.G. West (eds) *Studies in the Vegetational History of the British Isles*, 41-79. Cambridge University Press, Cambridge

Perring, D. 1991. The buildings. In D. Perring & S. Roskams, *The Archaeology of Roman London, Vol. 2: Early Development of Roman London West of the Walbrook*, 67-107. Museum of London/CBA, London

Pigott, C.D. & Huntley, J.P. 1981. Factors controlling the distribution of *Tilia cordata* at the northern limits of its geographical range. II. History in north-west England. *New Phytologist* 84, 145-64

Pilcher, J.R. & Hall, V.A. 1992. Towards a tephrochronology for the Holocene of the north of Ireland. *The Holocene* 2, 255-9

Pilcher, J.R. & Hall, V.A. 1996. Tephrochronological studies in northern England. *The Holocene* 6, 100-5

Pilcher, J.R., Hall, V.A. & McCormac, F.G. 1995. Dates of Holocene Icelandic volcanic eruptions from tephra layers in Irish peats. *The Holocene* 5, 103-10

Pilcher, J.R., Hall, V.A. & McCormac, F.G. 1996. An outline tephrochronology for the Holocene of the north of Ireland. *Journal of Quaternary Science* 11, 485-94

Punt, W. & Malotaux, M. 1984. Cannabaceae, Moraceae and Urticaceae. *Review of Palaeobotany and Palynology* 42, 23-44

Rackham, J. 1979. *Rattus rattus*: the introduction of the black rat into Britain. *Antiquity* 53, 112-20

Rackham, J. (ed.) 1994. *Environment and Economy in Anglo-Saxon England*. CBA Research Report 89, York

Rackham, O. 1977. Neolithic woodland management in the Somerset Levels: Garvin's, Walton Heath, and Rowland's Tracks. *Somerset Levels Papers* 3, 65-71

Rackham, O. 1980. *Ancient Woodland*. Arnold, London

Rackham, O. 1986. *The History of the Countryside*. Dent, London/Melbourne

Rackham, O. 1990. *Trees and Woodland in the British Landscape*. Revised edition. Dent, London

Rahtz, P. 1976. Buildings and rural settlement. In D.M. Wilson (ed.) *The Archaeology of Anglo-Saxon England*, 49-98. Cambridge University Press, Cambridge

Rampino, M.R., Self, S. & Stothers, R.B. 1988. Volcanic winters. *Annual Review of Earth Planet Science* 16, 73-99

Reece, R. 1980. Town and country: the end of Roman Britain. *World Archaeology* 12, 77-92

Rees, S.E. 1979. *Agricultural Implements in Prehistoric and Roman Britain*. BAR British Series 69, Oxford

Reid, C. 1903. Notes on the plant remains of Roman Silchester. In W.H. St J. Hope, excavations on the Site of the Roman City at Silchester, Hants, in 1902, 425-8. *Archaeologia* 58, 413-38

References

Renberg, I., Persson, M.W. & Emteryd, O. 1994. Pre-industrial atmospheric lead contamination detected in Swedish lake sediments. *Nature* 368, 323-6

Reynolds, D.M. 1982. Aspects of later timber construction in south-east Scotland. In D.W. Harding (ed.) *Later Prehistoric Settlement in South-East Scotland*, 44-56. University of Edinburgh Department of Archaeology Occasional Paper no. 8

Reynolds, P.J. 1981a. Deadstock and livestock. In R. Mercer (ed.) *Farming Practice in British Prehistory*, 97-122. Edinburgh University Press, Edinburgh

Reynolds, P.J. 1981b. New approaches to familiar problems. In M. Jones & G. Dimbleby (eds), *The Environment of Man: the Iron Age to the Anglo-Saxon Period*, 19-49. BAR British Series 87, Oxford

Reynolds, P.J. 1982. Substructure to superstructure. In P.J. Drury (ed.) *Structural Reconstruction. Approaches to the Interpretation of the Excavated Remains of Buildings*. BAR British Series 110, Oxford

Reynolds, P.J. 1995. Rural life and farming. In M.J. Green (ed.) *The Celtic World*, 176-209. Routledge, London

Reynolds, P.J. & Langley, J.K. 1980. Romano-British corn-drying oven: an experiment. *Archaeological Journal* 136, 27-42

Richards, J.D. 1991. *Viking Age England*. English Heritage/Batsford, London

Rippon, S. 1996. *Gwent Levels: the Evolution of a Wetland Landscape*. CBA, York

Ritchie, A. 1993. *Viking Scotland*. Batsford/Historic Scotland, London

Rivet, A.L.F. & Smith, C. 1979. *The Place-names of Roman Britain*. Batsford, London

Roberts, B.K., Turner, J. & Ward, P.F. 1973. Recent forest history and land use in Weardale, northern England. In H.J.B. Birks & R.G. West (eds) *Quaternary Plant Ecology*, 207-21. Blackwell, Oxford

Robinson, D.E. & Dickson, J.H. 1988. Vegetational history and land use: a radiocarbon-dated pollen diagram from Machrie Moor, Arran, Scotland. *New Phytologist* 109, 223-51

Robinson, M. 1979. Plants and invertebrates: methods and results. In G. Lambrick & M. Robinson, *Iron Age and Roman Riverside Settlements at Farmoor, Oxfordshire*, 77-103. CBA Research Report 32, Oxford Archaeological Unit/CBA, Oxford/London

Robinson, M. 1981. The Iron Age to Early Saxon environment of the upper Thames terraces. In M. Jones & G. Dimbleby (eds) *The Environment of Man: the Iron Age to the Anglo-Saxon Period*, 251-86. BAR British Series 87, Oxford

Robinson, M. 1986. Waterlogged plant and invertebrate evidence. In D. Miles (ed.) *Archaeology at Barton Court Farm, Abingdon, Oxon*, microfiche chapter 8. Oxford Archaeological Unit/CBA, Oxford/London

Robinson, M. 1992. Environment, archaeology and alluvium on the river gravels of the South Midlands. In S. Needham & M.G. Macklin (eds) *Alluvial Archaeology in Britain*, 197-208. Oxbow Monograph 27, Oxford

Robinson, M. & Hubbard, R.N.L.B. 1977. The transport of pollen in the bracts of hulled cereals. *Journal of Archaeological Science* 4, 197-9

Robinson, M. & Lambrick, G. 1984. Holocene alluviation and hydrology in the upper Thames basin. *Nature* 308, 809-14

Robinson, M. & Wilson, B. 1987. A survey of environmental archaeology in the south Midlands. In H.C.M. Keeley (ed.) *Environmental Archaeology: a Regional Review Vol II*, 16-99. HBMCE, London

Rowell, T.K. & Turner, J. 1985. Litho-, humic- and pollen stratigraphy at Quick Moss, Northumberland. *Journal of Ecology* 73, 11-25

Scaife, R.G. 1986. Pollen in human palaeofaeces; and a preliminary investigation of the stomach and gut contents of Lindow Man. In I.M. Stead, J.B. Bourke & D. Brothwell, *Lindow Man: the Body in the Bog*, 126-35. British Museum Publications, London

Scaife, R.G. & Burrin, P.J. 1983. Floodplain development in and the vegetational history of the Sussex High Weald and some archaeological implications. *Sussex Archaeological Collections* 121, 1-10

Scaife, R.G. & Burrin, P.J. 1985. The environmental impact of prehistoric man as recorded in the upper Cuckmere valley at Stream Farm, Chiddingly. *Sussex Archaeological Collections* 123, 27-34

Scaife, R.G. & Burrin, P.J. 1987. Further evidence for the environmental impact of prehistoric cultures in Sussex from alluvial fill deposits in the eastern Rother Valley. *Sussex Archaeological Collections* 125, 1-9

Sear, C.B., Kelly, P.M., Jones, P.D., & Goodess, C.M. 1987. Global surface-temperature responses to major volcanic eruptions. *Nature* 330, 365-7

Serjeantson, D. 1991. The bird bones. In B. Cunliffe & C. Poole, *Danebury: an Iron Age Hillfort in Hampshire Vol. 5: the Excavations, 1979-88: the Finds*, 479-81. CBA, London

Shennan, I. 1986. Flandrian sea-level changes in the Fenland. II: tendencies of sea-level movement, altitudinal changes, and local and regional factors. *Journal of Quaternary Science* 1, 155-79

Simmons, B.B. 1979. The Lincolnshire Car Dyke: navigation or drainage? *Britannia* 10, 183-96

Simmons, I.G. 1996. *The Environmental Impact of Later Mesolithic Cultures*. Edinburgh University Press, Edinburgh

Simmons, I.G., Atherden, M., Cloutman, E.W., Cundill, P.R., Innes, J.B. & Jones, R.L. 1993. Prehistoric environments. In D.A. Spratt (ed.) *Prehistoric and Roman Archaeology of North-East Yorkshire*, revised edition, 15-50. CBA Research Report 87, London

Simmons, I.G. & Tooley, M.J. 1981. *The Environment in British Prehistory*. Duckworth, London

Sims, R.E. 1978. Man and vegetation in Norfolk. In S. Limbrey & J.G. Evans (eds) *The Effect of Man on the Landscape: the Lowland Zone*, 57-62. CBA Research Report 21, London

Smith, A.G. & Green, C.A. 1995. Topogenous peat development and late-Flandrian vegetation history at a site in upland south Wales. *The Holocene* 5, 172-83

Smith, A.G. with Girling, M.A., Green, C.A., Hillman, G.C. & Limbrey, S. 1991. Buckbean Pond: the environmental evidence. In C.R. Musson with W.J. Britnell & A.G. Smith, *The Breiddin Hillfort. A Later Prehistoric Settlement in the Welsh Marches*, 95-111. CBA Research Report 73, London

Smith, A.H.V. 1996. Provenance of coals from Roman sites in U.K. counties bordering River Severn and its estuary and including Wiltshire. *Journal of Archaeological Science* 23, 373-89

Smith, A.H.V. 1997. Provenance of coals from Roman sites in England and Wales. *Britannia* 28, 297-324

Smith, K., Coppen, J., Wainwright, G.J. & Beckett, S. 1981. The Shaugh Moor Project: third report – settlement and environmental investigations. *Proceedings of the Prehistoric Society* 47, 205-73

Smyth, C. & Jennings, S. 1988. Mid- to late-Holocene forest composition and the effects of clearances in the Combe Haven Valley, East Sussex. *Sussex Archaeological Collections* 126, 1-20

Spain, R.J. 1985. Romano-British watermills. *Archaeologia Cantiana* 100 (1984), 101-28

References

Stace, C. 1991. *New Flora of the British Isles*. Cambridge University Press, Cambridge

Stead, I.M., Bourke, J.B. & Brothwell, D. 1986. *Lindow Man: the Body in the Bog*. British Museum Publications, London

Stevenson, A.C. & Harrison, R.J. 1992. Ancient forests in Spain: a model for land-use and dry forest management in south-west Spain from 4000 BC to 1900 AD. *Proceedings of the Prehistoric Society* 58, 227-47

Stirland, A. & Waldron, T. 1990. The earliest cases of tuberculosis in Britain. *Journal of Archaeological Science* 17, 221-30

Stothers, R.B. 1984. Mystery cloud of AD 536. *Nature* 307, 344-5

Stothers, R.B. & Rampino, M.R. 1983a. Historic volcanism, European dry fogs, and Greenland acid precipitation, 1500 BC to AD 1500. *Science* 222, 411-13

Stothers, R.B. & Rampino, M.R. 1983b. Volcanic eruptions in the Mediterranean before AD 630 from written and archaeological sources. *Journal of Geophysical Research* 88, 6357-71

Stuiver, M., Grootes, P.M. & Braziunas, T.F. 1995. The GISP2 δ^{18}O climate record of the past 16,500 years and the role of the sun, ocean, and volcanoes. *Quaternary Research* 44, 341-54

Stuiver, M. & Kra, R.S. (eds) 1986. Calibration Issue. Proceedings of the Twelfth International Radiocarbon Conference – Trondheim, Norway. *Radiocarbon* 28 (2B) 805-1030

Stuiver, M. & Pearson, G.W. 1986. High-precision calibration of the radiocarbon time scale, AD 1950-500 BC. *Radiocarbon* 28, 805-38

Stuiver, M. & Reimer, P.J. 1993. Extended ^{14}C data base and revised CALIB 3.0 ^{14}C age calibration program. In M. Stuiver, A. Long & R.S. Kra (eds) Calibration 1993. *Radiocarbon* 35, 215-30

Tallis, J.H. & Switsur, V.R. 1973. Studies in southern Pennine peats VI. A radiocarbon-dated pollen diagram from Featherbed Moss, Derbyshire. *Journal of Ecology* 61, 743-51

Thomas, C. 1985. *Exploration of a Drowned Landscape: Archaeology and History of the Isles of Scilly*. Batsford, London

Thomas, K.D. 1989. Vegetation of the British chalklands in the Flandrian period: a response to Bush. *Journal of Archaeological Science* 16, 549-53

Thompson, R. & Oldfield, F. 1986. *Environmental Magnetism*. Allen & Unwin, London

Thompson, R., Battarbee, R.W., O'Sullivan, P.E. & Oldfield, F. 1975. Magnetic susceptibility of lake sediments. *Limnology and Oceanography* 20, 687-98

Tinsley, H.M. & Smith, R.T. 1974. Surface pollen studies across a woodland/heath transition and their application to the interpretation of pollen diagrams. *New Phytologist* 73, 547-65

Tipping, R. 1992. The determination of cause in the generation of major prehistoric valley fills in the Cheviot Hills, Anglo-Scottish border. In S. Needham & M.G. Macklin (eds) *Alluvial Archaeology in Britain*, 111-21. Oxbow, Oxford

Tipping, R. 1994. The form and fate of Scotland's woodlands. *Proceedings of the Society of Antiquaries of Scotland* 124, 1-54

Tipping, R. 1995a. Holocene evolution of a lowland Scottish landscape: Kirkpatrick Fleming. Part I: peat- and pollen-stratigraphic evidence for raised moss development and climatic change. *The Holocene* 5, 69-81

Tipping, R. 1995b. Holocene evolution of a lowland Scottish landscape: Kirkpatrick Fleming. Part II: regional vegetation and land-use change. *The Holocene* 5, 83-96

References

Tipping, R. 1995c. Holocene landscape change at Carn Dubh, near Pitlochry, Perthshire, Scotland. *Journal of Quaternary Science* 10, 59-75

Tipping, R. 1997. Pollen analysis and the impact of Rome on native agriculture around Hadrian's Wall. In A. Gwilt & C. Haselgrove (eds) *Reconstructing Iron Age Societies*, 239-47. Oxbow Monograph 71, Oxford

Todd, M. 1987. *The South West to AD 1000*. Longman, London

Topping, P. 1989a. Early cultivation in Northumberland and the Borders. *Proceedings of the Prehistoric Society* 55, 161-79

Topping, P. 1989b. The context of cord rig cultivation in later prehistoric Northumberland. In M. Bowden, D. Mackay & P. Topping (eds) *From Cornwall to Caithness*, 145-57. BAR British Series 209, Oxford

Turner, J. 1964. The anthropogenic factor in vegetational history. I: Tregaron and Whixall Mosses. *New Phytologist* 63, 73-90

Turner, J. 1965. A contribution to the history of forest clearance. *Proceedings of the Royal Society of London* Series B 161, 343-53

Turner, J. 1979. The environment of north-east England during Roman times as shown by pollen analysis. *Journal of Archaeological Science* 6, 285-90

Turner, J. 1981. The vegetation. In M. Jones & G. Dimbleby (eds) *The Environment of Man: the Iron Age to the Anglo-Saxon Period*, 67-73. BAR British Series 87, Oxford

Turner, R.C. & Scaife, R.G. (eds) 1995. *Bog Bodies: New Discoveries and Perspectives*. British Museum, London

Twigger, S.N. & Haslam, C.J. 1991. Environmental change in Shropshire during the last 13,000 years. *Field Studies* 7, 743-58

Tyers, I. 1988. Environmental evidence from Southwark and Lambeth. In P. Hinton (ed.) *Excavations in Southwark 1973-76 Lambeth 1973-79*, 443-77. London and Middlesex Archaeological Society and Surrey Archaeological Society, London

Tyers, I., Hillam, J. & Groves, C. 1994. Trees and woodland in the Saxon period: the dendrochronological evidence. In J. Rackham (ed.) *Environment and Economy in Anglo-Saxon England*, 12-22. CBA Research Report 89, York

van Geel, B. 1986. Application of fungal and algal remains and other microfossils in palynological analysis. In B.E. Berglund (ed.) *Handbook of Holocene Palaeoecology and Palaeohydrology*, 497-505. John Wiley & Sons, Chichester

van der Veen, M. 1987. The plant remains. In D.H. Heslop, *The Excavation of an Iron Age Settlement at Thorpe Thewles, Cleveland, 1980-1982*. CBA Research Report 65, Cleveland County Council/CBA

van der Veen, M. 1992. *Crop Husbandry Regimes*. J.R. Collis Publications, Department of Archaeology and Prehistory, University of Sheffield, Sheffield

van der Veen, M. & O'Connor, T. 1998. The expansion of agricultural production in late Iron Age and Roman Britain. In J. Bayley (ed.) *Science in Archaeology: an Agenda for the Future*, 127-43. English Heritage, London

van der Veen, M. & Palmer, C. 1997. Environmental factors and the yield potential of ancient wheat crops. *Journal of Archaeological Science* 24, 163-82

Waddelove, A.C. & Waddelove, E. 1990. Archaeology and research into sea-level during the Roman era: towards a methodology based on highest astronomical tide. *Britannia* 21, 253-66

Wainwright, A. 1990. The mollusc and seed remains. In D.S. Neal, A. Wardle & J. Humm, *Excavation of the Iron Age, Roman and Medieval Settlement at Gorhambury, St Albans*, 213-18. HBMCE, London

Walker, M.J.C. 1993. Holocene (Flandrian) vegetation change and human activity in the Carneddau area of upland mid-Wales. In F.M. Chambers (ed.) *Climatic*

Change and Human Impact on the Landscape, 169-83. Chapman & Hall, London

Waller, M. 1993. Flandrian vegetational history of south-eastern England. Pollen data from Pannel Bridge, East Sussex. *New Phytologist* 124, 345-69

Waller, M. 1994a. *The Fenland Project, Number 9: Flandrian Environmental Change in Fenland*. East Anglian Archaeology Report 70, Cambridgeshire County Council, Cambridge

Waller, M. 1994b. Redmere. In M. Waller, *The Fenland Project, Number 9: Flandrian Environmental Change in Fenland*, 124-33. East Anglian Archaeology Report 70, Cambridgeshire County Council, Cambridge

Waller, M. 1994c. Willingham Mere. In M. Waller, *The Fenland Project, Number 9: Flandrian Environmental Change in Fenland*, 158-64. East Anglian Archaeology Report 70, Cambridgeshire County Council, Cambridge

Waller, M. 1994d. West-central Fens (Cambs). In M. Waller, *The Fenland Project, Number 9: Flandrian Environmental Change in Fenland*, 198-226. East Anglian Archaeology Report 70, Cambridgeshire County Council, Cambridge

Waller, M. 1994e. Eastern Fen Edge (Norfolk). In M. Waller, *The Fenland Project, Number 9: Flandrian Environmental Change in Fenland*, 251-67. East Anglian Archaeology Report 70, Cambridgeshire County Council, Cambridge

Waller, M. & Alderton, A. 1994. Swineshead. In M. Waller, *The Fenland Project, Number 9: Flandrian Environmental Change in Fenland*, 288-95. East Anglian Archaeology Report 70, Cambridgeshire County Council, Cambridge

Warner, R.B. 1990. The 'prehistoric' Irish annals: fable or history. *Archaeology Ireland* 4 (1), 30-3

Watkins, R. 1990. The postglacial vegetational history of lowland Gwynedd – Llyn Cororion. In K. Addison, M.J. Edge & R. Watkins (eds) *North Wales Field Guide*, 131-6. Quaternary Research Association, Coventry

Waton, P.V. 1982. Man's impact on the chalklands: some new pollen evidence. In M. Bell & S. Limbrey (eds) *Archaeological Aspects of Woodland Ecology*, 75-91. BAR International Series 146, Oxford

Waton, P.V. 1983. *A Palynological Study of the Impact of Man on the Landscape of Central Southern England, with Special Reference to the Chalklands*. Unpublished PhD thesis, University of Southampton

Webster, G. 1955. A note on the use of coal in Roman Britain. *Antiquaries Journal* 35, 199-217

Wells, C., Huckerby, E. & Hall, V. 1997. Mid- and late-Holocene vegetation history and tephra studies at Fenton Cottage, Lancashire, U.K. *Vegetation History and Archeobotany* 6, 153-66

Whittington, G. & Edwards, K.J. 1989. Problems in interpretation of Cannabaceae pollen in the stratigraphic record. *Pollen et Spores* 31, 79-96

Whittington, G. & Edwards, K.J. 1993. *Ubi solitudinem faciunt pacem appellant*: the Romans in Scotland, a palaeoenvironmental contribution. *Britannia* 24, 13-25

Whittington, G., Edwards, K.J. & Cundill, P.R. 1991. Late- and post-glacial vegetational change at Black Loch, Fife, eastern Scotland – a multiple core approach. *New Phytologist* 118, 147-66

Whittington, G. & Gordon, A.D. 1987. The differentiation of the pollen of *Cannabis sativa* L. from that of *Humulus lupulus* L. *Pollen et Spores* 29, 111-20

Whittington, G. & McManus, J. 1998. Dark Age agricultural practices and environmental change: evidence from Tentsmuir, Fife, eastern Scotland. In C.M. Mills & G. Coles (eds) *Life on the Edge: Human Settlement and Marginality*, 111-19. Oxbow Monograph 100, Oxford

Wik, M. & Natkanski, J. 1990. British and Scandinavian lake sediment records of carbonaceous particles from fossil-fuel combustion. *Philosophical Transactions of the Royal Society of London*, Series B, 327, 319-23

Willcox, G.H. 1978. Seeds from the late 2nd-century pit F28. In M.G. Dennis, 1-7 St Thomas Street, 411-13. In Southwark and Lambeth Archaeological Excavation Committee (ed.) *Southwark Excavations 1972-1974*, 291-422. London and Middlesex Archaeological Society/Surrey Archaeological Society, London

Williams, D. 1977. A consideration of the sub-fossil remains of *Vitis vinifera* L. as evidence for viticulture in Roman Britain. *Britannia* 8, 327-34

Williams, D. 1979. The plant remains. In H.K. Kenward & D. Williams, *Biological Evidence from the Roman Warehouses in Coney Street*, 52-62. CBA, London

Wilmott, T. 1997. *Birdoswald: Excavations of a Roman Fort on Hadrian's Wall and its Successor Settlements: 1987-1992*. English Heritage Archaeological Report 14, London

Wilson, B. 1986. Faunal remains: animals and marine shells. In D. Miles (ed.) *Archaeology at Barton Court Farm, Abingdon, Oxon*, microfiche chapter 6. Oxford Archaeological Unit/CBA, Oxford/London

Wilson, D.G. 1975. Plant remains from the Graveney Boat and the early history of *Humulus lupulus* L. in W. Europe. *New Phytologist* 75, 627-48

Wilson, D.G. & Connolly, A.P. 1978. Plant remains including the evidence for hops. In V. Fenwick (ed.) *The Graveney Boat*, 133-50. BAR British Series 53, Oxford

Wiltshire, P.E.J. 1997. The pre-Roman environment. In T. Wilmott, *Birdoswald: Excavations of a Roman fort on Hadrian's Wall and its successor settlements: 1987-92*, 25-40. English Heritage Archaeological Report 14, London

Young, C.J. 1977. *The Roman Pottery Industry of the Oxford Region*. BAR 43, Oxford

Younger, D.A. 1994. The small mammals from the forecourt granary and the south west fort ditch. In P. Bidwell and S. Speak (eds) *Excavations at South Shields Roman Fort. Volume 1*, 266-8. Society of Antiquaries of Newcastle upon Tyne, Newcastle

Yule, B. 1990. The 'dark earth' and late Roman London. *Antiquity* 64, 620-8

Zielinski, G.A. 1995. Stratospheric loading and optical depth estimates of explosive volcanism over the last 2100 years derived from the Greenland Ice Sheet Project 2 ice core. *Journal of Geophysical Research* 100, 20,937-55

Zielinski, G.A. & Germani, M.S. 1998. New ice-core evidence challenges the 1620s BC age for the Santorini (Minoan) eruption. *Journal of Archaeological Science* 25, 279-89

Zielinski, G.A., Germani, M.S., Larsen, G., Baillie, M.G.L., Whitlow, S., Twickler, M.S. & Taylor, K. 1995. Evidence of the Eldgja (Iceland) eruption in the GISP2 Greenland ice core: relationship to eruption processes and climatic conditions in the tenth century. *The Holocene* 5, 129-40

Zielinski, G.A., Mayewski, P.A., Meeker, L.D., Whitlow, S., Twickler, M.S., Morrison, M., Meese, D.A., Gow, A.J. & Alley, R.B. 1994. Record of volcanism since 7000 BC from the GISP2 Greenland ice core and implications for the volcano-climate system. *Science* 264, 948-52

Zielinski, G.A., Mayewski, P.A., Meeker, L.D., Whitlow, S., Twickler, M.S., Morrison, M., Meese, D.A., Gow, A.J. & Alley, R.B. 1995. The GISP ice core record of volcanism since 7000 BC. *Science* 267, 256-8

Index

Page numbers in italic refer to illustrations